Ethics

for

Behavior

Analysts

Ethics

for

Behavior Analysts

2nd Expanded Edition

by Jon Bailey & Mary Burch

Routledge
Taylor & Francis Group
New York   London

Routledge
Taylor & Francis Group
711 Third Avenue
New York, NY 10017

Routledge
Taylor & Francis Group
27 Church Road
Hove, East Sussex BN3 2FA

© 2011 by Taylor and Francis Group, LLC
Routledge is an imprint of Taylor & Francis Group, an Informa business

Printed in the United States of America on acid-free paper
10 9 8

International Standard Book Number: 978-0-415-88029-9 (Hardback) 978-0-415-88030-5 (Paperback)

Library of Congress Cataloging-in-Publication Data

Bailey, Jon S.
    Ethics for behavior analysts / by Jon S. Bailey and Mary R. Burch. -- 2nd expanded ed.
        p. cm.
    First published: Mahwah, N.J. : Lawrence Erlbaum Associates, 2005.
    Includes bibliographical references and index.
    ISBN 978-0-415-88029-9 (hardback : alk. paper) -- ISBN 978-0-415-88030-5 (pbk. : alk. paper)
    1. Behavioral assessment--Moral and ethical aspects--United States--Handbooks, manuals, etc. 2. Behavior analysts--Professional ethics--United States--Handbooks, manuals, etc. 3. Behavior analysts--Certification--United States--Handbooks, manuals, etc. I. Burch, Mary R. II. Title.

RC437.B43B355 2011
174.20973--dc22   2010035023

Visit the Taylor & Francis Web site at
http://www.taylorandfrancis.com

and the Routledge Web site at
http://www.routledgementalhealth.com

Contents

Preface

EVOLUTION OF THIS BOOK AND HOW TO USE IT

My first experience in ethics came when I was a graduate student in psychology in the late 1960s. I was working with a profoundly developmentally disabled young man who was confined to a heavy metal crib in the small ward of a private institution in Phoenix, Arizona. Blind, deaf, nonambulatory, and not toilet trained, my "subject" engaged in self-injurious behavior virtually all day long. His head-banging behavior against the metal bars could be heard 25 yards away and greeted me each time I entered his depressing, malodorous living unit. Day after day, I sat by his crib taking notes on a possible thesis concerning how one might try to reduce his chronic self-injurious behavior, or SIB (we called it *self-destructive behavior* in those days). After a few informal observation sessions, and reading through his medical chart, I had some ideas. I set up a meeting with one of my committee members, Dr. Lee Meyerson, who was supervising the research at the facility. "I'm observing a subject who engages in self-destructive behavior," I began. "He hits his head 10 to 15 times per minute throughout the day. I've taken informal data at different times of the day, and I don't see any consistent pattern," I offered. Dr. Meyerson let me go on for about 10 minutes, nodding and occasionally taking a puff on his pipe (smoking was allowed everywhere in those days). Then he stopped me abruptly and, gesturing with his pipe, began to ask me questions that I had never thought about. Did I know my "subject's" name? Did I have permission to observe and report on this individual? Who gave me permission to look at this medical record? Had I discussed this case with any of my graduate student colleagues or shown the data in class? I had no good answers to any of Dr. Meyerson's questions. I wasn't thinking of my "subject" as a person, only as a source of data for my thesis. It never dawned on me that "Billy" had rights to privacy and confidentiality and that he needed to be treated with dignity and respect, not as just another "subject" to help me complete a master's thesis. As it turns out, Dr. Meyerson was ahead of his time in grilling me with ethical questions that would not actually come up in legal circles for another 10 years (see Chapter 1). Dr. Meyerson's questions helped sensitize me to looking at what I was doing from an extra-experimental perspective. How would I like to be treated if I was a "subject" in someone's experiment? Or how would I want my mother or sister to be treated? "With kindness, compassion, and respect" is no doubt the quick response that most of us would offer. And so it is that ethics in psychology, and particularly in behavior analysis, can be easily personalized and made tangible if we will just stop and think about what we are doing.

Students today have a great advantage over my generation. We had no code of ethics or guidelines to follow; we had one foot in the animal lab and one in the real world, and we were trying to figure out how to transform powerful operant conditioning principles into effective treatments. It didn't dawn on us at the time that ethics was involved at all, until, of course, we encountered Dr. Lee Meyerson. Today, graduate students in behavior analysis have nearly 30 years of applied research and practice to fall back on (and to learn from and be held accountable for knowing). In addition, they have a wealth of resources on ethics including case law and precedent-setting legal findings. Finally, students today have a perfectly legitimate, thoroughly researched, and well-vetted set of guidelines specifically designed for our field: The Behavior Analyst Certification Board (BACB) Guidelines for Responsible Conduct. In teaching the graduate course Professional and Ethical Issues in Behavior Analysis for the past 10 years, I have learned a great deal about the ethical issues that appear to be unique to our field (see Chapter 3) and have been developing lectures and trying to discover ways of making ethics interesting, informative, and engaging for students who do not quite see the relevance or appreciate our cautious approach. One thing I've discovered is that although we now have an excellent set of Guidelines they are somewhat dry and by themselves do not convey the urgency and relevance that they should. Reading the Guidelines is something like reading instructions for computer software: it's clearly important, but you would rather just start using it.

A few years ago, I was scheduled to give a half-day workshop at Penn State on ethics with Dr. Jerry Shook. In the process of preparing my materials, I wondered what kind of ethical questions the participants might have. Dr. Shook arranged in advance to have each participant write and submit to us two questions or "scenarios" that he or she had confronted in the work setting. When I got the questions, I realized that reading the scenarios suddenly made the ethical issues jump right off the page. I began trying to look up the correct responses (according to the BACB Guidelines), and this turned out to be quite difficult. Something was missing; an index of some sort would help, but none was available that I could find. Several all-nighters later, I had developed one. By the time Dr. Shook and I traveled to the conference, I had a new approach to teaching ethics. It involved presenting scenarios, having the students look up the relevant sections in the Guidelines, and then present their proposed ethical actions. This approach teaches students that sometimes broad, ethical considerations always come down to some specific Guidelines. My experience in using this method over the past several years is that it brings the topic to life and generates excellent discussions of very relevant issues.

One troubling problem I encountered in teaching the Ethics for Behavior Analysis course was that specific code items were often very much out of context or were written in such stilted legalese that students did not understand why they were necessary or how they were relevant. I found myself often "translating" specific Guidelines into plain English. This process, along with providing some historic context and background about how and why certain items were important in our field, seemed to increase the level of understanding for the students.

This book, then, is the culmination of this attempt to present a practical, student-centered approach to teaching ethics in behavior analysis. All of the cases are based on real examples known to the authors but modified to avoid embarrassment or legal hassles. In addition, for each case, there is a question for students to consider followed by a response that can be found at the end of each chapter. In Appendix C, you will find 50 practice scenarios that can be used in class or as homework. You can, of course, develop your own scenarios based on the specific areas of application that you encounter in your practice of behavior analysis. Our examples lean heavily on our experience in autism, developmental disabilities, education, and organizational behavior management (OBM).

A final word about using this volume: this text is intended to be a practical handbook, and we specifically attempted to avoid making this an academic or theoretical work. Although we feel that it is quite comprehensive, it is not intended to be used alone but rather as a supplement to other texts or sources that you are currently using (see Suggested Reading in Section III). Many people teaching ethics courses will routinely have students read the U.S. Constitution, view *One Flew Over the Cuckoo's Nest*, and research their state laws on limits of treatment, requirements for keeping documents, maintaining confidentiality, and other relevant issues. My experience is that it takes some creative digging to find relevant readings. Exposing students to a variety of sources from

B. F. Skinner and Murray Sidman to Association for Behavior Analysis (ABA) position statements is useful in preparing them to tackle the world of ethical issues they will confront. I have tried to summarize what I consider the most important and pressing issues for new Board Certified Behavior Analysts (BCBAs) in Chapter 19: "A Dozen Practical Tips for Ethical Conduct on Your First Job." I hope you enjoy using this book and welcome input and dialogue on effective ways of teaching this most important topic.

Jon Bailey

Acknowledgments

We would like to thank Cristal Elwood for her insightful comments and helpful editing suggestions on an earlier draft of this manuscript for the first edition. We learned a great deal from the hundreds of people who attended our Ethics Workshops, and we thank you for the wide variety of scenarios you submitted, some of which appear in Appendix C. We would also like to thank the Professionalism and Ethics Subcommittee of the Suffolk County (NY) Committee on Preschool Special Education for submitting several new scenarios for Appendix C.

We are also indebted to Jerry Shook. Without him and the Behavior Analyst Certification Board, there would be no Guidelines. We would also like to thank the expert panel that worked on the revisions to the code, with special thanks to Margaret (Misty) Bloom, the BACB's very capable attorney.

Disclaimer

This book does not represent an official statement by the Behavior Analyst Certification Board, the Association for Behavior Analysis International, or any other behavior analysis organization. This text cannot be relied on as the only interpretation of the meaning of the Guidelines or their application to particular situations. Each Board Certified Behavior Analyst (BCBA), supervisor, or relevant agency must interpret and apply the Guidelines as it believes proper, given all of the circumstances.

The cases used in this book are based on the authors' combined 60 years of experience in behavior analysis. Some are nearly exact representations of actual events, whereas others are an amalgam of two or more incidents. In all cases, we have disguised the situations and used pseudonyms to protect the privacy of the parties and organizations involved. At the end of some of the chapters, we offer "Responses to Case Questions" as examples of real, or in some cases hypothetical, solutions to the ethical problems posed by the case. We do not hold these to be the only ethical solutions; rather, each response is an example of one ethical solution. We encourage instructors who use the text to create alternate solutions based on their own experiences. Finally, we hope that the responses offered here will stimulate discussion, debate, and thoughtful consideration about ways of handling what are by definition very delicate matters.

Evolution of the 2nd Expanded Edition

Not long after the publication of the first edition of *Ethics for Behavior Analysts,* we began receiving requests to give workshops on ethics at state association meetings and for other groups around the country. It was enlightening and educational to learn firsthand from practitioners about the ethics situations they were confronting on a daily basis. To facilitate our ability to refer to the participants' practical scenarios throughout the day, we began asking them to complete "Scenario Forms" before the workshop began. These scenarios generated lively discussions that gave practitioners a sounding board for the ethical challenges they were confronting in their jobs (see many new scenarios in Appendix C and in Chapter 4, "Most Frequent Ethical Problems.")

In role-playing exercises, we noticed that, while workshop attendees might know what a particular Guidelines item said, they had a hard time coming up with the words and actions needed to handle a situation. This led to another new chapter, "Delivering the Ethics Message Effectively" (Chapter 17). A key addition to the second edition came from a development at TxABA in 2005. It was there that Kathy Chovanec asked us why behavior analysts did not use a Declaration of Professional Services to help ward off problems presented by parents, teachers, and others. In collaboration with Kathy, we developed just such a document for behavior analysts, and it is newly added to this edition (see Chapter 18).

In the course of teaching ethics graduate classes, I've continued to learn about challenges that my students faced as they participated in practica and began to understand that their approach to ethics was homegrown. Some students had a difficult time giving up "personal ethics" and adopting our field's professional ethical guidelines. I soon began each class with this dramatic introduction: "Today is the last day of your civilian life. From this point forward, you are expected to join the ranks of Professional Behavior Analysts and to learn and use our Guidelines for Responsible Conduct." From this came the idea for Chapter 5, "Everyday Ethical Challenges for Average Citizens and Behavior Analysts."

In spring 2010, the BACB undertook a review of the Guidelines; an expert panel consisting of certificants Jon Bailey (chair), Jose Martinez-Diaz, Wayne Fuqua, Ellie Kazemi, Sharon Reeve, and Jerry Shook (chief executive officer of the board) was created. The panel recommended several changes to the Guidelines overall and did include some new procedures, including risk–benefit analysis. This topic is included in Chapter 16, "Conducting a Risk–Benefit Analysis."

I teach a semester-long graduate course each year called Ethics and Professional Issues for Behavior Analysts. I use *Ethics for Behavior Analysts* for the first half of the semester and *25 Essential Skills and Strategies for Professional Behavior Analysts* (Bailey & Burch, 2010) for the second half. By covering ethics first, I find that the students become sensitized to the new way of thinking about how they should conduct themselves, and then I introduce them to all the other professional skills they will need to be successful.

We hope that this second expanded edition of *Ethics for Behavior Analysts* will be useful as you learn about and teach others about ethics.

Jon Bailey

One

Background for Ethics in Behavior Analysis

1

How We Got Here

There is nothing more shocking and horrific than the abuse and maltreatment of innocent people who are unable to protect and defend themselves. Atrocious incidents of physical and emotional abuse toward animals, children, women, and people who are elderly occur every single day in our culture, and they are often reduced to a few lines in the local news of the daily paper.

Individuals who are developmentally disabled can also be the victims of abuse. The reprehensible mistreatment of children and adults with disabilities is especially disturbing when the abuses come at the hands of your chosen profession. But this is exactly what happened in Florida in the early 1970s. These abuses changed the course of history for behavior analysis and the treatment of people with disabilities.

The story of the evolution of guidelines for responsible conduct of behavior analysts began in the late 1960s when "behavior modification" was all the rage. Having started only in

> **Aversive consequences were used with abandon in informal reactions to self-injurious, destructive, and inappropriate behaviors.**

the mid-1960s (Krasner & Ullmann, 1965; Neuringer & Michael, 1970; Ullmann & Krasner, 1965), some of behavior modification's early promoters promised dramatic changes in behavior that were quick and easy to produce and could be carried out by almost anyone with an attendance certificate from a day-long "behavior mod" workshop. People calling themselves "behavior modifiers" offered rented-hotel-ballroom training sessions in abundance. There were no prerequisites for registering, and no questions were asked about the speaker's qualifications. The basic pitch was this: "You don't have to know why a behavior occurs (it was assumed to be learned—an 'operant behavior'); you need to know only how to manipulate consequences. Food is a primary reinforcer for almost everybody; just make it contingent on the behavior you want. For inappropriate or dangerous behavior, use consequences (punishers) to 'decelerate' the behavior." There was no consideration given to the notion of "causes" of behavior or that there might be a connection between a likely cause and an effective treatment. Further, no thought was given to possible side effects of using food (e.g., food allergies, weight gain) or how the food, often candy, might be handled. Indeed, Cheerios®, M&Ms®, pretzels, and other bite-sized snacks and treats were loaded in the pockets of the "behavior specialist" in the morning and used throughout the day as needed (a hungry behavior specialist might even have a few from time to time). Likewise, aversive consequences were used with abandon in informal, impromptu, and spontaneous reactions to self-injurious, destructive, and inappropriate behaviors. Some staff members were urged to "be creative" in coming up with consequences. As a result, hot pepper sauces such as Tabasco and undiluted lemon juice might be seen in the jacket pockets of staff members who were on their way to work on "the behavior unit."

In the early 1970s, "the unit" was frequently a residential facility for developmentally disabled individuals who had moderate to severe mental retardation, some physical disabilities, and troublesome behaviors. It was most likely a former veterans' or tuberculosis (TB) hospital, which might house 300 to 1,500 "patients." Custodial care was the norm until "behavior mod" came along and offered dramatic treatment for severe behavior problems.

With no guidelines and essentially no restrictions, this "treatment" quickly drifted into flat-out abuse.

THE SUNLAND MIAMI SCANDAL

The Sunland Training Center in Miami became "ground zero" for an abuse investigation that rocked the state of Florida in 1972. The center had been plagued by high turnover rates since it opened in 1965, resulting in frequent understaffing and low-quality training. Surprisingly, the majority of students serving as "cottage parents" were college students. In 1969, the superintendent resigned under pressure from an investigation into "allegations of resident abuse." It seems that he confined two residents in a "cell improvised from a large trailer" (McAllister, 1972, p. 2). Then, in April 1971, the Florida Division of Mental Retardation and the Dade County Attorney's Office began an intensive investigation of resident abuse that concluded after a 6-month inquiry regarding allegations of "infrequent and isolated cases of abuse" (p. 2) and that the superintendent had dealt with the employees involved and taken appropriate disciplinary action. One of those professional employees, Dr. E., challenged his reassignment, and a grievance committee then uncovered what it considered to be a "highly explosive situation" involving resident abuse with the apparent knowledge and approval of top administrators. As a result, seven individuals were immediately suspended, including the superintendent, the director of Cottage Life, the staff psychologist, three cottage supervisors, and a cottage parent. Each was charged with "misfeasance, malfeasance, negligence, and contributing to the abuse of residents" (p. 4). Subsequent to this, Jack McAllister, the director of the State Health and Rehabilitative Services (HRS) Division of Retardation, formed a nine-member Blue Ribbon Panel "Resident Abuse Investigating Committee" composed of experts in retardation as well as an attorney, a social worker, a client advocate, and two behavior analysts (Dr. Jack May, Jr., and Dr. Todd Risley).

Interviews were set up with more than 70 individuals, including current staff members, former employees, residents, and relatives of residents (including one whose son died at Sunland Miami), with some interviews lasting as long as 10 hours. The committee also examined original logs, internal memoranda, a personal diary, and personnel records.

It seems that Dr. E., a psychologist who presented himself as an expert in behavior modification and joined the staff in 1971, had set up a truly ironically named program called the "Achievement Division" in three cottages, allegedly to study "some rather esoteric questions of statistical models for economic analysis" (McAllister, 1972, p. 15). Dr. E., over a period of the next year, established a "treatment" program that consisted of, or evolved into, abusive incidents, including the following: forced public masturbation (for residents caught masturbating), forced public homosexual acts (again for those caught in the act), forced washing of the mouth with soap (as punishment for lying, abusive language, or simply speaking at all), beatings with wooden paddle (10 "licks" for running away); and excessive use of restraints, including one resident who was restrained for more than 24 hours and another who was forced to sit in a bathtub for 2 days. Restraints were routinely used as punishment rather than an emergency method of preventing self-injury. As if this were not enough, the list of horrific, systematic abuses goes on: a male client required to wear women's underpants; excessive use of lengthy (e.g., 4-hour) seclusions in barren and unpadded rooms with no permission to leave to use the bathroom; public shaming by forcing a resident to wear a sign that

> Dr. E. established a "treatment" program that consisted of forced public masturbation, forced public homosexual acts, forced washing of the mouth with soap, beatings with a wooden paddle, and excessive use of restraints.

said "The Thief"; food or sleep withheld as a form of punishment; another resident forced to hold feces-stained underwear under his nose for 10 minutes as punishment for incontinence; and another resident forced to lay on urine-soaked sheets for repeated incontinence (pp. 10–11).

The "milieu" of the Achievement Division consisted of an utter lack of programmed activities, which resulted in "profound boredom and deterioration, unattractive surroundings, complete lack of privacy, public humiliation, nakedness …, and lack of any means of residents to express their grievances" (McAllister, 1972, p. 13). One resident died from dehydration, and another drowned in a nearby canal in his futile attempt to escape his cottage at Sunland Miami.

At first glance it might appear that such abuses would certainly have to be the work of a few frustrated, angry, poorly trained employees bent on sadistic acts. However, the investigation revealed the contrary: these revolting acts of abuse were the result of an

These revolting acts of abuse were the result of an attempt by Dr. E. to create a "superb behavior modification program."

attempt by Dr. E. to create a "superb behavior modification program" (McAllister, 1972, p. 14) using routine "behavior shaping devices" (p. 15). The committee's explanation was that this program "degenerated … into a bizarre, abusive, and ineffective system of punishment" (p. 17). In the Achievement Division, these procedures were systematically applied, condoned by supervisors and professional staff, and recorded in daily living unit logs. The procedures not only were used openly but also were, at least initially, well researched. A token program, for example, had been modeled after one first developed in Parsons, Kansas, by Dr. James Lent, a well-respected expert in behavioral treatment. One key ingredient was left out of this and other aspects of the Achievement Division: monitoring of individual resident behavior. Rather, the emphasis was on guidelines for treatment that gave the otherwise poorly trained employees a great deal of latitude in their reactions. The three guidelines were as follows: (1) emphasize "natural consequences of behavior"; (2) devise your own immediate response to problem behaviors that might crop up where no other instructions apply; and (3) do not threaten—if you verbalize a consequence to a resident, "follow through on every contingency."

The investigating committee was adamant in its observation that none of the cruel and abusive procedures employed in the Achievement Division had any basis in the behavior modification literature or "any other modern therapeutic or educational methodology." They went on to suggest that because the cottage where the abuses took place was totally isolated from outside monitoring it was entirely possible for "well meaning but poorly trained personnel" to try some mild form of these procedures and then gradually escalate to the bizarre applications that were ultimately achieved. Each instance was, as noted previously, in a daily log book, and, given no corrective action or response, a cottage parent would naturally assume tacit approval and then perhaps employ a "slightly more extreme form" of the procedure. "In this way, quite extreme procedures evolved in gradual steps from spontaneous initiation of less extreme procedures by the cottage staff, until ... a pattern had been established of dealing with recurrent problems by escalating the intensity of whatever procedures happened to be in use for a particular resident" (pp. 17–18). This natural tendency toward "behavior drift" on the part of the staff is certainly not uncommon in residential treatment facilities. In the case of Sunland Miami, it was facilitated by a nearly total lack of monitoring by upper-level management. The written policies at Sunland Miami clearly prohibited abusive practices, but there was no evidence that these were "forcefully communicated" to employees, and recall that the facility suffered from chronic turnover of staff so that ongoing staff training was superficial at best.

Another concern of the investigating committee had to do with the training and credentials of Dr. E. As it turns out, he had recently graduated with his doctoral degree from the University of Florida and then had completed some postdoctoral work at Johns Hopkins University. He claimed to have worked with some of the biggest names in the field. However, when the committee contacted them, these eminent researchers "vaguely remembered a brash young man who visited their laboratories on several occasions," but none would claim him as his student (McAllister, 1972, p. 19). It must be remembered that Dr. E. was trained in the late 1960s when the field was in its infancy, and it appeared that the sky was the limit as far as behavior modification was concerned. The *Journal of Applied Behavior Analysis,* the professional journal of behavior analysis, had first been published only in 1968, so there was very little research on the application of behavior principles and there was no code of ethics for behavioral researchers or practitioners.

RECOMMENDATIONS OF THE BLUE RIBBON COMMITTEE

The investigating committee took on itself the additional responsibility of making recommendations to hopefully prevent any future systematic abuses in the name of behavior modification in the state of Florida. These included strong support for a statewide advocacy program in which staff members would be allowed to make unannounced visits to residential institutions and to collect information from key personnel as well as residents, parents, staff, and concerned citizens. In addition, the committee recommended professional peer review of all behavior programs to ensure that treatment was derived from the literature and that no procedures would be used that were considered "experimental." Experimental programs would come under standard review for human experimentation in the HRS Division of Retardation. Other recommendations of the committee included the following: (1) the prohibition of certain bizarre examples of punishment; and (2) abandoning seclusion in favor of "positive and appropriate 'time out' techniques" (McAllister, 1972, p. 31).

FOLLOW-UP

In most cases, a report such as that produced by the Blue Ribbon Committee would simply find its way to the shelves of state bureaucrats and languish with no lasting effect. Such was not the case in Florida. The Florida Association for Retarded Children (now the Association for Retarded Citizens of Florida) took up the cause of humane treatment and ultimately endorsed the notion of supporting data-based, behavioral treatment,

> Charles Cox instituted reforms including setting up both statewide and local peer review committees for behavior modification programming in facilities throughout Florida.

using strict guidelines, under close supervision by properly trained professionals. The Division of Retardation, under the guidance of Charles Cox, instituted reforms including setting up both statewide and local peer review committees for behavior modification programming in facilities throughout Florida. The Statewide Peer Review Committee for Behavior Modification (PRC) then established a set of guidelines for the use of behavioral procedures, which were subsequently adopted by the National Association for Retarded Citizens (MR Research, 1976) and by the Florida Division of Retardation as Health and Rehabilitative Services Manual (HRSM) 160–4 (May et al., 1976). The state-funded PRC proceeded to make visits to institutions around the state over the next several years educating staff members about the guidelines and making recommendations for more ethical treatment. By 1980, the PRC reached a consensus that it was time to encourage all the institutions, group homes, and smaller residential facilities to begin networking with one another and to begin to bring some sense of professionalism to behavior analysis in Florida. The "First Florida Work Session on Behavior Analysis in Retardation" was held in September 1980 and drew nearly 300 administrators, treatment specialists, behavior analysts, and direct care staff to the 2-day conference held in Orlando. At this historic conference, a meeting was held to organize an official state association. The first annual conference of the Florida Association for Behavior Analysis (FABA) was held in 1981, again in Orlando. None other than B. F. Skinner was the keynote speaker. The formation of FABA marked a turning point in behavior analysis, not only in Florida but also in the rest of the country. It was now possible to set high expectations for behavioral treatment because leaders in the field were routinely being brought to state conference to present their latest applied behavioral research, and practitioners had an opportunity to see firsthand what others were doing in other parts of the country to solve some of the most intractable behavior problems of the day. Administrators from state government and private facilities were able to see that behavior analysis was not just some local phenomenon but rather was an approach to treatment that was legitimate, effective, and humane. The PRC, in conjunction with FABA, began the process of certifying behavior analysts via a testing program sponsored by the Division of Retardation. In 1988, FABA membership adopted the FABA Code of Ethics, the first state association to do so.

THE SUNLAND MIAMI LEGACY

In retrospect, the horrific abuses at Sunland Miami in the early 1970s were probably necessary for half-baked, unregulated behavior modification to evolve into professional, respected, behavior analysis. Without the abuses, there would have been no Blue Ribbon Committee formed to think seriously about how to protect developmentally disabled individuals from

The pain and suffering of the individuals with developmental disabilities involved in the abuses amplified the need to think clearly about the ethics of treatment.

systematic abuse of behavioral procedures. The headlines resulted in the intense scrutiny of a treatment mode that was in its infancy and that needed guidelines and oversight. The pain and suffering of the individuals with developmental disabilities involved in the abuses amplified the need to think clearly about the ethics of treatment. Although it would have been easier to prohibit behavior modification altogether, the Blue Ribbon Committee was convinced by its two behavioral advocates, Drs. May and Risley, that a better alternative was to establish strict guidelines for treatment and to set up an infrastructure for oversight involving community citizens who would bring their values, common sense, and good judgment to evaluate behavioral treatment strategies on an ongoing basis. The notion of oversight by both human rights and peer review committees gave teeth to the public appraisal of behavior analysis. These actions, plus the development of a state-endorsed mechanism of certification, the evolution of a strong state professional organization, and its promotion of a Code of Ethics for Behavior Analysts, put in place all the necessary elements of control and management to prevent future abuses. And ethics, after all, is concerned primarily with the edict to "do no harm." In the Florida case, we saw how great harm could be done by well-meaning people and that when appropriate, comprehensive strategies were adopted, abuse was prevented. Although ethics is usually seen as an individual professional engaging in responsible behavior of his or her own volition, the Florida case suggests that responsible conduct can be encouraged by other means as well. It is certainly painful and embarrassing for a profession to undergo such public scrutiny and scorn, but it was clearly warranted in this case. Indeed, it is hard to imagine such powerful procedures as behavioral treatments being used consistently across the board in the absence of such obvious forms of oversight and control.

It is also clear that, even given these mechanisms, the behavior analyst faces numerous questions every day about the appropriateness of treatment decisions. What is fair? What is right? Am I qualified to administer this treatment? Can I do no harm? Am I taking enough data? Am I interpreting it correctly? Would my client be better off with no treatment? It is the purpose of this volume to try to elucidate the current Behavior Analyst Certification Board (BACB) Guidelines for Responsible Conduct to assist the behavior analyst in making right choices on a daily basis.

2

Core Ethical Principles

Behavior analysts are part of a culture of caring individuals who seek to improve the lives of others. They carry with them a set of core ethical values that are derived from thousands of years of compassionate practices dating back to the Greeks. (Ethics comes from the Greek word *ethos,* meaning moral character.) As a field, ethics can be divided into three divisions: normative ethics, meta-ethics, and practical ethics. Although it is the purpose of this volume to focus on practical ethics in behavior analysis, we first need to discuss some basic moral principles that underlie our culture at large. These core ethical principles guide our everyday lives and play a significant role in basic decision making in the practice of our profession.

In 1998 in their book *Ethics in Psychology,* Koocher and Keith-Spiegel outlined nine ethical principles for psychologists. These principles can be applied to ethics in many areas, including psychology, the teaching of children, and the training of animals. Koocher and Keith-Spiegel's nine core ethical principles are so basic, yet often go unstated, that we listed them, following, with explanations of how they relate to behavior analysis.

DO NO HARM

The expression "First, do no harm" is usually attributed to Hippocrates, a Greek physician in the fourth century B.C. Commonly written as "Do no harm," the phrase is typically referred to as appearing in the Hippocratic Oath that is taken by physicians. However, there is some debate on this issue (Eliot, 1910). Hippocrates did say, "As to diseases, make a habit of two things—to help, or at least to do no harm." The Hippocratic Oath states, "I will follow that system of regimen which, according to my ability and judgment, I consider for the benefit of my patients, and abstain from whatever is deleterious and mischievous."

Although no behavior analyst would knowingly do harm, it can come in subtle forms that need to be attended to carefully. One obvious example is that of a behavior analyst who is practicing outside his or her area of expertise.

> A behavior analyst who has been trained to work with adolescents accepts the case of a preschool child who is having severe tantrums at school. His initial impression is that the child is "noncompliant," and he prepares a behavior program based on extinction of tantrum behaviors plus a DRO for compliance.

Another form of "harm" might come in a more subtle case of the behavior analyst who does not develop a responsible data collection system and misses the significance of a behavior.

> A Board Certified Behavior Analyst (BCBA) consulting with a group home receives a referral for a young developmentally disabled man who is described as engaging in "self-stimulatory behavior." He asks the staff to begin data collection, which involves counting the number of incidents per day. Two weeks later he reviews the baseline data and tells staff members that they do not have a significant problem and not to worry because the behavior is occurring only two to three

times per day. On his next visit, the BCBA inquires about the client only to discover that he was taken to the emergency room with lacerations to his scalp requiring six stitches. A review of the case determined that the BCBA failed to inquire about the severity of the behaviors and failed to ask the nursing staff to perform skin ratings.

Behavior analysts often work with staff members who are not at all well versed in human behavior and who will not necessarily think to offer all the information necessary to operate ethically.

Herman was referred for his combative behavior when being guided toward the shower each morning in a residential facility for the developmentally disabled. He was reluctant to take a shower and showed his displeasure by pushing and shoving the staff and trying to escape. This resulted in at least two staff injuries, one in the shower itself that left the training instructor unable to work for 2 weeks. Clearly, this was a case of aggressive behavior that needed treatment. In light of the danger involved, the staff strongly recommended restraint as an immediate consequence for Herman's refusal to cooperate with his morning bathing routine. This program was nearly implemented when the behavior analyst inquired about how long this problem had been going on. The answer turned the treatment in a totally different direction. It turned out that Herman had previously been allowed to take his bath at night and was assisted by an aide who helped him by filling up the tub, getting just the right temperature for the water, providing his favorite towel, and in general recreating the conditions his mother used at home. When this staff member quit the facility, it was determined that Herman should take a shower in the morning, which, as we came to understand, he detested. Although it was possible that a behavior program could have been written to essentially force Herman to take a morning shower, it was determined that this would cause more harm than good. The ethical solution for this case was to train another staff member to reinstate Herman's evening bath.

RESPECTING AUTONOMY

To respect one's autonomy means to promote his or her independence or self-sufficiency. Clearly, the basic procedures of behavior analysis are designed to do just this: prompting, shaping, chaining, fading and the use of conditioned reinforcers, token economies, and prosthetic environments are all designed to change behavior in such a way that the person can deliver his or her own reinforcers rather than depend on a mediator. Clashes can occur, of course, when it is determined that someone actually prefers to keep another under his or her control. This can produce very difficult situations for the behavior analyst who is often hired by that person.

> Molly was a cute, dimple-cheeked 4-year-old with language delay. She was receiving one-on-one therapy each day from a certified assistant behavior analyst. The therapist was making progress in teaching Molly basic sounds for common objects. The mother, who was clearly not happy with the treatment, confronted her. It seems that Molly now knew the names for milk, cookie, snack, draw, play with blocks, and a few other words and was beginning to generalize these requests to the mother. The mother's position was that Molly would get snacks only when she wanted her to have them. By learning to request these items, the mother was afraid that Molly would become pushy and demanding. "The next thing you know she will think that she can just get in the fridge and get her own drinks," said Molly's mother.

Autonomy can also bring risks that cannot always be foreseen. A behavior analyst who advocates for a person to acquire a skill that will provide greater independence has to recognize that this may put the person in harm's way.

> Marie was a geriatric patient in a nursing home. She spent most of her day in bed refusing to participate in most activities. The goal of the facility was to encourage patients to ambulate independently when possible and to attend the wide variety of social and cultural events that were offered. The behavior

analyst reviewed Marie's case and determined that she was capable of walking with assistance but got more reinforcement from refusing. After determining Marie's reinforcers, the behavior analyst arranged to make them contingent on first walking with assistance and then, after approval of the physical therapist, walking on her own. The case was considered a success until Marie fell and broke a hip. Marie's family considered the behavior analyst responsible for this accident. One family member said, "Why didn't you just leave well enough alone? She preferred to stay in bed, but you had to meddle in her affairs."

Behavior analysts often work in educational or business settings where they consult in the areas of classroom management or performance management. In these settings, the notion of autonomy can also produce some ethical issues. For example, teachers are frequently reinforced by the students who stay in their seats and follow instructions; business managers and supervisors may desire that their employees simply "follow directions" and do what they are told.

Rory supervised 15 employees in a small machine shop that fabricated specialized exhaust systems for racing cars. His employees were well paid and creative in coming up with solutions for the increasingly complex demands of their elite customers. After attending a conference on performance management, Rory contacted one of the speakers and asked for help. What he wanted was for his employees to follow the manual that he had written a few years earlier. "These young guys think they know it all. They are coming up with completely new designs and telling our customers that my methods are outdated."

BENEFITING OTHERS

It almost goes without saying that the primary role of behavior analysts is to benefit others in whatever setting or situation they may work. This principle can often put the behavior analyst at odds with other professionals and requires frequent checks on "who is the client?" in any given situation.

> *Tamara was referred to the behavior analyst by her teacher. Tamara's problem was that she caused frequent disturbances in the classroom. Her teacher, Ms. Harris, provided a data sheet showing date, time, and type of disturbance going back 2 weeks. Ms. Harris requested help in setting up a time-out booth for Tamara. Although Ms. Harris was the person requesting help, the behavior analyst quickly determined that Tamara was her client, and she decided to take her own data. This required several visits to the school, which was quite a distance from the rest of the behavior analyst's cases. Tamara benefited from this extra effort on the part of the behavior analyst because it was discovered that her classroom disturbances were due to a hearing problem and not "willfulness," as alleged by the teacher.*

BEING JUST

This principle is very basic and is directly derived from the "Golden Rule" or the Ethic of Reciprocity (Ontario Consultants on Religious Tolerance, 2004). Being just means that you should treat others as you would like to be treated. This has special meaning in behavior analysis because there is some potential for the use of uncomfortable stimuli or stressful contingencies in treatment. A further refinement of the ethic might ask, "How would I like my mother or my child to be treated in similar circumstances?" Questions of just treatment arise often in behavior analysis because there is often so little known about the origins of a particular behavior, and functional relationships often assumed are yet to be determined.

> *A senior behavior analyst was asked to consult on the case of a client who was engaging in persistent self-injurious behavior—arm and face scratching. Ignoring had been*

tried without effect, and a fairly dense DRO with block-
ing was not proving effective either. The behavior analyst
was puzzled but asked himself, "How would I like to be
treated?" and realized that he had been treated for just
such a behavior about 2 years prior. He had been diag-
nosed with a case of hives (his scratching looked a lot like
self-injurious behavior [SIB]) and felt fortunate to receive
medication rather than a DRO plus blocking. The behavior
analysts' attention then turned to medical diagnosis of the
client's SIB.

BEING TRUTHFUL

Well-respected professionals attain their reputation based on the trust placed in them by others. Those who are loyal, trustworthy, and honest are sought out as dependable and reliable sources of wise counsel and effective, ethical treatment. Being truthful and honest with clients, colleagues, and administrators provides the basis for long-term relationships that make for a successful career.

Dr. B., an experienced behavior analyst, was consulting at a
residential facility for clients with behavior problems that were
severe enough to prevent them from living at home or in the
community. One day, as soon as Dr. B. arrived at the facility,
the administrator approached him and began congratulating
him on successfully treating one of the most intransient cases
in the facility. After discussions with the behavior specialist
and Board Certified assistant Behavior Analyst (BCaBA), Dr. B.
met with the administrator to explain that no credit was due.
In fact, baseline was still under way, and the treatment plan
had not yet been executed.

ACCORDING DIGNITY

Many of the clients we serve are not able to effectively represent themselves. They may be nonverbal or simply unable to get some-one to listen to them. If their wishes are unknown and they are unable to make choices, they may become depressed and present behavior problems that come to the attention of a behavior analyst. Although it is not a "behavioral" term, low self-esteem seems to capture the essence of a person who has not been afforded dignity. As behavior analysts, our job is to make sure that every client is treated with dignity and respect. Behaviorally this means that we would work with clients on acquisition skills to make sure that they are able to voice or signal their needs to those around them. A good behavior analyst would also push for all staff to undergo the training necessary to learn to communicate with the clients who are nonverbal. These persons should be given choices throughout the day and allowed to exercise their preferences for food, clothing, roommate, activities, and living conditions. Other more subtle ways of according dignity involve the language we use to talk to or about clients. If you want to know how Bertha feels about her treatment plan, you could ask the staff or family, or you could ask Bertha herself. Clients should be addressed by name in a friendly fashion using eye contact and a pleasant smile—the kind of treatment you expect when you are receiving services from someone in your business community.

> *Thomas was a nonverbal, developmentally disabled young man who was referred for his aggressive and sometimes self-injurious behavior. The incidents seemed to occur in the afternoon when he returned to his group home from his sheltered work setting. It often took two staff members to drag him from his bedroom to the living room where there were group activities. Before being taken to the living room, he had to be dressed because he was frequently found sitting in his underwear on the floor rocking and listening to music on his headset. After some considerable investigation and discussion with staff, family, nurses, and social workers, the behavior analyst prevailed in his position that Thomas should be given his choice of activities in the afternoon. He was to be offered the option of joining the group each day, but if he chose to stay in his room and listen to music his choice was respected. Given this*

resolution there was no need to develop a behavior treatment program because the aggressive and self-injurious behavior ceased to exist.

TREATING OTHERS WITH CARING AND COMPASSION

Many of the previous ethical principles relate to this ethical principle. If, as a behavior analyst, you respect the autonomy of clients, work to benefit them, and devise programs that accord them dignity, you will automatically be treating clients with care and compassion. This value also suggests not only that clients be given choices but also that interpersonal relationships should demonstrate sympathy and concern.

Terrence hated getting up in the morning to go to work. He would fight with staff members, throw shoes at them, and pull the bed covers up over his head. One staff member who reported no such reaction when she was on duty described her method of getting Terrence up. "Basically I try to treat him like my dad who lives with us. He's on medication just like Terrence, and I know that it makes him groggy in the morning. So, I have to show some patience with Terrence. What I do is I go in his room and say in my sweetest voice, 'Terrence, honey, it's almost time to get up,' and I open the curtains about halfway and then leave his room. Then I come back about 15 minutes later and open the curtains the rest of the way and go to Terrence and gently rub his arm and say, 'How you doin', Terrence? It's almost time to get up. We've got some fresh coffee brewing, and I've set out your favorite work clothes. I'll be back to get you in a few minutes.' Then about 15 minutes after that I come back, and if he's not up I turn on his clock radio and say, 'Terrence, sweetheart, it's time to get up now. Let me help you get dressed.' I know this takes extra effort. But this is the way I would like to be treated, and it's the way I treat my dad so I don't mind. And it works. By the time I turn on the radio he's swinging out of bed and has that little half-grin on his face that says, 'Thank you for being so understanding.'"

PURSUIT OF EXCELLENCE

Behavior analysis is a rapidly growing field. Behavior analysts need to stay current with new developments as well as constantly updated rules and regulations. Excellence in this profession means being aware of the latest research in the field and in your specialty and incorporating the most up-to-date methods and procedures in your practice of behavior analysis. It is a given that you will subscribe to the key journals in the field and attend your state association meeting as well as the annual meeting of the Association for Behavior Analysis. To stay at the top of your game, you may also want to watch for specialty workshops offered in your area or consider taking graduate seminars offered at a nearby university. The Behavior Analysis Certification Board (BACB) requires BCBAs to acquire continuing education each year. Continuing education hours required by the BACB are a minimum, and the behavior analyst who wants to maintain excellence will set aside 2 to 4 hours each week to read the latest journals and newest reference works.

> *Nora received her master's degree in psychology with a specialty in applied behavior analysis in the mid-1990s. Since then she has gone to a few conferences but does not find them exciting enough to maintain her interest. She was embarrassed recently at a local peer review meeting when a newly minted PhD began questioning her proposed treatment plans. She had not been aware of new standards for functional assessment and was surprised to find that she was so out of touch.*

ACCEPTING RESPONSIBILITY

Behavior analysts have an awesome responsibility in analyzing the behavior of a client and then making recommendations to implement a program to change a target behavior. In pursuing excellence, you will want to make sure that everything you have done in making your diagnosis is of the highest standard. By presenting your conclusions to colleagues and other professionals, you are responsible for making sure that the proposed treatment is proper, justified, and worthy of consideration. And, when your treatments fail, you must take responsibility, accepting blame and making corrections to satisfy the consumer and other related parties. Behavior analysts who are better at making excuses than analyzing behavior do the profession no favor. Those who do not take the time to research the problem they are working on and arrive at hasty conclusions will find themselves constantly in the line of fire.

> *Clara had been on her job for only 3 months when she found herself at the center of a serious discussion at an Individual Education Plan (IEP) meeting at one of the schools where she worked. She developed a token economy for one of the teachers to use with a student. The program involved the teacher giving the student points for quietly doing her work. Unfortunately, Clara failed to take into account the issue of quality when writing up the child's program, and now the teacher was very irritated at Clara, claiming that "she has created a monster who cares nothing for the work and just scribbles away on her papers so that she can get her stupid points." Rather than point out the rather obvious fact that the teacher could have easily made the decision to reward only quality work, Clara accepted responsibility, apologized to the teacher, and rewrote the program.*

Behavior analysts do not begin their ethical training in graduate school. A person's ethical training begins long before the college years. Developmental psychologists would argue that one's ethical standards are fairly well set by the time a child ventures into junior high school. Personal ethical situations confront people every day, and there is probably a tendency to generalize from these everyday occurrences to professional life. Persons who advance their personal interests above others, avoid conflict, and do not take responsibility for their actions are unlikely to immediately take account of ethical standards in their profession. It is for these reasons that a Code of Responsible Conduct has been developed for behavior analysts. It is our hope that by reviewing these principles and examining the code carefully, behavior analysts will come to see the value in adopting a set of responsible behaviors that will advance the profession and provide respect to this important new field of psychology.

3

What Makes Behavior Analysis Unique?

In many respects, the practice of behavior analysis is unique compared with those of the other helping professions. Although other fields may represent that they base their treatment methods on science, behavior analysis is the only human services approach to actually take the next step and require that the treatment itself use these methods. This is possible because the methodology is founded on single-subject design research, where individuals serve as their own control (Bailey & Burch, 2002). In research studies, this means that baseline data are collected for each participant and that interventions are applied and evaluated for each person. This strategy is maintained in the therapy that is derived from the science; that is, each client is evaluated individually, custom-tailored measurement is designed for each person based on the referred behavior, and online evaluation of the intervention is made continuously until the case is terminated. To complicate matters, the field of behavior analysis encompasses a very wide range of clients (some call them *consumers*) that have to be served ranging from very low-functioning, multiply physically handicapped, developmentally disabled individuals to high-functioning children with autism and adults, to corporate supervisors, managers, and chief executive officers. There are perhaps a dozen specialized journals that publish research in the various areas of behavior analysis. Ethical behavior analysts have to keep up with the latest developments in their specialty to meet the expectation of "excellence" embodied in the Behavior Analyst Certification Board (BACB) Guidelines.

In addition to the methodology requirement, there is a further commitment to the science in that there must be a scientific basis for the treatment itself. Behavior analysts require of themselves and their profession

> Although "evidence-based treatment" has recently become a catch phrase in psychology and medicine, it has been standard procedure in behavior analysis for over 40 years.

that practitioners keep up with the research literature and apply procedures that only have first been proven effective in the laboratory or other controlled settings. Furthermore, all modifications in treatment must be based on the online data collected as the treatment progresses. Although "evidence-based treatment" has recently become a catch phrase in psychology and medicine, it has been standard procedure in behavior analysis for over 40 years. To be included in the library of possible procedures, a study must meet rigorous peer-review standards of excellence. Perhaps the most rigorous standard is that a clear demonstration of experimental control must be shown; simple correlations need not apply. Behavior analyst practitioners rely on this solid foundation for their treatment ideas and need a good deal of confidence that a given procedure will, in fact, produce a specific outcome. Some considerable degree of judgment is required, however, in adapting each procedure to each client. A review of the literature may not reveal an intervention with exactly the population or client characteristics that are being treated at the time, or a treatment may seem appropriate but some features may need to be changed, such as the type of reinforcer or schedule of reinforcement.

Another aspect of treatment that makes behavior analysis unique is that, to a great extent, treatments are carried out by others, often paraprofessionals, under the supervision of a certified professional. For example, Board Certified Behavior Analysts

(BCBAs) may be working with caregivers, parents, or teachers, for example, in the treatment of a child behavior problem. The BCBA is responsible for determining the seriousness of the behavior, establishing baseline data collection, doing the necessary background work, and carrying out a functional assessment. Once the BCBA has determined what the controlling variables are, a treatment plan is designed, approved, and put in place. This latter step may involve the behavior analyst demonstrating to the rest of the "team" how a procedure should be carried out and then carefully training them to do so reliably and with precision. The behavior analyst is bound by the ethics code to use this approach; to do less than thorough training or to allow unqualified persons to use the procedures would essentially be unethical.

Traditionally the clinical psychologist carries out therapy in a clinic setting, one on one with patients who self-select for treatment. When the session is over, the "patient" leaves the clinic under his or her own steam and drives home or goes to work. With the vast majority of behavior analysis treatment, the work is done in the setting where the behavior problem actually occurs. Our clients are likely to have been referred by someone else for treatment, and often the behavior is severe enough that

> This combination of working in real-world settings, with severe behavior problems, certainly makes behavior analysis unique and presents a special set of ethical problems.

the person must be under some sort of supervision, possibly in a residential setting. This combination of working in real-world settings, with severe behavior problems, certainly makes behavior analysis unique and presents a special set of ethical problems.

First, because the person being treated was likely referred by someone else, we need to be especially careful to respect the rights of the client. We need to make sure that the referring person, often referred to as "the third party," has not made the referral for treatment based on mere convenience. It could happen, for example, in a residential setting, that staff members might refer a client for treatment of screaming or running away. The behavior analyst must be careful to respect the rights of the client who was referred because that individual may be yelling and screaming or trying to leave the setting because he or she is being mistreated in some way. To establish a program to simply suppress the screaming or stop the running would be unethical.

Second, working in full view of other professionals, staff, and administrators can present additional ethical dilemmas. Special care must be taken not to stigmatize the client with obtrusive observation systems or methods of data collection, yet the data need to be reliable and valid. Walking this fine line presents the ethical behavior analyst with challenges every working day.

Finally, the behavior analyst is often found working with vulnerable populations who are unable to protect themselves from harm. In contrast to the clinical patient who drives home after a 1-hour talk-therapy session, our clients often cannot speak or ambulate. The ethical behavior analyst must do everything possible to make sure that the client's rights are not violated in the process of receiving treatment. A 25-year-old person who is developmentally disabled, nonverbal, and nonambulatory who engages in self-injurious behavior (SIB) still has a right to privacy, a right to be treated with dignity and respect, and a right to effective treatment, for example. The individual cannot simply be restrained, isolated, or overmedicated to stop the behavior. Analyzing the behavior while trying to protect the client's rights is a tall order but is required by our code of ethics. Although in this example the referral involved only a request that a behavior be reduced (SIB), the behavior analyst has an additional requirement to determine how greater independence might be given to the client to possibly prevent future occurrences of the challenging behavior. The aforementioned developmentally disabled adult may have been screaming because he was in pain or because he was trying to signal that he was thirsty or needed attention. The ethical behavior analyst is required to carry out a functional assessment to determine such possible causes and to develop appropriate interventions, such as teaching a less dangerous method of signaling staff of his needs. Clearly, an intervention of this nature is more ethically appropriate than the use of a punisher, such as time-out, to reduce the referred behavior of screaming.

Behavior analysts are often called in to work on cases where the behavior is not only quite severe but also amazingly complex in nature. As determinists, we assume that the behavior we see has a causal basis, and we believe that doing a functional analysis will help yield information that will produce valid, ethical treatments. However, arriving at the point of treatment involves myriad variables that are difficult to access. The SIB alluded to earlier may have had its cause in some medical condition that occurred years earlier (e.g., the client had a chronic sore that went untreated), but the variables that maintain the behavior might be completely different (e.g., staff attention). Other complexities might include the occurrence of conditioned reinforcers or complex schedules of intermittent reinforcement, which are operating to maintain the behavior, establishing operations that provide motivation from time to time, or discriminative stimuli and setting events, which also set the occasion for the behavior. The ethical behavior analyst must examine all these possibilities and determine which are most salient in arriving at a treatment approach.

> Behavior analysts are often called in to work on cases where the behavior is not only quite severe but also amazingly complex in nature.

One hallmark of behavior analysis from its earliest days remains the role of consequences in modifying behavior. In the beginning, although most other helping professions relied on counseling or "talk therapy" to change attitudes or feelings, "behavior modification" put an emphasis on consequences, often aversive consequences. And, combined with a lack of clear ethical or professional guidelines, some tragic results tarnished the field and gave us a reputation that was difficult to shake. Many of the advances in ethical controls for behavior analysis came out of this era.

Aversive consequences would currently be considered "more restrictive" procedures and would be recommended only after reinforcement procedures had been tried, and if aversive procedures were to be used the client or his or her surrogate would have to give approval. It is further recommended that, if any punishment procedures are used, reinforcement for alternative behaviors is also included in the program. Clearly, ethical behavior analysts have their work cut out for them on the use of consequences. Staying on the side of positive reinforcement must be balanced with the client's right to effective treatment.

One final way that behavior analysis is unique involves the way behavior analysts are employed. Currently we are likely to be working for either a state agency or a private consulting firm: the employer is a third party. When the service is paid directly by the patient, presumably there is sufficient countercontrol to prevent abuses, to ensure that the service meets the needs of the consumer, and to prevent the sort of harm that was seen in the Sunland Miami case. Agencies not only must be diligent in hiring qualified behavior analysts but also must assume responsibility for their actions on a day-to-day basis. Whether state or private, some entity or organization has to keep tabs on their professionals' performance, to assume a monitoring function, and to exert some form of quality assurance.

> The responsibility for ethical conduct goes to the behavior analyst, who must uphold the highest standards to avoid harming clients or tarnishing the reputation of the employer.

This can be a tall order when we live in a culture where role models, from college coaches to American presidents, are regularly accused of unethical conduct. In practice, this means that the employer must be fully aware of the Guidelines for Responsible Conduct. The employer must be prepared to keep tabs on the activities of the behavior analysts who are working in the field under very little, if any, supervision. Here again, the responsibility for ethical conduct goes to the behavior analyst, who must uphold the highest standards to avoid harming clients or tarnishing the reputation of the employer. Not often mentioned is the problem of the employer, who may push the behavior analyst to engage in unseemly or possibly unethical behavior. In this instance, the behavior analyst's pledge to support the Guidelines must supersede the desire of the employer to cut corners or increase profits. Myriad complexities that are encountered when the behavior analyst works for a third party presents perhaps the most difficult challenges of all, because to deny an employer's request may result in termination. This is clearly a high price to pay for ethical conduct.

The behavior analyst has the potential to do great good for clients and society by analyzing complex problematic behaviors, finding humane and effective solutions, implementing programs that work, and ensuring the least restrictive, most effective evidence-based treatments possible given limited resources. It is the goal of the BACB Guidelines to ensure that this outcome is consistently achieved while protecting clients' rights at all times.

4

Most Frequent Ethical Problems

Life is hectic for graduate students who are finishing up the last of their courses, taking tests for their classes, and preparing for the Behavior Analysis Certification Board (BACB) comprehensive exam. Looking forward to commencement and the next phase of their professional lives, many have questions about what they are likely to encounter in their first jobs. Eager and ready to take on new challenges, they often ask, "What's it like out there?"

There do not appear to have been any official, systematic surveys of behavioral practitioners to determine the most frequently occurring ethical problems, but as a result of conducting ethics workshops we have some idea of the ethical concerns facing practitioners. After conducting workshops from New York to California over a 5-year period, we asked participants to describe ethical problems for which they needed help resolving in their setting. Participants wrote their scenarios for us before the workshops began and they had received ethics training. We gathered 500 scenarios and sorted them according to the item of the BACB Guidelines to which they best related. While this was not a scientific study, it provided a quick snapshot of the issues and concerns faced by practitioners across the country. We believe the scenarios collected over 5 years in multiple states show the most significant ethical concerns and problems that we face as a profession.

RIGHT TO EFFECTIVE TREATMENT (2.10B)

By a wide margin, the most frequently submitted concern was with our clients' right to effective treatment. The right to effective treatment can be compromised in a number of ways, which participants wrote about in some detail.

Funding

Practitioners expressed considerable concern over the lack of funding to provide effective treatment. They complained that administrators did not want to pay for Association of Behavior Analysis (ABA) treatment even though the money was available, and they felt helpless to do anything about this. In many cases they were aware that the funding was simply not available in their district so that the administrator had little choice. Finally, as many professionals working with children on the autism spectrum are fully aware, most insurance companies are not reimbursing for ABA services. In all these cases, the right to effective treatment is hollow when funds are not available.

Data Taking and Data Faking

We rely on data collection to determine if our methods are working, and it becomes a stumbling block if a parent or teacher refuses. "I just don't have time for that" is a familiar refrain. Practitioners also run into other professionals who say they "do not believe that data are the answer" and prefer to use their own judgments about treatment outcomes. If these nonbehavioral professionals are in leadership positions, they often get their way. A number of participants mentioned the problem of someone in the setting faking the data that were then presented to the group as valid.

Alternative Nonevidence-Based Treatments Are Preferred

"Choice" is an important factor in treatment, and many parents do not feel that they are comfortable putting all their eggs in one ABA basket. There is just something about special diets, hugging, or sensory stimulation that appeals to them, and no amount of rational conversation seems to make a difference. Our practitioners find this frustrating, particularly when alternative treatments take a lot of time and prevent the effective implementation of behavioral services.

Competing Lines of Authority

In some settings, the BCBA is operating as a member of a treatment team but a psychiatrist is essentially in charge. Our participants inform us that this can completely undermine the "right to treatment" since the authority's position is that he is in charge of treatment and the treatment will be medication.

RESPONSIBILITY TO RECOMMEND SCIENTIFICALLY SUPPORTED AND MOST EFFECTIVE TREATMENTS (2.10A)

The second most frequently cited area of ethical concern relates to the behavior analyst's responsibility to recommend scientifically supported treatments. As the number of children receiving services for autism has continued to expand, so have the number and types of alternative treatments.

Choice

So why do parents and professionals buy into unvalidated approaches? "Choice" appears to be one reason. Parents want to feel that they are doing the best they possibly can for their children, and they find it hard to believe that there is only one valid approach. Strong recommendations that they commit to one therapeutic approach seems wrong to them, especially if they are hearing from another parent that chiropractic adjustments or megavitamins worked for her child. This is compounded by pronouncements from celebrities such as the high-profile former *Playboy Playmate* who successfully transformed herself into a game show host and then "pseudo scientist" who says, "Try

Everything." One participant expressed the attitude this way: "If you try everything, something is bound to work. Supporting multiple approaches seems like the best bet for a desperate parent with little background in science. That parent wants hope." Some parents, our participants reported, like variety and want to use multiple approaches because they get bored. Others seem to think treatment approaches are like movie or restaurant reviews—it doesn't hurt to try a new movie or restaurant, so why not try every new thing that comes along in the therapy world?

Competing Professions and Their Theories

On a cloudy afternoon toward the end of a 6-hour workshop in the southeast, a clinical psychologist who was also a BCBA described her aggravation in dealing with therapists from other related areas. As she explained, "The background for some fields of study may be oriented toward certain treatments, such as occupational therapists recommending sensory integration or a physical therapist requesting trampoline time as part of the treatment. Some of these therapists have strong opinions about how exercise is important and jumping on a trampoline can build balance and muscles. They have no data to show this will reduce maladaptive behaviors, but they advocate sensory integration as the primary therapy."

BEHAVIOR ANALYSTS ASSESSMENTS ARE SUFFICIENT TO PROVIDE APPROPRIATE SUBSTANTIATION FOR THEIR FINDINGS (3.0A)

The need for proper use of assessments was the third most frequently identified Guideline item mentioned in our informal survey. Behavior analysts make decisions based on data, not opinion, or secondhand anecdotes. BACBs and Board Certified Association Behavior Analysts (BCaBAs) were given strong feedback by other participants in the workshop discussions for indicating in role plays and written scenarios that they had not done sufficient assessments before moving ahead with a treatment. We are led to believe from this input that it is not uncommon for behavior analysts to start an intervention without conducting any assessment whatsoever. Another complaint was about behavior analysts who developed their recommendations without ever observing the client. One scenario described a behavior analyst in the school system who routinely referred children to other special classrooms to relieve the teacher of problem children.

DUAL RELATIONSHIPS AND CONFLICTS OF INTEREST (1.06A,B)

Dual relationships (in which a therapist interacts with a client in any capacity beyond the role as a therapist) were the fourth most frequent area of concern for behavior analysis practitioners who attended our ethics workshops. Behavior analysts recounted story after story of being drawn into dual relationships by innocent offers of gifts, drinks, or snacks. Most denied that it impaired their objectivity; however, during discussions it was clear they felt a *quid pro quo* had been established after a while where they felt they "needed to cut the family some slack" on billing or comply with their requests regarding the continued requirement for services.

Most behavior analysts understand that accepting large, expensive gifts or trips would be a problem. Where the confusion comes in is deciding where to draw the line. "I know I can't accept a $200 bottle of wine, but a $10 gift and card is okay, right?" or, "Of course I wouldn't go to Europe with the client's family, but going to her birthday party isn't a problem, is it?"

FUNCTIONAL ASSESSMENT (3.02)

"The behavior analyst conducts a functional assessment to provide the necessary data to develop an effective behavior plan." Of the top five concerns for practitioners who attended our workshops, ethical problems related to the need for conducting functional assessments (to determine the controlling variables related to a behavior problem) were cited as the fifth most frequent area related to the Guidelines. Many of the comments spoke of a lack of resources to do a proper experimental functional assessment, and participants indicated in discussions that they felt other forms of assessment were not adequate. Some said they just skipped doing functional assessments in favor of using their professional judgment, whereas others said they felt comfortable using descriptive assessments.

After the top five ethical concerns, the consultants in our workshops expressed five additional concerns that rounded out the top 10:

Least restrictive procedures (4.10)
Responsible for appraisal of alternative treatments (2.10c)
Responsibility to all parties affected by behavioral services (primarily families) (2.03)
Reinforcement/punishment (reinforcement when possible) (4.05)
Environmental conditions that hamper implementation (4.03)

As the level of professionalism grows in behavior analysis, practitioners are becoming more knowledgeable about the Guidelines for Responsible Conduct, and they are able to cite the relevant areas of the Guidelines related to ethical problems. Once an ethical issue is identified, the next step is knowing how to handle the situation. Chapter 17, "Delivering the Ethics Message Effectively," will show you how to respond to the most common ethical issues.

5

Everyday Ethical Challenges for Average Citizens and Behavior Analysts

As they travel down the bumpy, pothole-riddled road to adulthood, children absorb the rules of their communities, religions, and cultures. Over a surprisingly short time, parents, relatives, teachers, and the occasional Scoutmaster pave the way for future ethical conduct. These unsuspecting adults may not realize that every day they are playing a key role in stating rules and delivering the consequences that will determine future adult behavior.

In any event, from the time people are young children we can safely say that there is no consistent set of rules of ethical conduct for all citizens. If a junior high school student cheats on a test and does not get caught, he may come to believe that cheating is okay regardless of what his parent or religious leader says. A

> When students decide to enter a graduate program in behavior analysis, they are entering a world where suddenly the rules are different.

pattern can develop where "don't get caught" becomes the rule rather than "don't cheat." A child who routinely fails to do her after-school chores, makes excuses, and is forgiven may grow up to be an adult who learns to make up elaborate stories about why she was late to work or why her quarterly report was sloppy and not turned in on deadline. Over time, the cumulative result of these childhood-through-adulthood experiences produces individuals with loosely formed rules, referred to as *personal ethics*. Cheating on one's spouse, lying about why you can't visit your elderly parents, and illegally using someone else's Internet connection are all examples related to personal ethics. Personal ethics can be contrasted with *professional ethics*. When students decide to enter a graduate program in behavior analysis, they are entering a world where suddenly the rules are different—and explicit. To understand the possible conflicts that budding professional behavior analysts face, consider the following comparisons.

FAVORS

Friends often ask each other for favors. A favor might range from sharing a DVD or watching a friend's house while she is on vacation to borrowing a lawn mower. The longer the friendship, the more intimate or complex the favors can become. "Could you tell me the name of a good counselor? My husband and I are having some personal problems," or, "If my wife asks, could you tell her I went bowling with you and the guys on Thursday night?" If a citizen who is accustomed to asking for and returning favors then begins receiving in-home services from a behavior analyst three times a week, it would not be unexpected to also ask the behavior analyst for favors. "Could you run the therapy session for Jimmy in the car today while we drive? I have to take my older son to soccer practice." This request might sound odd, but this actually happened to one of the first author's master's degree students. Falling back on her own history of personal ethics—people do favors for each other—the student agreed. Soon it became an everyday routine. Of course, the language training was totally ineffective in the distracting backseat microenvironment of a minivan weaving through 5 o'clock traffic.

GOSSIP

If you pause briefly at the checkout counter of any grocery store, you will find yourself coming in contact with gossip—and not just any gossip, but juicy gossip, complete with in-depth, full-color, Photoshop-enhanced pictures. Between magazines at

> The general thinking seems to be that gossip is fun and entertaining, so what is the harm?

the checkout counter and reality television shows, not only is gossip one of the recognized coins of the popular cultural and commercial realm, but it is also accepted by average citizens as normal in our society. The general thinking seems to be that gossip is fun and entertaining, so what is the harm? This attitude is so pervasive that a person refusing to participate may be seen as peculiar.

In the professional setting, behavior analysts encounter daily temptations. Consultants frequently report that parents will ask about someone else's child. "How is Maggie doing? I heard she was having some problems," a parent of another child will ask, without realizing that we cannot talk about clients or their families or reveal confidential information. To the person who wants to inquire about a client, the request seems harmless. Rather than consider the information "confidential," the person wanting to get the scoop on someone else's child views the question as just a part of the daily harvesting of bite-sized nuggets of tasty information. Talking about other people like this is gossip.

"WHITE LIES"

In an attempt to avoid conflict or censure, it has become common in our culture for people to cover up their motives, mistakes, or other personal shortcomings with "white lies." Rather than tell a friend she doesn't want to join her for coffee because she is gossipy, the sensitive person who doesn't like conflict will offer up, "I've got to go shopping for my niece's birthday party; I'm sorry." And, of course, she will get caught. "Oh, that sounds like fun; can I join you?" Now the little-white-lying culprit will have to make additional, perhaps even more dramatic, excuses. "Well, actually, I have a lot of boxes in my car, since I have to drop off Sam's brochures at Easy Mail before I go shopping." "Oh, I can help you with that," replies the doesn't-take-a-hint friend, "We can take my new SUV; it has lots of room for boxes, and I can help you unload them." One theory says that, because people so commonly use evasive tactics rather than telling the truth, they are suspicious of other people's explanations. At the other extreme, there are also plenty of people who can't read your subtle signals and will try to help you overcome every lying excuse you can offer.

APPRECIATION

Although there might be some variation from one part of the country to the other, it appears that there is a universal tendency for consumers, especially in-home clients, to give gifts to their favorite loveable, friendly, polite, kind, and gentle behavior analyst. After all, considering the behavior analyst is the life-saver who has transformed the

> Exchanging gifts creates a dual-role relationship; the client and the behavior analyst now become friends, and the BCBA is expected to return the favor at the right time.

child and given the parents hope, it seems only reasonable to give this valued person some tangible form of appreciation. This might range from homemade cookies to leftover spaghetti ("It's my secret family recipe.") or an invitation to go with the family to the beach for a weekend ("It will be fun; you can play with Damon and see what he is like when he sits and plays in the sand."). In the civilian world, people give gifts regularly including cash for the doorman, hairdresser, and newspaper delivery person at Christmas or a bottle of wine for a friend who is having an open house. Wily clients have been known to do their own research to find out when their BCBA's birthday is and surprise the consultant with a gift that is sure to please. Team logo ball caps, sports tickets, books, DVDs, expensive wine, baby gifts, new CDs, and loaded gift cards are all reported gifts given to behavior analysts who have attended our workshops. Exchanging gifts creates a dual-role relationship; the client and the behavior analyst now become friends, and the BCBA is expected to return the favor at the right time.

ADVICE

Citizens ask for and give advice to one another freely. They will recommend a movie, restaurant, babysitter, and maybe even a doctor without blinking. Their advice is often based on personal experience, unspecified biases, and undisclosed relationships. "There is a new carpet store out on Broadway West; I got a really good deal there." Full disclosure might reveal that the brother-in-law of the person who made the recommendation owns the store. Just as they will ask a friend or neighbor to recommend a school or a realtor, many people will ask their behavior analyst what he thinks is the best way to handle a smart-aleck teen or a lazy husband.

Prior to their professional training, behavior analysts were once citizens who probably freely asked for and gave advice on a variety of topics from what psychology course to take or where to apply for graduate school. However, once one becomes a Board Certified Behavior Analyst, the rules change considerably. As a professional, with a whole host of professional ethics to soak up, the BCBA must be careful about how and what is said to others when it comes to giving advice.

A teacher has gotten to know the behavior analyst who visits her classroom twice a week to check on Janie's progress. In the middle of a conversation about Janie's data, the teacher says, "What do you think I should do with Nunzio? You've seen him act out. I think he's got some kind of behavior disorder. What do you think?" Having one's behavior guided by a professional code of ethics is a whole new experience for many behavior analysts. While there may be a tendency to give a quick and clever retort or to toss off one-liners, the correct response is, "I'm sorry; I can't comment. He's not my client, and it would not be appropriate" (BACB Guidelines for Responsible Conduct, 1.05 a).

RESPONSIBILITY

Passing the buck when something goes wrong, staging cover-ups to avoid embarrassment, and concealing evidence of incompetence have become national pastimes among our political leaders, movie stars, and sports personalities. The average person gets desensitized, and unethical behavior seeps into the general population to the point that admitting error and confessing have become a lost art. The parents who do not take responsibility for their child's school vandalism often deny their failure to supervise effectively. Some parents go so far as to provide an alibi or excuse for the child's behavior ("He couldn't help it. He has been so sick, and his father had a drinking problem."). Such actions teach children an interesting set of rules: if negative consequences are prevented, both parties are reinforced for tactics to avoid responsibility. Behavior analysts must be aware of the possibility that there are indeed clients who have histories like this and take the necessary steps to ensure that agreements with parents are followed through. This is especially the case with parent-administered consequences in the home (e.g., Good Behavior Plans) where the child is earning points or privileges for reinforcers.

SUMMARY

When it comes to ethics, behavior analysts have to make the difficult but important transition from "civilian" to professional.

If standards from one's prebehavior analysis life are at cross-purposes with what is expected of a BCBA, they must be abandoned and replaced with our field's rather strict Guidelines for Responsible Conduct and ethical behaviors. Furthermore, on a daily basis, the BCBA and BCaBA will make contact with clients, paraprofessionals, and other professionals who will engage in "unethical" behaviors, possibly tempting them or even mocking them for their straight-laced approach.

The potential conflict of a history of personal ethics versus newly learned professional ethics and our Guidelines for Responsible Conduct is a worthy challenge for our field and one that is worth engaging in for the benefits and integrity that it will bring to our profession.

Two

Understanding and Following the Behavior Analyst Certification Board Guidelines for Responsible Conduct

In Section II, Chapters 6 through 15 address each of the 10 sections of the BACB Guidelines. In these chapters, the actual text of the Guidelines is italicized. Our explanatory comments "in plain English" follow in plain text. We developed the cases, and they are not a part of the BACB Guidelines.

6

Responsible Conduct of a Behavior Analyst (Guideline 1)

As a profession, behavior analysis has evolved in a unique way compared with the other "helping professions." We have a relatively short history, going back only to the mid-1960s, and our roots are firmly planted in the experimental analysis of behavior. The original behavior analysts were often experimental psychologists who recognized how their animal lab procedures could be applied to help the human condition. The original applications with humans (Ayllon & Michael, 1959; Wolf, Risley, & Mees, 1964) were almost direct replications of experimental (animal lab) procedures. These procedures were used with populations that were abandoned by the other service professionals at the time. This was also a time in which questions about the ethics of treatment were not raised. Well-trained, responsible, experimental psychologists used their own conscience, common sense, and respect for human values to create new treatments. Based on learning theory, it was believed that these treatments might work to relieve

> Based on learning theory, it was believed that these treatments might work to relieve suffering or dramatically improve the quality of life.

suffering or dramatically improve the quality of life for institutionalized individuals who were not receiving any other forms of effective treatment. There were no "guidelines for responsible conduct," and there was no oversight of these PhD researchers turned leading-edge therapists. Their work was done in the public eye with full knowledge of parents or guardians, and a review of the work today would find little to fault in terms of ethical conduct. It was only much later that some poorly prepared and insensitive behavior analysts would run into ethical problems creating the scandals described in Chapter 1.

Today, as a field, we have very high expectations for practicing behavior analysts, and Guideline 1.0 addresses this concern for overall responsible conduct. This guideline expresses the value system of our field, which states that those professionals who want to call themselves behavior analysts must conduct themselves in a way that reflects positively on the field—very positively, in fact. Guideline 1.01 emphasizes our roots in the science of behavior (Skinner, 1953) and reminds behavior analysts that the decisions they make from day to day must be tied to this science. This is actually a very tall order

> **Professionals who want to call themselves behavior analysts must conduct themselves in a way that reflects positively on the field.**

given the thousands of applied behavioral studies that have been conducted in the last 40 years. Currently, nearly two dozen journals worldwide publish behavioral research (APA, 2001), so the ethical behavior analyst has an obligation to keep in touch with quite a bit of "scientific knowledge." Another expectation is that the behavior analyst remains "proficient in professional practice." This is another demanding standard given the constantly improving methodology of our relatively young field. In the early years of behavior analysis, there was an emphasis on the use of aversive procedures to change behavior, which unfortunately set the stage for considerable backlash on the part of advocate and consumer groups. An "antiaversives" movement began and still exists that has portrayed our field as prone to the use of punishment although we have long since passed into another level of professionalism. As happens in many fields, some practitioners seem to become frozen in time with regard to their skills. It is possible even now to run into someone who got a PhD in 1975 who has not remained current with the trends in the field. This guideline was meant as a wake-up call to such individuals for them to get back in touch with current standards before they hurt innocent people and damage the reputations of legitimate, up-to-date behavior analysts.

It does not seem too much to ask of professionals that they recognize the legal code of their community and maintain high moral principles. To do otherwise is to put a stain on the good reputation of others. Even although not practicing behavior analysis, the community will identify you as a member

> Our goal as a profession is to gradually emerge onto the scene with a terrific reputation for truth, honesty, and reliability.

of that group if something goes amiss. None of us wants to see a headline like, "Behavior analyst caught dealing drugs at local high school," but that is exactly how a headline would read. As a new profession with a complex two-part name, we are not on the radar screens of most Americans. Our goal as a profession is to gradually emerge onto the scene with a terrific reputation for truth, honesty, and reliability. What we do not want is to end up on the "Ten Least Respected Professions" list along with journalists and government employees (BBC Radio, 1999). So our admonition to those of you entering behavior analysis is to monitor your behavior, make sure that in your dealings with your clients and the public your conduct is above reproach and well within the law, and be recognized by those around you as an exemplary citizen.

When behavior analysts are operating professionally, others are observing and making judgments about their conduct. Are

> If we are to advance our field, we must, as a new profession, gain the respect of all those we work with by our responsible conduct.

they forthright and honest or somewhat devious and deceptive? Do they talk down to their professional colleagues or treat them with respect? Do they demean the work of others or attempt to collaborate and educate? If we are to advance our field, we must, as a new profession, gain the respect of all those we work with by our "responsible conduct" every day, and many aspects of this behavior are discussed in Guideline 1.05. We discourage all behavior analysts from becoming "shade tree mechanics" (Guideline 1.05a) and to translate their suggested treatment plan into plain English for clients, consumers, and other professionals (1.05b), saving the jargon for behavioral colleagues at conferences.

A major personal commitment that we ask of behavior analysts is to shed and ultimately reject any biases they may have grown up with in their families or communities and learn to deal with people of different genders, race, ethnicity, or national origin in a totally accepting and nondiscriminating manner. It is unacceptable that behavior analysts would treat a person of a different race or socioeconomic status any different from someone of their own race or status. This may be quite a stretch for some newcomers to our field, and it could present major challenges, depending on your commitment to another value system (strength of your

> If you are a graduate student and see any problems related to your values, now is the time to reflect on your situation and approach one of your professors for a frank talk about this issue and the implications for your future success in the field.

conditioning history). If you are a graduate student and see any problems related to your values, now is the time to reflect on your situation and approach one of your professors for a frank talk about this issue and the implications for your future success in the field.

Sexual harassment is a blight on our culture that will not go away. Over 13,000 charges are filed each year, 85% of which are made by women, and with fines reaching $50 million each year to resolve the conflicts (U.S. EEOC, 2004). Sexual harassment is a form of sex discrimination that violates Title VII of the Civil Rights Act of 1964. One would think that most professionals would be aware of this. However, even attorneys have engaged in this despicable form of abuse, as noted in the case of Anita Hill in her testimony against Clarence Thomas (Hill, 1998). This form of conduct includes unwelcome advances, requests for sexual favors, and any form of behavior that is sufficiently severe and pervasive and produces an abusive working environment (Binder, 1992).

Even behavior analysts may develop problems in their personal lives. Chronic illness, a messy divorce, or alcohol addiction can bring most anyone down, and, as in the case of any professional, your obligation is to make sure that personal issues do not interfere with your ability to deliver quality services (Guideline 1.05f). This is probably best handled via the "trusted colleague" model described in Chapter 1 in which you develop a relationship with a person on whom you can rely to be straight and honest with you on a range of matters that affect your professional life. If you in any way feel that you might not be fulfilling your obligations to your clients or in your workplace, it is time to have a heart-to-heart talk with a trusted colleague to determine his or her perceptions and to help you sort out

> If you in any way feel that you might not be fulfilling your obligations to your clients, it is time to have a heart-to-heart talk with a trusted colleague.

your options. Some of those will probably involve taking a leave of absence for a period of time while you get your life back in order. During this time, you need to make sure that you have made arrangements with other behavior analysts to cover your clients and sit for you on committees.

> A behavior analyst who freely gives advice to a relative runs the risk of alienating that person if the program goes bad.

Effective behavior analysts wear many hats in their community, and it is easy for them to encounter situations where some conflict of interest might arise (Guideline 1.06). Such conflicts come about because busy, effective behavior analysts who have a full client caseload might also have other responsibilities such as serving on the peer review committee, being an elected representative of their state association, and possibly having some responsibility with their local Parent–Teacher Organization. More personal conflicts of interest can arise when a neighbor asks for help with a child behavior problem or a visiting relative clearly needs help resolving a personal issue. A behavior analyst who is a government employee, elected to a position with a state organization, may find that the position the organization takes on an issue is at odds with his or her employer. Behavior analysts who freely give advice to a relative run the risk of alienating that person if the program goes bad or their advice is contrary to what the school psychologist or counselor recommended. The best solution is to avoid such situations on the front end, but the Guidelines require the behavior analyst to resolve them before any harm is done (Guideline 1.06c).

> Parties on both sides need to be aware of the potential for exploitation when one person is in control, even if the person is a behavior analyst.

As our profession has grown over the past 40 years, behavior analysts have increasingly been respected for their skills and have moved into positions of authority where they wield some considerable power and influence. Whereas in the beginning they served only as therapists or unit directors, many behavior analysts are now chairs of psychology departments, superintendents of large residential facilities, or owners of major consulting firms. In such positions, even the most ethically sensitive behavior analysts may find that they can call the shots without anyone else's approval. The PhD president of a consulting firm can direct his or her master's-level consultants to advocate a certain procedure, to promote overbilling, or to encourage snooping on the competition while on the job. We would hope that the ethical master's-level consultant would resist such pressure, but the differential in power allows supervisees to be exploited if care is not taken. Supervisors could extract favors from students in exchange for a good grade in practicum, and, theoretically, behavioral faculty could do the same. Or, as has occasionally been reported, students may offer favors for a good grade. Thus, parties on both sides need to be equally aware of the potential for exploitation when one person is in control, even if the person is a behavior analyst.

RESPONSIBLE CONDUCT OF A BEHAVIOR ANALYST (1.0)

The behavior analyst maintains the high standards of professional behavior of the professional organization.

Professional behavior here is distinguished from private or everyday behavior. This means that when you are at work or serving on a committee where you are representing your profession or organization you must uphold the standards expected by the profession. These are understood to include honesty, integrity, reliability, confidentiality, and trustworthiness.

• • • • • • •

CASE 1.0: POLITICS AS USUAL

Jane P., a Board Certified assistant Behavior Analyst (BCaBA) who serves on a state association nominating committee, very much wants her colleague Dr. Elaine J. to be elected. Jane begins by talking to the Board Certified Behavior Analysts (BCBAs) she knows and tells them that Dr. J. is absolutely the best person for the job. Jane realizes she will gain influence on the Board if her friend Dr. J. is elected.

Why are there ethical problems associated with Jane's political strategy?

• • • • • • •

RELIANCE ON SCIENTIFIC KNOWLEDGE (1.01)

Behavior analysts rely on scientifically and professionally derived knowledge when making scientific or professional judgments in human service provision, or when engaging in scholarly or professional endeavors.

One of the characteristics of behavior analysis that makes it unique is the reliance on scientific evidence as a basis for our practice. As a general rule, we expect to base our methods of assessment on systematic observation of behavior and one of several methods of functional assessment. Although we might seek input from family or caregivers during an intake process, the behavior analyst depends on objective data that are sufficient to allow some conclusion. This same data collection system is used along with treatment data to determine if a change in behavior has occurred. When presenting findings at a conference or for publication, it is essential that you maintain the highest standards of integrity for description of your method and results that you obtained.

COMPETENCE (1.02)

(a) Behavior analysts provide services, teach, and conduct research only within the boundaries of their competence, based on their education, training, supervised experience, or appropriate professional experience.

Boundaries of competence in behavior analysis are sometimes difficult to discern. However, you are obligated to practice only in those areas where you have had formal training.

• • • • • • •

CASE 1.02A: CHILD PSYCHOLOGY

Dr. Sandra F., a professor at a small Midwestern college, is asked to teach a course in child psychology. Dr. F. is a Doctoral-level Board Certified Behavior Analyst (BCBA-D) with a PhD from a major university, and although she did her dissertation on children with phobias she has never taken a graduate course or seminar specifically on this topic.
How should Dr. F. handle this request?

• • • • • • •

(b) Behavior analysts provide services, teach, or conduct research in new areas or involving new techniques only after first undertaking appropriate study, training, supervision, and/or consultation from persons who are competent in those areas or techniques.

When you feel it is necessary to practice outside the areas in which you were trained, you are required to seek further training in the new area.

PROFESSIONAL DEVELOPMENT (1.03)

Behavior analysts who engage in assessment, therapy, teaching, research, organizational consulting, or other professional activities maintain a reasonable level of awareness of current scientific and professional information in their fields of activity, and undertake ongoing efforts to maintain competence in the skills they use.

As a behavior analyst, you are required to stay current in your specialty area. This means you should subscribe to and read the relevant journals in your specialty and attend conferences and workshops that are specific to your area of practice, research, or therapy.

• • • • • • •

CASE 1.03: OLD SCHOOL IS NOT COOL

Tony H., a BCBA chair of a local behavioral review committee, has noticed that in the last several meetings one of the presenters is very much behind on current behavioral treatment. The presenter, also a BCBA, has many years experience and is well thought of in the community. Other committee members have begun to make occasional embarrassing comments about this person behind his back at the end of the meetings.

What are some suggestions for how Tony could handle this situation in a professional and tactful manner?

• • • • • • •

INTEGRITY (1.04)

(a) Behavior analysts are truthful and honest. Behavior analysts follow through on obligations and professional commitments with high quality work and refrain from making professional commitments that they cannot keep.

It seems so simple: just be honest with your clients, and tell the truth. If you are overloaded and cannot get to their home before the end of the day, say so. If you think that it is going to require several weeks of verbal behavior therapy before little Holly begins speaking in three-word phrases, let the parents know. And set a personal standard for yourself to carry out every promise that you make.

(b) The behavior analyst's behavior conforms to the legal and moral codes of the social and professional community of which the behavior analyst is a member.

You are required to be aware of legal issues pertaining to the delivery of services in your state, and you need to be cognizant of moral and social values in your community. Although behavioral procedures have been shown to work in a vast array of circumstances and settings, it is only because the behavior analyst gained the confidence of key members of the community and worked within the informal social codes of conduct that were prescribed by the professional community.

• • • • • • •

CASE 1.04: THE MISSING LINK

Dr. J. recently was recruited to teach at a major university where he was expected to set up a laboratory to study self-injurious behavior (SIB). His previous research emphasized the effectiveness of certain aversive stimuli that, when made contingent on early responses in the SIB chain, greatly reduced the probability of the final members of the chain being emitted. The work had been published in prestigious journals. Dr. J. was shocked when one of the BCaBAs he hired to work in the lab said that this research was prohibited by a state law that had been passed about 10 years earlier.

What corrective steps does Dr. J. need to take now?

• • • • • • •

(c) The activity of a behavior analyst falls under these Guidelines only if the activity is part of his or her work-related functions or the activity is behavior analytic in nature.

These Guidelines cover your activities when you are at work and when you are engaged in other activities that involve basic principles of behavior.

(d) If behavior analysts' ethical responsibilities conflict with law, behavior analysts make known their commitment to these Guidelines and take steps to resolve the conflict in a responsible manner in accordance with law.

If you find yourself in a situation where it appears there is a conflict between these Guidelines and some state statute, you will need to resolve the issue without breaking the law. The most common example of a law that ethical behavior analysts may feel the need to question would be a state law pertaining to confidentiality. In some cases, the behavior analyst may feel conflicted if the client's safety is at risk and someone needs to be told.

PROFESSIONAL AND SCIENTIFIC RELATIONSHIPS (1.05)

(a) Behavior analysts provide behavioral diagnostic, therapeutic, teaching, research, supervisory, consultative, or other behavior analytic services only in the context of a defined, remunerated professional or scientific relationship or role.

You should not "volunteer" to treat someone without some authority to do so. If you do pro bono work for a family or an agency, your role and responsibility must be clearly specified. They must be informed of your credentials and competence. It is recommended that you have something in writing to document this relationship.

(b) When behavior analysts provide assessment, evaluation, treatment, counseling, supervision, teaching, consultation, research, or other behavior analytic services to an individual, a group, or an organization, they use language that is fully understandable to the recipient of those services. They provide appropriate information prior to service delivery about the nature of such services and appropriate information later about results and conclusions.

When you are working with laypeople, speak English, and be diligent in making sure they understand what you are doing both prior to intervention and in follow-up.

• • • • • • •

CASE 1.05: NOT IMPRESSED

Matthew T. was a BCaBA who had just recently graduated from college and was taking his first job as a behavior analyst. He wanted to impress his clients with his newfound knowledge, so he sprinkled terms like tact, mand, autoclitic, and control procedures liberally in his meetings with parents. His supervisor received complaints from the parents saying, "We have no idea what he is talking about, but it sounds scary to us."

What should the supervisor do about this BCaBA and his technical way of talking about things?

• • • • • • •

(c) Where differences of age, gender, race, ethnicity, national origin, religion, sexual orientation, disability, language, or socioeconomic status significantly affect behavior analysts' work concerning particular individuals or groups, behavior analysts obtain the training, experience, consultation, or supervision necessary to ensure the competence of their services, or they make appropriate referrals.

If you are working with individuals different from those to whom you are accustomed, you should seek guidance from another professional. Alternatively, you may consider referring the clients to another behavior analyst.

(d) In their work-related activities, behavior analysts do not engage in discrimination against individuals or groups based on age, gender, race, ethnicity, national origin, religion, sexual orientation, disability, socioeconomic status, or any basis proscribed by law.

It is unethical to discriminate against others in your work-related activities for any reason. You may not treat people unfairly or provide less or unsatisfactory treatment just because they are different from you.

• • • • • • •

CASE 1.05D: RELIGIOUS DILEMMA

Ahmed had always been fascinated by psychology and took a special undergraduate track that prepared him to sit for the assistants test offered by the BACB. He earned good grades and excelled at doing descriptive functional assessments in his practicum. When he got his first job, he discovered that one of his student clients in an elementary school was a Sunni Muslim. Ahmed mentioned this to his parents, who were irate and insisted that he refuse to associate in any way with this student of a rival religious sect.

Ahmed is in a very sensitive situation. How should he handle this?

• • • • • • •

(e) Behavior analysts do not knowingly engage in behavior that is harassing or demeaning to persons with whom they interact in their work based on factors such as those persons' age, gender, race, ethnicity, national origin, religion, sexual orientation, disability, language, or socioeconomic, status in accordance with law.

As a behavior analyst, you should be sensitive to the reaction others have to your behavior. It is inappropriate to make sexual advances to others ("flirting") or to tease or make demeaning comments about their size, weight, sexual orientation, age, or any other noticeable feature.

(f) Behavior analysts recognize that their personal problems and conflicts may interfere with their effectiveness. Behavior analysts refrain from providing services when their personal circumstances may compromise delivering services to the best of their abilities.

As a behavior analyst, you have an obligation to monitor your own behavior and recognize when stress, changes in life situation (e.g., death in the family, divorce), or some conflict negatively affect your professional performance. In such cases, you will need to make arrangements for another behavior analyst to serve your clients until you recover.

• • • • • • •

CASE 1.05F: LEFT

A 40-something-year-old BCBA, Stella V., came home after a long day of analyzing behavior to discover that her husband had left her. His note said he was unhappy with never seeing his wife, that she had changed since their marriage 10 years earlier, and that he was going on a "voyage of self-exploration." Although she denied to everyone that it bothered her, Stella's work became erratic and appeared to be unusually prickly about feedback on her functional assessments. She walked out in the middle of one parent meeting saying, "I just can't take this anymore." Stella's colleagues were worried about her, and they were very concerned about her recent performance.

Should the behavioral colleagues get involved in Stella's personal business?

• • • • • • •

DUAL RELATIONSHIPS AND CONFLICTS OF INTEREST (1.06)

(a) In many communities and situations, it may not be feasible or reasonable for behavior analysts to avoid social or other non-professional contacts with persons such as clients, students, supervisees, or research participants. Behavior analysts must always be sensitive to the potential harmful effects of other contacts on their work and on those persons with whom they deal.

You should strive to avoid social contacts with your clients because it might interfere with your objectivity as a behavior analyst or possibly harm or exploit them. With supervisees, students, or research participants, it is also a good idea to avoid any more than casual contact as this might be construed as showing favoritism in the case of students or supervisees or bias their participation in the case of research participants.

• • • • • • •

CASE 1.06: A SMALL-TOWN BCBA

A BCBA who lives in a small town was asked by her sister to develop an Association of Behavior Analysis (ABA) program for her son. There are no other behavior analysts available, and the BCBA has issues with the sister that would be complicated by her taking the case.

What is the BCBA's most appropriate course of action?

• • • • • • •

(b) A behavior analyst refrains from entering into or promising a personal, scientific, professional, financial, or other relationship with any such person if it appears likely that such a relationship reasonably might impair the behavior analyst's objectivity or otherwise interfere with the behavior analyst's ability to effectively perform his or her functions as a behavior analyst, or might harm or exploit the other party.

It is best to avoid dual relationships with others (e.g., student and business associate) if it appears that this will negatively affect your ability to be effective as a behavior analyst or might in some way harm the other person.

(c) If a behavior analyst finds that, due to unforeseen factors, a potentially harmful multiple relationship has arisen (i.e., one in which the reasonable possibility of conflict of interest or undue influence is present), the behavior analyst attempts to resolve it with due regard for the best interests of the affected person and maximal compliance with these Guidelines.

If you find that you have become involved in a harmful dual relationship with a client or other professional, you are required to resolve the situation in the best interests of the person and with due regard for these Guidelines.

EXPLOITATIVE RELATIONSHIPS (1.07)

(a) Behavior analysts do not exploit persons over whom they have supervisory, evaluative, or other authority such as students, supervisees, employees, research participants, and clients.

Behavior analysts do not use or take advantage of anyone regardless of whether the behavior analysts supervise them or have some sort of authority over them.

(b) Behavior analysts do not engage in sexual relationships with clients, students, or supervisees in training over whom the behavior analyst has evaluative or direct authority, because such relationships easily impair judgment or become exploitative.

Do not become involved in sexual relationships with clients, students, or supervisees because such relationships can impair your judgment. Also, you may be exploited or find that you are taken advantage of by the other party.

• • • • • • •

CASE 1.07B: SINGLES MINGLING

Bill was a 30-year-old, single BCBA who worked with clients and conducted research in a large state institution. He had a good working relationship with the local university's psychology and special education programs. One semester, Bill found himself attracted to Kristi, one of the college students he was supervising. The attraction seemed mutual because Kristi made it a point to let Bill know that she was single and available for dating.

Because the feelings seemed to be mutual and they were both adults, was there any problem with Bill asking Kristi for a date?

• • • • • • •

(c) Behavior analysts are cautioned against bartering with clients because it is often (1) clinically contraindicated, and (2) prone to formation of an exploitative relationship.

Bartering is the exchange of goods or services in lieu of payment. It is strongly discouraged because it can easily go awry when one party feels that he or she has not received an equal return according to the agreement.

• • • • • • •

CASE 1.07C: "WILL WORK FOR FOOD"

Julie S. was a BCBA who provided behavioral services to families and their children. Julie was working in the home with two of the children of Rosita and Manny G. Rosita and Manny were the owners of a very popular Mexican restaurant. On one visit, Rosita suggested to Julie that instead of paying for behavioral services with a check, she and Manny would like to trade out food at their restaurant.

Julie was a fan of Rosita's guacamole cheese crisps, blue corn tamales, and especially the margaritas. As long as she kept a close watch on her billable hours versus restaurant tab, would this mutually agreed on system be within the Guidelines?

• • • • • • •

RESPONSES TO CASES

CASE 1.0: POLITICS AS USUAL

Jane is in violation of 1.0 of the Guidelines; she is not maintaining high standards for professional behavior. She is trying to influence her friends to vote for someone for her own gain. She has a hidden agenda, and she is not being honest. As a board member, she is also violating her role as a person who is supposed to be objective and impartial. She should not be trying to influence the way that other BCBAs vote if she is on the board.

CASE 1.02A: CHILD PSYCHOLOGY

The professor meets with the chair of the department to explain that she would be reluctant to teach the course because she has not had formal training in this area and that the BACB code requires that behavior analysts operate within their "boundaries of competence." The professor suggests the course be called Behavior Analysis and Therapy With Children. This suggestion was approved by the department chair.

CASE 1.03: OLD SCHOOL IS NOT COOL

Tony asks the BCBA to stay after one of the meetings and begins a low-key conversation about a speaker he heard at a recent conference that he attended, looking for some sign of recognition or interest. When this was not forthcoming, he became a little bolder, asking that the BCBA consider looking into some recent articles on behavioral treatment that seemed quite relevant. Again, seeing no sign of interest, Tony said, "I'm concerned about your clients. I'm not sure they are getting the best treatment available."

Tony H. is professional and tactful as he points out the 1.02 standard in the BACB Guidelines.

CASE 1.04: THE MISSING LINK

In some states, the "use of noxious and painful stimuli" is not allowed in the treatment of developmentally disabled individuals or others who receive services from state agencies. Dr. J. was required to change the focus of his treatment to a different type of question regarding the use of noncontingent reinforcement (NCR), a topic in which he also had a strong interest.

CASE 1.05: NOT IMPRESSED

The supervisor met with the BCaBA and reminded him about translating his technical terminology into closely equivalent English words. He gave the BCaBA a list of common terms that could be interchanged with behavioral terminology and urged him to practice using them. After the next meeting, the supervisor checked with the family to see if they felt any more comfortable with the BCaBA.

CASE 1.05D: RELIGIOUS DILEMMA

Refusing to provide treatment of a person based on religion, ethnicity, or national origin is considered a form of discrimination, is not condoned by the BACB Guidelines, and is illegal as well. This means Ahmed cannot discriminate against the child and refuse treatment just to satisfy his parents. If he cannot be totally unbiased, he must make a referral to another BCBA (1.05c and 1.05f). In addition, Ahmed needs to rethink his commitment to his chosen field.

CASE 1.05F: LEFT

Although specifically trained as behavioral observers, behavior analysts may still not be able to put their own behavior in perspective and see how it affects others. Someone close to Stella needs to take her aside and offer her some assistance. Ideally, this would be a colleague but might also be her supervisor. The main point of this ethical problem is that you have an obligation to talk to a colleague whose performance is not up to standard. In this case, the supervisor might suggest a leave of absence for Stella to give her a chance to focus on getting her life under control.

CASE 1.06A: SMALL-TOWN BCBA

The BCBA decides not to take the case and contacts her state association to locate someone who would be willing to work with her sister. She also contacts the local school system to determine if there are services available there. If this is, for example, a very rural area where there is absolutely no one else who can provide behavioral services, it may be necessary for a non-BCBA to work with the child. The BCBA may wish to begin training other professionals on behavioral skills (e.g., a talented teacher), and it might be possible that someone else could work with the family.

CASE 1.07B: SINGLES MINGLING

Behavior analysts do not engage in sexual relationships with clients, students, or supervisees; such a relationship could impair their judgment and constitute a form of exploitation as well. Dating is also in this category. If Bill believes Kristi is the woman of his dreams, he should wait until her internship is over to have nonprofessional contact with her. Depending on the nature of the interactions, it might be appropriate to find someone else to supervise Kristi.

CASE 1.07C: "WILL WORK FOR FOOD"

The Guidelines caution behavior analysts against bartering because it is often clinically contraindicated and can result in the forming of exploitative relationships. The potential for a perceived imbalance or unfairness by either party is also great. If Rosita and Manny feel that the therapy is not going well and that progress is slow with their children, they may provide less stellar service to Julie in their restaurant. Julie, on the other hand, may feel that the extra hours she puts in should be worth an extra margarita now and then. The possibilities are endless for squabbling, and such an arrangement has little to do with Julie providing quality behavioral services to her client.

7

The Behavior Analyst's Responsibility to Clients (Guideline 2)

In the early days, when our field consisted of experimental psychologists applying the principles of behavior to "subjects" they encountered in the residential units of institutions, there was no question about where the responsibility lay; it was clearly with the employer. These pioneer behavior analysts most often had no training in clinical psychology. They believed that behavior could be changed using procedures derived from learning theory. The "client" (although that term was not used initially) was their employer. In some cases, the parents of a child were the "clients."

It was not until 1974 that issues of a client's "right to treatment" would surface as an issue in the landmark *Wyatt v. Stickney* (1971) case in Alabama. In this case, it was argued that institutionalized mental patients had a right to receive individual treatment or be discharged to the community. Although the case really did not have anything directly to do with treatment per se (e.g., it dictated increases in professional staff, improvements in the physical plant, and how many showers a patient should receive per week), it blasted

> *Wyatt v. Stickney* (1971) put behavior analysts on notice that a paradigm shift had occurred.

the term *right to treatment* into the legal arena and put all psychologists, including behavior analysts, on notice that a paradigm shift had occurred. In behavior analysis, we immediately became sensitive to the possibility that our "client" might be harmed by our procedures, and in a short period of time, "clients' rights" were the new watchwords. The original trial judge, Frank M. Johnson, Jr., set forth what later became known as the Wyatt Standards. This case set a precedent and put all mental health and retardation professionals on notice that their services had to be delivered in humane environments, where there were sufficient qualified staff members and individualized treatment plans, and that the treatment had to be delivered in the least restrictive environment.

Following the Wyatt decision, if you were assigned to work with a client in a residential facility, it was clear that you had not only an obligation to the facility to do your best work but also a responsibility to the person on the receiving end of the treatment to make sure he or she was not harmed. There was concern in the beginning that "behavioral specialists" (they were not yet called behavior analysts)

> Following the *Wyatt* decision, it was clear that you had a responsibility to the person on the receiving end of treatment.

would manipulate "client" behavior just for the convenience of the staff, such as punishing clients who were incontinent so that staff members would not have to change their diapers. Over time it became clear that, ethically speaking, it was only right to consider the needs of the actual client along with anyone else who might be affected by the procedures (e.g., staff, parents or guardian, other residents). This immediately made the behavior specialist job far more difficult. By the end of the 1970s, behavior analysis was becoming more widespread and visible, and behavior analysts found themselves working with other professionals on "habilitation teams" to determine the right treatment for clients. Thus, the beginning of issues concerning consultation and cooperation with other professionals arose. In addition, there began to be differentiation of the roles of the entities, and concerns developed about "third party" involvement. If a client (first party) hires a behavior analyst (second party), presumably there is no conflict of interest, and the client can fire the behavior analyst if he or she is not satisfied with the services. Likewise, the behavior analyst will do his or her best to satisfy the client's needs so that the behavior analyst will be paid for his or her services. This arrangement has built-in checks and balances. But if the behavior analyst is hired by a third party (e.g., a facility) to treat the behavior of one of its residents (first party), there is a presumption that the behavior analyst will work to satisfy the needs of the third party to keep his or her job. The Guidelines address this issue in some detail in 2.04.

By the 1980s, behavior analysis was much more visible in mental retardation treatment circles and was accepted by many as a viable strategy for habilitation. It was around this time that the further trappings of service delivery had to be accommodated. It was clear that clients had rights (both under the U.S. Constitution and the Wyatt Standards) and that everyone, including the behavior analyst, had to respect them and certainly to be informed of them prior to treatment. Furthermore, with behavior

> In the late 1980s, the Association for Behavior Analysis convened a blue-ribbon panel of experts to reach consensus on right to treatment.

analysis approaching the mainstream of accepted approaches, other protections had to be put in place. Clients had a right to privacy, and arrangements had to be made to protect their privacy and confidentiality. Records had to be stored and transferred in a way that maintained these rights, and behavior analysts had the same obligation as other professionals to obtain consent to disclose the information. By the late 1980s, the time had come for behavior analysts to speak out on the issue of right to treatment, and the Association for Behavior Analysis (ABA) convened a blue-ribbon panel of experts to reach some consensus on the topic. A consensus was reached and ultimately approved by the governing body of the ABA, which essentially stated that clients had a right to a "therapeutic environment" where their personal welfare would be of paramount importance and where they had a right to treatment by a "competent behavior analyst" who would conduct a behavioral assessment, teach functional skills, and evaluate the treatments. The ABA panel finally concluded that clients had a right to "the most effective treatments available" (Van Houten et al., 1988). This reference to effective treatments set the stage for behavior analysts to redouble their efforts to make a direct connection between the published research and the application of empirically tested interventions.

Guideline 2.0 provides a clear and detailed list of the obligations that behavior analysts have if they undertake to treat any client using behavioral procedures. By accepting these responsibilities and taking them seriously, we can guarantee that our clients will receive the first-class treatment they deserve and that as a profession we will have demonstrated our respect for their rights even as we provide state-of-the-art behavioral interventions.

THE BEHAVIOR ANALYST'S RESPONSIBILITY TO CLIENTS (2.0)

The behavior analyst has a responsibility to operate in the best interest of clients.

Although this may seem a truism, it is nonetheless a bedrock value of behavior analysis. As a service provider, you will make many decisions each day that will affect the quality of the treatment you provide. On a day-to-day basis, it is possible for service providers to make small decisions that are not in the best interest of the client. Deciding to cut short a discrete-trial language session so that you can make it to the dry cleaners before it closes or dropping a client simply because it is somewhat inconvenient to get to his home when the traffic is bad are examples of not upholding your responsibility to your client. "Clients" include individuals as well as programs and agencies. On a larger scale, a behavior analyst could persuade an administrator to budget more hours than are really needed for the behavior analyst to make increased profit. This action would harm multiple clients by depleting the budget, thereby possibly depriving others of services. By always asking yourself, "What is in the best interest of my client?" you will make better decisions in the long run.

• • • • • • •

CASE 2.0: SAVING MONEY FOR THE SCHOOL

Betsy was a Board Certified Behavior Analyst who provided services for a school-based autism program. She was contracted for 20 hours per week. Betsy did great work, and she was well liked by teachers and school administrators. She had a reputation for being very good at her job and for having the ability to get results. Betsy received an offer to provide part-time consulting at a private school. Betsy decided to go to the principal of the school with the autism program and to tell her that she would like to cut back to 10 hours per week. Betsy explained that this would help the principal come in under budget but did not reveal that she had taken a position with a private school.

If this principal was okay with this proposal, were there any problems with it?

• • • • • • •

DEFINITION OF CLIENT (2.01)

The term client as used here is broadly applicable to whomever the behavior analyst provides services whether an individual person (service recipient), parent or guardian of a service recipient, an institutional representative, a public or private agency, a firm or corporation.

Your client is the person or agency for whom you are providing services. Clients may be individuals, parents, agencies such as schools and developmental disability (DD) facilities, or businesses. It is generally accepted in human services that the most vulnerable individuals in the chain of services are your primary clients, the persons who cannot advocate for themselves.

• • • • • • •

CASE 2.01: PARENTS WHO DON'T WANT HELP

Allan was a 10-year-old with developmental disabilities. He had a number of behavior problems that included noncompliance and tantrums, and he was beginning to be aggressive when placed in demand situations. The behavior analyst in Allan's classroom was making good progress, but there were still high rates of inappropriate behaviors at home. Monica was the BCBA assigned to Allan's home. She had completed a functional analysis and was ready to begin taking baseline. On the evening Monica went to the home to explain the program to Allan's mother, she was surprised to have Mom start the meeting by saying, "I've really had a lot going on. I've given it a lot of thought, and I would like to stop services at home. I think Allan can get everything he needs at school." Monica didn't agree with this because Allan's mother had shaped a lot of the behavior problems. When Monica told her supervisor (the owner of the consulting firm) what happened, his reply was, "The mother has the right to terminate services. Allen is a minor who is not competent. His mother has the right to make the decisions here. We can use the hours to serve someone who wants our help."

• • • • • • •

ACCEPTING CLIENTS (2.02)

The behavior analyst accepts as clients only those individuals or entities (agencies, firms, etc.) whose behavior problems or requested services are commensurate with the behavior analyst's education, training, and experience. In lieu of these conditions, the behavior analyst must function under the supervision of or in consultation with a behavior analyst whose credentials permit working with such behavior problems or services.

Behavior analysts understand and acknowledge the limitations of their expertise. If they are working on cases beyond their range of experience and training, behavior analysts will seek supervision from someone with proper credentials to ensure that they are operating ethically and to avoid doing any harm.

• • • • • • •

CASE 2.02: QUESTIONABLE REPERTOIRE

Martin was a BCBA who moved to a new city to work at a large state hospital for persons with mental health problems. This was a new area of expertise for Martin; his past experience was limited to clients who were profoundly mentally and physically disabled. One of the clients Martin was assigned to was Dan, a 23-year-old man who had a severe head injury. Dan engaged in violent and unpredictable outbursts of aggression. Dan's dangerous outbursts resulted in more than one staff person being rushed to the emergency room for medical treatment. Martin was eager to treat Dan, and he began reading everything he could about head injury. He felt that the state hospital hired him to do a job and assigned him to this client, and he was committed to getting Dan's behavior under control.

Is Martin ready to take on this case?

• • • • • • •

RESPONSIBILITY (2.03)

The behavior analyst's responsibility is to all parties affected by behavioral services.

In addition to the client, you are responsible to others who might also be affected by your services. For example, if a school retains you to work with a behaviorally disordered second grader, you have an obligation to make sure that all principles of ethics extend to the child, the parents, and even other children in the student's classroom.

• • • • • • •

CASE 2.03: TEACHER'S PET

Terry was a BCBA providing behavioral services to Brianna, an elementary school student who was extremely disruptive in the classroom. Terry had some good things going for her as far as implementing a behavior plan went. First, Brianna loved attention. She also liked toys, trinkets, and stickers of various types. Terry knew that everyone in the class, including the other students, suffered when Brianna was causing a ruckus. Terry decided to let everyone get involved to help Brianna. Terry designed a behavior plan that involved Brianna getting a sticker on a chart for each hour that she had exhibited no inappropriate behaviors. Then, at the end of every good day, the teacher gave Brianna a small toy and said to the class, "Let's all clap for Brianna. She had a great day!" The program worked very well—for Brianna. Her behavior was coming under control. The problem was that the other children began to make comments about the teacher having favorites and how the system wasn't fair.

Terry explained to the teacher that, in a matter of time, when Brianna's behavior was well under control the program could be faded. Since progress was occurring so quickly, should Terry continue the program?

• • • • • • •

CONSULTATION (2.04)

(a) Behavior analysts arrange for appropriate consultations and referrals based principally on the best interests of their clients, with appropriate consent, and subject to other relevant considerations, including applicable law and contractual obligations.

If the behavior problem you are working on exceeds your level of competence or needs help in an area in which you are not trained, you should seek assistance (consultation from another professional) or make a referral (pass the case to another behavior analyst). This must be done with your client's full knowledge. When considering making a referral to another professional, you must take the client's needs and interests into account. Be careful about referring to your friends as this could violate the prohibition of conflict of interest.

> (b) When indicated and professionally appropriate, behavior analysts cooperate with other professionals in order to serve their clients effectively and appropriately. Behavior analysts recognize that other professions have ethical codes that may differ in their specific requirements from these Guidelines.

You will find that it is often necessary to cooperate with non-behavioral professionals to meet your client's needs. When interacting with a nonbehavioral professional about one of your clients, keep in mind that other professionals have ethical guidelines that may differ from the BACB Guidelines you need to follow.

• • • • • • •

CASE 2.04: SEX THERAPY

Dr. M., a Doctoral-level BCBA (BCBA-D), was providing behavioral services to Jerry, a 16-year-old who was disruptive at school. Dr. M. had been working in the field of behavior analysis for 20 years and was very well read in other forms of treatment and psychology. During several of Dr. M.'s visits, Jerry began to talk about issues related to sex. Jerry was clearly confused and troubled about these intimate issues. Dr. M. determined that this fell in the general category of verbal behavior, one of his areas of expertise, and decided to teach Jerry to "verbalize" his sex-related issues.

Is this acceptable as long as Dr. M. documents this work and does not refer to it as behavior analysis?

• • • • • • •

THIRD-PARTY REQUESTS FOR SERVICES (2.05)

(a) When a behavior analyst agrees to provide services to a person or entity at the request of a third party, the behavior analyst clarifies to the extent feasible, at the outset of the service, the nature of the relationship with each party. This clarification includes the role of the behavior analyst (such as therapist, organizational consultant, or expert witness), the probable uses of the services provided or the information obtained, and the fact that there may be limits to confidentiality.

If you are asked by a third party (e.g., school system) to treat a child client, for example, you must clarify your relationship to the child, the parent, the teacher, and the school. You must explain your role (e.g., therapist, trainer, consultant) and how you think the information you provide can be used, and remind each one of issues of confidentiality. In a case involving the school, parents, and a child, the parent must give consent for the child to be observed by the behavior analyst on the school grounds and in the classroom. The parent must also give consent for the teacher to see the data. If anyone else requests information on the case, such as the school counselor, the parent must give consent for this, too.

(b) If there is a foreseeable risk of the behavior analyst being called upon to perform conflicting roles because of the involvement of a third party, the behavior analyst clarifies the nature and direction of his or her responsibilities, keeps all parties appropriately informed as matters develop, and resolves the situation in accordance with these Guidelines.

If there is some chance that you will be called on to perform a service for the third party (e.g., testify at a hearing), you must clarify this with the second party at the outset of the consultation. If a conflict arises, you must resolve the situation according to the BACB Guidelines.

• • • • • • •

CASE 2.05B: FULL DISCLOSURE?

Dr. B. was hired as an organizational consultant by the state office Department of Developmental Disabilities. He was assigned to an older, large residential facility for children and adults with developmental disabilities. His job was to help staff develop behavior programs for clients and to provide facility-wide program consultation. Some of the staff thought that Dr. B. was simply a new behavior analyst who was working with clients. They were unaware of the connection with the state office, and as a result, they were often observed to be off-task including talking on their cell phones when they were supposed to be working with clients.

The administrators knew, of course, that Dr. B. was sent by the state office. As time went on, the facility administrator began to pressure Dr. B. not to report facility problems to the Department of Developmental Disabilities.

What are some procedures Dr. B. could implement to manage this situation?

• • • • • • •

RIGHTS AND PREROGATIVES OF CLIENTS (2.06)

(a) The behavior analyst supports individual rights under the law.

As a behavior analyst, you must support the constitutional rights of your clients. In some states, client rights have become expanded to include additional rights such as to certain kinds of treatment, to hold and keep possessions, and to sexual activities. It is important to explore this issue for each state where you practice.

(b) The client must be provided on request an accurate, current set of the behavior analyst's credentials.

If your client wants to know about your background and train-ing, you should be eager to share an updated vita. This document should be a straightforward, honest, and accurate portrayal of your experience and training. Embellishment is not allowed.

> (c) Permission for electronic recording of interviews and service deliv-ery sessions is secured from clients and all other settings. Consent for different uses must be obtained specifically and separately.

If you find that you need to make audio or video electronic record-ings of interviews or behavioral observations or treatment, you must get permission from each client individually and from the administrators of each setting (e.g., parents, school administrator, case manager, group home director) as well. If you plan to use the recordings for some purpose other than therapy, you must obtain permission each time to use the recordings.

• • • • • • •

CASE 2.06C: VIDEO BACKLASH

Susan P. was a graduate student working as a behavior spe-cialist. Susan planned to do her doctoral dissertation on ado-lescents who were physically abused. By coincidence, Susan was assigned to work with Sara, an interesting, verbal 14-year-old, who was more than happy to describe her history of abuse for anyone who would listen. Susan videotaped an interview with Sara and 1 year later used this tape as part of a local conference presentation. As it turned out, one of the people in the audience recognized Sara. The friend told the mother about the video—the mother was extremely upset. She called Susan in a fury. Susan explained to the mother that this was an acceptable practice because she did not reveal Sara's last name.

> *If the identify of clients is protected (i.e., their names are not used), is it acceptable to present their cases, videotapes, or audiotapes?*

• • • • • • •

(d) Clients must be informed of their rights, and about procedures to complain about professional practices of the behavior analyst.

Your clients should be told of their rights to confidentiality. They should also be advised they have the right to withdraw from treatment or a research project at any time. Additionally, you must inform clients about how to voice any complaints regarding your services to your supervisor or to the BACB (see also 2.13). This information can be included in your declaration of professional services as described in Chapter 18.

MAINTAINING CONFIDENTIALITY (2.07)

(a) Behavior analysts have a primary obligation and take reasonable precautions to respect the confidentiality of those with whom they work or consult, recognizing that confidentiality may be established by law, institutional rules, or professional or scientific relationships.

It is very important that you respect and protect the confidentiality of your clients. You may not talk about or share data with regard to your clients with anyone without their explicit consent. Further, clients often don't want others to know about the nature of their disabilities or that they or their family members are receiving treatment. Clients have the right to confidentiality, and as a behavior analyst you are responsible for understanding the law regarding confidentiality.

(b) Clients have a right to confidentiality. Unless it is not feasible or is contraindicated, the discussion of confidentiality occurs at the outset of the relationship and thereafter as new circumstances may warrant.

You should discuss your client's right to confidentiality with the client and guardian at the onset of your professional relationship. If circumstances change, it is necessary to again remind the client of his or her right to confidentiality.

(c) In order to minimize intrusions on privacy, behavior analysts include only information germane to the purpose for which the communication is made in written and oral reports, consultations, and the like.

To protect your client's right to privacy, you should include information in your verbal and written reports only that is directly relevant to the behavior change under consideration.

(d) Behavior analysts discuss confidential information obtained in clinical or consulting relationships, or evaluative data concerning patients, individual or organizational clients, students, research participants, supervisees, and employees, only for appropriate scientific or professional purposes and only with persons clearly concerned with such matters.

You may share confidential information (fictitious names, location, and other identifying information should replace actual information) only with other professionals who may benefit in a scientific sense.

• • • • • • •

CASE 2.07D: PRYING PARISHIONERS

Dr. Elizabeth C. was a BCBA-D who worked with a number of children in her small community. Dr. C. most often provided treatment in the children's homes after school hours. Two of Dr. C.'s clients, Jason and Jessica, were brother and sister. Their alcoholic father was in and out of the home, and the father had abused their mother in the past. Dr. C. attended a church where several members of the congregation knew the family. They cared very much about the children and would ask how they were doing. These caring people would often tell Dr. C. what they knew about the family, and they would ask how the children were getting along in school and what kinds of things she worked on when she went to the home. The women from the church had donated clothing to the family in the past, and they always had the children on the list to receive Christmas gifts from the church.

With regard to maintaining confidentiality, how much information about the children should Dr. C. give these caring church members?

• • • • • • •

MAINTAINING RECORDS (2.08)

Behavior analysts maintain appropriate confidentiality in creating, storing, accessing, transferring, and disposing of records under their control, whether these are written, automated, or in any other medium. Behavior analysts maintain and dispose of records in accordance with applicable federal or state law or regulation, and corporate policy, and in a manner that permits compliance with the requirements of these Guidelines.

You are primarily responsible for any and all records that you create, use, or store. You will need to be current with current federal Health Insurance Portability and Accountability Act (HIPAA) legislation (HHS, 2003).

• • • • • • •

CASE 2.08: SAFE ENOUGH?

Steven J. is a BCBA who works with clients who live in a group home. He also works with the clients in the sheltered workshop they attend during the day. Steven takes data on vocational skills as well as any inappropriate behaviors occurring in the work setting. He is responsible for the behavioral component of the annual Habilitation Plan, and he updates annual assessments. Steven does not have an office in his home so he has been given some file drawers in the special education teacher's classroom at the sheltered workshop. He keeps all of his assessment results and raw data there. The teacher locks her classroom door when she leaves for the day so that the file drawers are safe.

Does Steven's system for keeping records meet the Guidelines?

• • • • • • •

DISCLOSURES (2.09)

(a) Behavior analysts disclose confidential information without the consent of the individual only as mandated by law, or where permitted by law for a valid purpose, such as (1) to provide needed professional services to the individual or organizational client, (2) to obtain appropriate professional consultations, (3) to protect the client or others from harm, or (4) to obtain payment for services, in which instance disclosure is limited to the minimum that is necessary to achieve the purpose.

Unless your client has signed a consent form, you should not release any information about the client unless required by law. Certain circumstances may require you to release information to provide needed services for the person, to make a referral, or to collect for services rendered.

(b) Behavior analysts also may disclose confidential information with the appropriate consent of the individual or organizational client (or of another legally authorized person on behalf of the client), unless prohibited by law.

If you have written consent from your client, you may disclose confidential information.

• • • • • • •

CASE 2.09B: JUST TAKING DATA

Dr. Connie G. was working in a school system's prekindergarten classrooms for developmentally disabled children. Billy was a 4-year-old whose parents were divorced. Billy spent alternating weeks with each of his parents. The teacher had a theory that Billy's maladaptive behaviors, including tantrums and disruption, greatly increased on the first few days after a visit to his mother's house, so Dr. G. began taking data to test this theory. She felt that this sort of evaluation was simply part of her job description and did not inform the parents. At the end

of the month, she submitted her time sheet indicating 3 hours
for an "evaluation of parent-induced behavior disorder."
Is this a violation of the Guidelines?

• • • • • • •

TREATMENT EFFICACY (2.10)

(a) The behavior analyst always has the responsibility to recommend scientifically supported most effective treatment procedures. Effective treatment procedures have been validated as having both long-term and short-term benefits to clients and society.

You should always recommend evidence-based treatments that have been shown scientifically to be effective in both the short- and long-term.

(b) Clients have a right to effective treatment (i.e., based on the research literature and adapted to the individual client).

It is an article of faith of behavior analysis that our clients have a right to effective treatment that has been so demonstrated in the research literature. It is the job of the behavior analyst to adapt that treatment for each individual client and then to make sure it is effective for him or her. If the data show it is not working, there is an obligation to search for another method.

(c) Behavior analysts are responsible for review and appraisal of likely effects of all alternative treatments, including those provided by other disciplines and no intervention.

If your client is receiving "alternative" treatment, you are responsible for determining if there is research to support it. This may include behaviorally based treatments for which there is no evidence as well as nonbehavioral treatments that are not supported in any scientific literature. You should also be prepared to evaluate the effects of no intervention being provided. A good model for this is illustrated in Kay and Vyse's (2005) excellent chapter, "Helping Parents Separate the Wheat From the Chaff: Putting Autism Treatments to the Test." They describe simple, elegant research designs by which BCBAs working with parents can help them determine, with data, whether "alternative" treatments are having any significant impact on behavior.

• • • • • • •

CASE 2.10C: OUTNUMBERED

Kevin is a 6-year-old with a developmental disability who continues to bang his head. Robert is a BCBA who has been recently assigned to Kevin's classroom. Robert's functional analysis of Kevin's behavior shows that it is related to attention from his parents and teachers. An occupational therapist (OT) has developed the current treatment plan that includes sensory integration training, joint compression, and sessions three times a week to jump on a trampoline to "use up this pent-up energy." The speech therapist recommended sign language. The physical therapist recommended a helmet. Kevin continued to bang his head with the helmet, and he also started biting his fingers. The OT is very sure that her plan will eventually work, and she explains at every treatment team meeting that everyone needs to be patient and give the sensory integration program time to work. The special education teacher has been, and continues to be, supportive of the OT's program.

Robert, the BCBA, is clearly outnumbered here. How should he proceed?

• • • • • • •

(d) In those instances where more than one scientifically supported treatment has been established, additional factors may be considered in selecting interventions, including, but not limited to, efficiency and cost-effectiveness, risks and side-effects of the interventions, client preference, and practitioner experience and training.

As behavior analysts we are obligated to use evidence-based treatments, but in some, perhaps many, cases there might be a dozen journal articles supporting somewhat different treatments. What's a practitioner to do? This new guideline puts the responsibility squarely in the lap of the practitioner and says essentially, that you should choose, based on your training and experience and client preference. If you were trained to use procedure A and have a lot of experience with it (evidence-based, of course) and you find an article supporting procedure B (equally effective), then you may decide to go with A based on experience. Or, your client may have a strong choice for B in which case you will need to get up to speed on B so that you can respect her wishes. Conducting a risk–benefit analysis (Chapter 16) is also recommended.

• • • • • • •

CASE 2.10D: POSITIVELY TRUMPED

Farah knew how to design classroom token economies and had done so all over the school district. She was a positive person and had been since grade school when she won her first spelling bee. Farah's token economies reflected her personality: they were positive; that is, the teacher gave out tokens for appropriate behavior from the time the first bell rang until lunch, and the students in Mrs. Boyle's class could cash them in for preferred activities in the afternoon. It worked for the first week, although Mrs. Boyle seemed stressed by having to keep track of five different appropriate behaviors. "I don't have any time to teach; all I do is hand out points," she muttered on Friday. To her surprise Farah found a copy of an article comparing "positive and negative" point systems in her mailbox on Monday morning with a note, "Can we talk?" signed by Mrs. Boyle. She had spent the weekend on the Internet and had come across the Journal of Applied Behavior Analysis (JABA) Web site with an article she wanted to talk about with Farah. It showed that a response–cost-based point system was just as good as a positive

*system and that some teachers preferred it because it was easier
to administer.*

What is Farah's next move?

• • • • • • • •

DOCUMENTING OF PROFESSIONAL AND SCIENTIFIC WORK (2.11)

(a) Behavior analysts appropriately document their professional
and scientific work in order to facilitate provision of services later
by them or by other professionals, to ensure accountability, and to
meet other requirements of institutions or the law.

You must maintain written records of your work product so that
at some later time other professionals may use the documentation
to assist your client and to ensure accountability. Keep your raw
data sheets, spreadsheets, and written summaries and reports in a
secure location as required by law.

(b) When behavior analysts have reason to believe that records
of their professional services will be used in legal proceedings
involving recipients of or participants in their work, they have a
responsibility to create and maintain documentation in the kind
of detail and quality that would be consistent with reasonable
scrutiny in an adjudicative forum.

If there is some chance that information regarding your professional behavioral services will become part of a court case, you
have an obligation to make sure that the records are complete.

• • • • • • • •

CASE 2.11B: DATA KEEPER

*Dr. M. is a BCBA-D who is providing behavioral services to
a school system that has limited services for children with
autism. She has been hired to do a very limited number
of consulting hours with several children with a diagnosis of*

autism. Dr. M. keeps the standard data expected of a behavior analyst, including baseline and treatment data. A teacher's aide collects the data twice a week. It is beginning to look like a lawsuit will be filed against the school district on behalf of its students with autism.

Considering this, what kind of records should Dr. M. be keeping to ensure the she is accountable if subpoenaed?

• • • • • • •

(c) Behavior analysts obtain and document (1) Institutional Review Board (IRB) and/or local human research committee approval and/or (2) confirmation of compliance with institutional requirements when data gathered during their professional services will be submitted to professional conferences and peer reviewed journals.

This important addition to the Guidelines in 2010 expands protections to clients for data collected during the normal provision of professional services. All behavior analysts collect and analyze data while providing treatment; it is required to understand what is effective and how treatments work. Some practitioners present this data at state and local conferences, and they will now be required to obtain and document that they are in compliance with "institutional requirements." Presumably this means that they will have to plan ahead and get permission to gather and use data for public professional audiences.

• • • • • • •

CASE 2.11C: DATA DIFFICULTIES

As a BCBA who worked with many individual client cases, Dr. C. had a lot of data from his work with students with autism. Quickly becoming recognized as a leader in the field, Dr. C. had developed some unique protocols for teaching language. Each year, he presented the data of his clients at state and national conferences. Recently, a colleague told Dr. C. that the new revision to the Guidelines was going to make it more difficult to present client data at conferences. Dr. C.'s response was that Institutional Review Board (IRB) approval pertains only to college students and university faculty, and as long as names were changed so that clients could not be identified there would be no problems with his presentations.

Was Dr. C. interpreting the change to 2.11c correctly?

• • • • • • •

RECORDS AND DATA (2.12)

Behavior analysts create, maintain, disseminate, store, retain, and dispose of records and data relating to their research, practice, and other work in accordance with applicable federal and state laws or regulations and corporate policy and in a manner that permits compliance with the requirements of these Guidelines.

You will need to keep your records relating to your research and practice. This may range from 90 days to 12 years, depending on the type of records and specific regulations for state and federal laws. You will need to be in compliance with these guidelines, and check with your agency or university for specific requirements in your area.

• • • • • • •

CASE 2.12: TIGHT SPACE

Barbara is a BCBA graduate student on a limited budget. She has a typical student's apartment—small, cramped, not much storage space—and she shares it with three roommates. Barbara keeps the data for her clients for about 3 months, and then she throws them away, but only after attending a monthly meeting where she turns in copies of her data to her supervisor.

Barbara certainly seems justified in her handling of records given her living conditions. Is she living within the Guidelines?

• • • • • • •

FEES, FINANCIAL ARRANGEMENTS, AND TERMS OF CONSULTATION (2.13)

(a) As early as is feasible in a professional or scientific relationship, the behavior analyst and the client or other appropriate recipient of behavior analytic services reach an agreement specifying the compensation and the billing arrangements.

As soon as you establish a professional relationship with a client (i.e., the client or his or her representative has asked you to take the case), you should inform the client (or agency) of your fees and payment policy. Although this may make you uncomfortable, it is necessary for everyone involved to avoid embarrassment, and possibly worse, later.

• • • • • • •

CASE 2.13A: CERTAINLY A LEARNING EXPERIENCE

Glenda was a fourth-year graduate student in a prestigious doctoral program in behavior analysis. When she got a call from the associate chair of the department about an unusual case, she jumped at the chance to get the experience and make some extra money. She was so excited about meeting the family and the child who was referred that she neglected to bring up her fee expectation. She was thinking along the lines of $75 per hour because she was nearly "a doctor," and this case did require some special expertise.

At the end of the month, when Glenda asked the associate chair where she should send her bill, she was shocked and stunned to learn that this was considered a charity case.

• • • • • • •

(b) Behavior analysts' fee practices are consistent with law and behavior analysts do not misrepresent their fees. If limitations to services can be anticipated because of limitations in financing, this is discussed with the patient, client, or other appropriate recipient of services as early as is feasible.

If state or federal law sets your fees, obey the law and clearly present your fee schedule to your client. If the client has limited funding and this will limit behavioral services, the issue should be discussed as soon as possible to avoid any confusion or charge of misrepresentation. Keep in mind that for a child in a school system, the "client" may be the school system.

• • • • • • •

CASE 2.13B: WAYNE'S WORLD

Wayne is an 8-year-old who has moved into a new school system in the last few weeks of the school year. He was diagnosed as severely emotionally disturbed (SED) and he has shown some serious behavior problems in his new classroom. Wayne will be enrolled in the district's summer school program, and Jean, a BCBA part-time employee of the district, has been asked to work with him. The principal and teacher met with Jean and explained to her that funding for behavioral services during summer school is very limited, but considering the severity of Wayne's problems they hoped that she would agree to take the case and do whatever she needs to do to meet Wayne's needs. It is clear to Jean, after some initial observations, that the funding is not adequate to provide the level of service Wayne needs.

How should Jean handle her consulting fees and the financial arrangements for this case?

• • • • • • •

(c) Prior to the implementation of services, the behavior analyst will provide in writing the terms of consultation with regard to specific requirements for providing services and the responsibilities of all parties (a contract or Declaration of Professional Services).

Other professions have for years used a contract or declaration describing their professional services at the onset of each case. If used consistently it will prevent many problems that inevitably come up in the course of months-long treatment for behavior problems. This is a new idea for most behavior analysts, but it should help with issues regarding access to the behavior analyst during off-hours, handling of missed appointments, and awkward situations involving gifts, invitations to dinner or birthdays, and other questions that come up in the course of long-term treatment. A complete description of the declaration of professional services can be found in Chapter 18, "Avoiding the 'Slippery Slope' of Ethical Problems by Using a Declaration of Professional Services."

ACCURACY IN REPORTS TO THOSE WHO PAY FOR SERVICES (2.14)

In their reports to those who pay for services or sources of research, project, or program funding, behavior analysts accurately state the nature of the research or service provided, the fees or charges, and where applicable, the identity of the provider, the findings, and other required descriptive data.

When handling billing information, always honestly and accurately present the necessary details regarding work completed, hours of service, and any other necessary data.

• • • • • • •

CASE 2.14: A+ BILLING

The A+ Behavior Consulting Group has a contract to provide behavioral services for five intermediate care facility/mental retardation (ICF/MR) group homes owned by the same company. A+ has several consultants who provide the services to the group homes. Depending on scheduling, any one of several consultants may come to sit in on Habilitation Plan meetings, do assessments, and so forth. When the billing is submitted to the company owning the group homes, the name of the consultant is on the bill, the date service was provided, and the number of hours the consultant was at the facility.

Is there any other information that should be provided with the billing?

• • • • • • •

REFERRALS AND FEES (2.15)

When a behavior analyst pays, receives payment from, or divides fees with another professional other than in an employer–employee relationship, the referral shall be disclosed to the client.

Do not make it a practice to accept any form of payment for a referral. Those who do so put their reputation at risk and must disclose this information immediately to the client.

• • • • • • •

CASE 2.15: PAYOLA

A large consulting firm of clinical psychologists has several psychologists on staff who specialize in psychological testing. Barry S., a BCBA, knows some of the psychologists through work he has done in the schools. One of the clinical psychologists in this group approached Barry and told him that the firm would pay him $25 for each client he referred to the group for testing. Barry is an ethical BCBA who would refer only clients who needed a psychological work-up.

Because he knows these psychologists and respects their diagnostic skills, under what conditions would this arrangement be acceptable?

• • • • • • •

INTERRUPTING OR TERMINATING SERVICES (2.16)

(a) Behavior analysts make reasonable efforts to plan for facilitating care in the event that behavior analytic services are interrupted by factors such as the behavior analyst's illness, impending death, unavailability, or relocation or by the client's relocation or financial limitations.

For each of your clients, you should have a plan to provide coverage in the event that you are no longer able to do so. Interruption of service applies to temporarily stopping services by the behavior analyst, often due to the behavior analyst's health or family problems. Interrupting services does not mean canceling sessions for a short time, as when the behavior analyst has the flu or takes a vacation. The interruption of services refers to stopping services for an extended period of time, such as a month or longer.

(b) When entering into employment or contractual relationships, behavior analysts provide for orderly and appropriate resolution of responsibility for client care in the event that the employment or contractual relationship ends, with paramount consideration given to the welfare of the client.

If you are working through an agency that has a contract with clients for services, read the contract carefully so you understand what will happen to the clients if you are unable to provide consulting for an extended period of time. The welfare of each client should be of utmost importance to you should this occur.

• • • • • • •

CASE 2.16B: FURLOUGH

Dr. D. has been providing behavioral services to the six young women who live in a group home. Dr. D. has developed a health problem requiring surgery and a lengthy recovery period. Dr. D. is attached to these young women and does not want to give up this contract, but her surgery and follow-up recovery are not optional. She would like to resume her consulting when she is better. Her best estimate is that she would be away from the group home for about 3 months.

Because she will be gone so long, does Dr. D. need to resign from this job in the best interest of the clients?

• • • • • • •

(c) Behavior analysts do not abandon clients. Behavior analysts terminate a professional relationship when it becomes reasonably clear that the client no longer needs the service, is not benefiting, or is being harmed by continued service.

Do not walk away from your clients without notice. You may terminate a professional relationship when (a) it is clear that the client no longer needs your service, (b) you determine that the client is not benefiting, or (c) you establish that the client is actually being harmed in some way by your service.

(d) Prior to termination for whatever reason, except where precluded by the client's conduct, the behavior analyst discusses the client's views and needs, provides appropriate pre-termination services, suggests alternative service providers as appropriate, and takes other reasonable steps to facilitate transfer of responsibility to another provider if the client needs one immediately.

If you need to terminate your service, you should discuss the client's needs with the relevant parties (e.g., parents, guardian, agency director, school administrator) and suggest other professionals who can provide assistance.

• • • • • • •

CASE 2.16D: TOUGH CHOICE

Marcus is a 10-year-old from a divorced family who was physically and verbally abused while living with his alcoholic mother. Protective Services removed him from the home and placed him with his biological father. A BCBA has been assigned to work in the home several hours per week. Marcus has been prescribed medication for hyperactivity, but his dad does not give it to him on a consistent basis. The dad recognizes Marcus's behavior problems, including running away and noncompliance, but has refused parent training. He says he does not need anyone telling him how to handle his child's behavior. When the BCBA comes to the home, the dad uses the visit as a chance to have a free babysitter and will go work in the garage and he has even gone to the store.

It feels like it is impossible to get any cooperation with behavioral services in this home, but can the BCBA justify leaving this child?

• • • • • • •

RESPONSES TO CASES

CASE 2.0: SAVING MONEY FOR THE SCHOOL

Helping the principal come in under budget should not be Betsy's primary concern. Betsy's first concern and responsibility is to the students. The primary issue here is whether a reduction in hours would mean that a client would not receive the ideal level of behavioral services. The question would arise as to whether too many hours had been contracted for in the first place or if enough progress had been made that 20 hours per week were no longer needed.

CASE 2.01: PARENTS WHO DON'T WANT HELP

While a child's parent could also be considered the "client," Allan is the most vulnerable party in this situation. Monica needs to be an advocate for Allan and the services he needs. Monica might start by asking Mom if there is anything that can be done (e.g., a schedule change) to make it easier for her to be available for Allan's behavioral treatment in the home. In case the mother has decided she just doesn't like Monica and doesn't have the nerve to say this, Monica's supervisor may want to talk to the mother to determine if there would be a consultant who was a better match for this parent. Monica and her supervisor might also want to get Allan's case manager involved as soon as possible.

CASE 2.02: QUESTIONABLE REPERTOIRE

Because behavior analysts should accept only clients whose behavior problems are commensurate with the behavior analyst's skill level, Martin needs to consult with an expert specifically in the treatment of head injury with unpredictable aggressive behavior. If there is no such person at the facility, he needs to find someone in the area to supervise him. There can be liability issues if he does not.

CASE 2.03: TEACHER'S PET

Since the behavior analyst's responsibility is to all parties affected by behavioral services, Terry needs to modify her behavior plan immediately. Even though Brianna's behavior is improving, Terry's plan has started damaging the relationship between the teacher and the other children.

Further, it is not ethical to require other students to be a part of reinforcing Terry when they have no chance to earn reinforcers themselves.

CASE 2.04: SEX THERAPY

No, Dr. M. is a BCBA-D, and although he may be widely read he is not trained as a sex therapist or counselor. Teaching Jerry "to verbalize about sex-related issues" does not make this a behavioral problem. With appropriate consent from Jerry and his parents, Dr. M. should refer Jerry to a properly trained and certified counselor who can help him sort through his problems.

CASE 2.05B: FULL DISCLOSURE?

On his arrival at the facility, Dr. B. should have a meeting with the administrator to clarify his relationship with the Developmental Disability Department and his role at the facility. He should set up some routine reporting procedures such as weekly meetings with key administrators, including brief written reports of his findings. He has taken this position because he believes he can help the facility, but everyone needs to be aware of for whom he is actually working, and attempts to influence his judgment need to be turned away.

CASE 2.06C: VIDEO BACKLASH

The behavior analyst must support the rights of clients. At any time a client is recorded (audio or video), consent must be granted. Further, if you get permission to tape a session for one purpose and then decide to do something additional with the tape, you must again obtain permission. At the beginning of working with any client (and his or her family or guardian, in the case of a minor), the BCBA should inform that client of procedures to complain about the professional practices of the behavior analyst. Susan, although not a BCBA, clearly violated the spirit of these Guidelines and should apologize to the mother and report to her major professor about this incident.

CASE 2.07D: PRYING PARISHIONERS

Behavior analysts have an obligation to respect the confidentiality of those with whom they work. When asked about the children, Dr. C. should politely tell anyone who asks that she cannot discuss her work with her clients. She should then politely change the subject.

CASE 2.08: SAFE ENOUGH?

Although keeping records in the office of another professional is a frequent practice, this should not be done unless the BCBA has file drawers to which he has the only keys. Although the teacher locks her classroom door at the end of the day, when Steven is not at the facility the teacher, her aide, or anyone with access to the classroom could view the confidential information in the records.

CASE 2.09B: JUST TAKING DATA

Although 2.07 addresses confidentiality, 2.09 gives the behavior analyst the right to disclose information without the consent of the client to obtain payment for services. A key distinction here is that disclosure is limited to the minimum necessary information to achieve the purpose. This means that Dr. C. should not include confidential information in her report other than the minimum amount of information required for billing.

CASE 2.10C: OUTNUMBERED

Robert should explain to the team that clients have a right to effective treatment. His professional responsibility is to review and evaluate alternative treatments, and he should request empirically based articles from these other professionals and critique them. A baseline should be started as soon as possible. Emergency procedures should be used if Kevin is hurting himself. Interventions for SIB should be based on the research literature, and if Robert is not satisfied that these "other" treatments are supported by empirical evidence he should say so at the next habilitation team meeting.

CASE 2.10D: POSITIVELY TRUMPED

Farah should probably have done a better job of "qualifying" Mrs. Boyle when she began working in her classroom. It appears that she took the route of doing what was easy for her but not necessarily a good choice for her client. Farah was actually caught a little off guard by the JABA article and had to confess that she had not seen it before, but she read it carefully and then had to agree with Mrs. Boyle that it could be done.

CASE 2.11B: DATA KEEPER

The Guidelines say that work should be documented to ensure account-ability and to meet other requirements. Therefore, at a minimum, Dr. M. would want to have data as described in 3.0 (Assessment) and 4.0 (Behavior Change Programs) of the Guidelines. Further, Dr. M. should be sure that she has collected some sample of the data herself. In addition to data, detailed case notes would be helpful. If there are any observations related to students being affected by a lack of services or resources, this should be noted with relevant specifics.

CASE 2.11C: DATA DIFFICULTIES

No, Dr. C. missed the point of this new addition to the Guidelines. 2.11c adds another level of privacy for clients; now behavior analyst practitioners must seek permission to use any data collected in the course of providing treatment. Presumably this means that clients must give permission as well as any funding agencies that are supporting the therapy. A behavior analyst working in the schools would need permission in writing from the school and perhaps even the school board to use data collected there as part of treatment.

CASE 2.12: TIGHT SPACE

Barbara is keeping records in her apartment. Can the roommates see the records? The records should be locked so that she has the only access. Throwing client records in the trash is not a good idea. Sometimes trashcans are knocked over, sanitation workers can drop things when emptying cans into the truck, and the next thing you know your tossed papers are flying down the street. Client records that are thrown away should be shredded. Three months is not long enough to keep records. Barbara should be complying with state laws and other relevant (e.g., Medicaid) requirements. In most states, records should be kept for at least 3 years. Finally, if a consulting firm hires Barbara, this firm should have an office or storage location where records can be maintained appropriately. This is especially important for companies that retain the services of graduate students who are likely to graduate and move away.

CASE 2.13A: CERTAINLY A LEARNING EXPERIENCE

Had Glenda inquired about her payment for taking this case on the front end, she might not have gotten it. It was a valuable experience, and it did enhance the departments' image as a caring organization that can help out those in need in a pinch. And it was a valuable lesson for Glenda that she would not soon forget as she prepared to take comps and move into the real world.

CASE 2.13B: WAYNE'S WORLD

Jean and the principal can quickly make an appeal to the district and other support services for getting additional hours approved for behavioral services. If this doesn't work, Jean needs to estimate the number of hours she can work given the funding in the budget. She needs to discuss and put in writing the limitations to services. As a last resort, Jean can start training a school staff person to assist with the services she is providing. She may be able to be on-site less if someone else who has the appropriate skill level can assist with Wayne's behavioral program.

CASE 2.14: A+ BILLING

The billing should also include the specific nature of the service provided, the findings, and any recommendations.

CASE 2.15: PAYOLA

The Guidelines state that referral fees can be accepted, but they must be disclosed with the client or agency. In this case, to remain within the Guidelines, Barry would have to tell the school that he was suggesting that this firm do the testing and that he would receive referral fees. Depending on how this was handled and how often it happened, this situation could border on a conflict of interest. The safest bet for the ethical behavior analyst is to never accept referral fees.

CASE 2.16B: FURLOUGH

It is acceptable for behavior analysts to interrupt their services as long as they provide for the orderly and systematic care of the clients. Dr. D. needs to talk with the agency as soon as possible, to tell the appropriate personnel she would like to continue, and to give the timelines expected for her recovery. Dr. D. can suggest someone to cover for her while she is out on leave, and she can develop a plan for that person to use while she is gone. When she is feeling better, she can check in by phone.

CASE 2.16D: TOUGH CHOICE

This is clearly a very sad situation for Marcus. However, it is reasonably clear that given the current situation Marcus is not benefiting from the behavioral services at this time. The BCBA needs to terminate this relationship. She should document everything she has tried to do and the noncompliance on the dad's part. The documentation should be provided to Protective Services as well as the other relevant agencies.

8

Assessing Behavior (Guideline 3)

It is a bedrock principle of behavior analysis that it is necessary to "take a baseline" before any treatment is contemplated. The reasons are not so obvious to outsiders, and the methodology by which it is accomplished is out of the reach of most other professions. For us, taking a baseline means many things, including the following:

- A referral has been made of a behavior that is problematic.
- The behavior is observable and has been operationally defined in some manner that allows quantification.
- A trained observer has visited the setting where the behavior occurs and has documented the occurrence and the circumstances under which it occurs (this indicates that the referral is legitimate, that the problem is measurable, and that the behavior may or may not require treatment, depending on what the graphs of the data show).

Behavior analysts do not work on rumor or hearsay. They want to see the problem for themselves, to get some sense of the variability from day to day, and to determine if there is any trending, and, finally, they want to understand the circumstances under

> **Behavior analysts do not work on rumor or hearsay. They want to see the problems for themselves.**

which the behavior occurs and to get some sense of the function of the behavior.

"This kid is driving me crazy, he is constantly out of his seat, talking with the other children, and he never completes an assignment that I hand out. I spend all my time sending him back to his seat and telling him to sit down." This referral from a very frustrated third-grade teacher would be the stimulus for a behavior analyst to go to the classroom and observe exactly what is going on. (The teacher, meanwhile, was thinking that she would like to get this "brat" out of her classroom.) Although the assistant principal, school counselor, or school psychologist might immediately start giving the teacher some advice on what to do or schedule a battery of IQ and personality tests, the behavior analyst insists that some assessment of the behavior occur first. How much time is the student out of his seat? What was the stimulus for this behavior? What kinds of assignments are given, and how many does he actually complete? The behavior analyst will also be interested in knowing what kind of prompts the teacher uses for each of the behaviors and what type of reinforcement she currently uses to maintain the behavior (if any). Another question that might come up has to do with the appropriateness of the class assignments for the student. Is there any chance that they are too difficult or that the instructions are inadequate? And finally, the behavior analyst, while observing the referred student, will also be assessing the degree of peer involvement in this child's behavior. The astute and ethical behavior analyst will take enough baseline to ensure that there is indeed a problem that needs solving and will have some preliminary ideas as to the variables that might be operating. One final point is that these baseline data will be graphed and used in an evaluation of treatment effects. Imagine how this would work if there was no rule about

> The astute and ethical behavior analyst will take enough baseline to ensure that there is indeed a problem that needs solving.

taking a baseline first. The behavior analyst would have to rely on an untrained, possibly biased person's estimate of the frequency of the target behaviors, would have to take this person's opinion of likely causal variables seriously, and would have no basis for evaluation of any suggestions made. Viewed in this light, it is downright unethical to operate in this fashion, yet this scenario is probably the mode for what passes as behavior consulting in America by nonbehavioral "professionals."

In Guideline 3.0, Assessing Behavior, the Behavior Analysis Certification Board (BACB) Guidelines clearly specify what goes into a behavioral assessment and further (in Guideline 4.0) includes an even broader obligation to explain to the client (e.g., the teacher, principal, and parents) the conditions necessary for the intervention to work (4.01) and those that might prevent it from being properly implemented (4.02, 4.03). If the ethical behavior analyst determines what the controlling variables are through a functional assessment (see Iwata, Dorsey, Slifer, Bauman, & Richman, 1982, for the original study on this method), he or she is obligated to spell this out for the clients and to explain the limiting conditions for treatment. This latter concept, limiting conditions, is critical

> The concept of limiting conditions is critical to an understanding of how behavior analysis works.

to an understanding of how behavior analysis works in applied settings. To take a simple example, if we want to use a reinforcer to strengthen the sitting-in-seat behavior of the third grader described earlier, we have to find out what is the reinforcer. If, for some reason, we are not able to find a reinforcer, then this limiting condition has been exceeded. Or, if we discover what the reinforcer is but are not allowed to use it, or if the teacher refuses to use the reinforcer even if we know what it is, we have exceeded one of the limiting conditions of treatment. If the reinforcer is some sort of snack (discovered through a reinforcer assessment) but the teacher "doesn't believe in using snacks," then it will be difficult to change this child's behavior through this means. Or if the behavior analyst determines that a daily report card is the best solution for the child but the parents refuse to cooperate by delivering contingent reinforcers at home, we have run headlong into a limiting condition of treatment.

As a final note on assessment, it is so important that behavior analysts explain to the client what the data mean (probably using actual working graphs to illustrate the key points), that we have determined that it should be included in the Guidelines. There, in Guideline 3.03, it is clearly stated that as a behavior analyst, you have an obligation to explain the baseline data, functional assessment, reinforcement assessment, or other forms of behavioral data collection to the client, in plain English, so he or she can understand what is involved. This includes, of course, the results of any interventions to show actual measured effects of what was tried and what worked. Besides keeping the client, guardian, or advocate apprised of our interventions, this requirement also probably serves some public relations function. It teaches the client that what we do is transparent and understandable, that we are objective in our approach, and that we use data for decision making. One hoped-for result is that clients and client-surrogates so educated will begin to ask questions of other professionals about the basis for their interventions. One fairly major change is a requirement to seek a medical consultation in cases where a behavior may be a result of a "medication side effect or some biological cause." Most well-trained behavior analysts have been doing this for years, but now this is made explicit in our Guidelines.

> **As a behavior analyst, you have an obligation to explain your data in plain English.**

ASSESSING BEHAVIOR (3.0)

Behavior analysts who use behavioral assessment techniques do so for purposes that are appropriate in light of the research. Behavior analysts recommend seeking a medical consultation if there is any reasonable possibility that a referred behavior is a result of a medication side effect or some biological cause.

This statement refers to those behavior analysts who perhaps use more standardized behavioral assessments than simply taking a baseline. The thrust of this recommendation is that the behavior analyst is obligated to learn about the research associated with the assessment and to make sure that it is used within the boundaries of reliability and validity that have been established for the assessment. Additionally, there is an obligation to consider the possibility that a specific behavior referral might be caused by or affected by some biological factor or by a medication side effect. If you have any doubt about the origin of a behavior it is best to make a referral to a physician. And, of course, it makes sense to consult a medical professional for any behavior that could obviously cause physical harm to the individual. Head banging; eye gouging; arm, leg, or head scratching; and lip biting are all dangerous behaviors that can be modified by behavioral procedures so a consult is essential before proceeding. Head banging could be a result of severe headaches; scratching could be a symptom of allergies. As an ethical behavior analyst you have an obligation to be open to the possibility of biological causes of behaviors that you are required to deal with.

(a) Behavior analysts' assessments, recommendations, reports, and evaluative statements are based on information and techniques sufficient to provide appropriate substantiation for their findings.

Behavior analysts present their findings based on assessment tools that are up to the task scientifically. This means knowing precisely how the standardization sample compares with the client being evaluated and being able to interpret the results using the test manual and associated research that may have been done with the assessment.

(b) Behavior analysts refrain from misuse of assessment techniques, interventions, results, and interpretations and take reasonable steps to prevent others from misusing the information these techniques provide.

The most likely form of misuse of an assessment is to go beyond the data that are actually collected. We do not overstate the results of our assessment results and discourage others from doing so.

> (c) Behavior analysts recognize limits to the certainty with which judgments or predictions can be made about individuals.

As behavioral scientists, we stay very close to the data rather than make unsubstantiated predictions about behavior. We frequently use qualifiers such as "my best judgment is" or "it seems to me that...," and we usually acknowledge that our assessment is not perfect or definitive. For example, we might say, "Based on three days of observation, I would say that Carl's behavior is more likely to occur when he is asked to do math problems," rather than "Carl is math phobic." In cases where nonbehavioral assessments are provided to a behavior analyst, the behavior analyst conducts behavior assessments (i.e., functional analysis, data collection, direct observation of behaviors) before planning a behavior program.

• • • • • • •

CASE 3.0C: BACK TO BASICS

Theresa, a Board Certified Behavior Analyst (BCBA) who was providing behavioral consultation for adults who were profoundly mentally retarded, was provided with assessment materials for Charlie, a new client at a residential facility. His folder included the results from Stanford Binet and Wechsler IQ tests. Charlie was a verbal client, and he appeared to have good self-help and social skills. However, because his IQ test scores were listed as "untestable," the facility administrator felt that Charlie should start in basic training classes at the facility rather than in the sheltered workshop setting. The administrator said if Charlie "proved himself," he could transition to sheltered work in a few months.

Theresa felt very uneasy about the test results, but she was not sure if she should question the work of another professional and the administrator. What do you think?

• • • • • • •

(d) Behavior analysts do not promote the use of behavioral assessment techniques by unqualified persons, i.e., those who are unsupervised by experienced professionals and have not demonstrated valid and reliable assessment skills.

Behavior analysts are very particular about data collection and insist that only those who are well trained should be involved in this aspect of assessment. Work that is done by a Board Certified assistant Behavior Analyst (BCaBA) should be supervised by a BCBA.

• • • • • • • •

CASE 3.0D: PROCEED WITH CAUTION

In the aforementioned scenario, after calling the previous facility, Theresa received some assessment information that was behavior analytic in nature. She was relieved to see a functional analysis. The functional analysis and other behavioral assessments were done by a BCaBA. Theresa called the facility again to ask if there was any additional assessment information or data and to get the name of the BCBA who supervised the BCaBA. It seems that the facility did not have a BCBA and that the BCaBA was doing the best she knew how to provide behavioral assessments and treatment for clients.

In light of this information, how should Theresa proceed? Is she ready to start an intervention?

• • • • • • • •

BEHAVIORAL ASSESSMENT APPROVAL (3.01)

The behavior analyst must obtain the client's or client-surrogate's approval in writing of the behavior assessment procedures before implementing them. As used here, client-surrogate refers to someone legally empowered to make decisions for the person(s) whose behavior the program is intended to change; examples of client-surrogates include parents of minors, guardians, and legally designated representatives.

FUNCTIONAL ASSESSMENT (3.02)

(a) The behavior analyst conducts a functional assessment, as defined below, to provide the necessary data to develop an effective behavior change program.

It is considered "best practice" for behavior analysis to determine the function of a behavior prior to writing a behavior program. Some common functions include attention, escape from demands, or tangible reinforcers; the behavior analyst should not make assumptions or operate on simple hearsay but rather should strive to determine causal environmental variables. Some recent research even suggests that the same behavior may have different functions in different environments.

(b) Functional assessment includes a variety of systematic information-gathering activities regarding factors influencing the occurrence of a behavior (e.g., antecedents, consequences, setting events, or motivating operations) including interview, direct observation, and experimental analysis.

Functional assessment may range from an informal descriptive analysis (based on interviews and informal observations) to a more formal data-based observation system to an actual experimental functional assessment, as is often seen in the *Journal of Applied Behavior Analysis* (*JABA*). The goal of a functional assessment is to determine what the controlling variables are for the behavior in question. Sometimes this is obvious just from watching the individual for a few sessions; in other cases, it is necessary to interview staff members or teachers to get some inkling of what motivates the behavior. Finally, in some cases, the controlling variables are so subtle that it takes an experimental protocol to discover an effective independent variable.

• • • • • • •

CASE 3.02B: NOW WHAT?

Florence worked as a supervisor in a residential facility for multiply handicapped individuals. One of her residents, Sondra, had a strange behavior that involved pulling at her hair at various times during the day. She had clear bald spots, and her scalp was often red and tender. Using what she learned about functional analysis from workshops at a state convention of behavior analysts, Florence started some informal obser- vations. She concluded that Sondra's hair pulling was more likely to occur right before meals and was perhaps a "frus- tration response" to not being able to eat when she wanted. Florence arranged for Sondra to have nutritious snacks while the meal was being prepared and for her to eat first to elimi- nate the frustration. After a month, it appeared that Sondra's hair pulling was unaffected. Next, Florence called in her BCBA and asked for help. She showed the BCBA her data and told him about the informal functional assessment. The BCBA then began time sampling several times per day to produce a more precise descriptive analysis. The BCBA's data showed that although some of the hair pulling occurred before meals even more was occurring after Sondra went to bed. He felt that the source of the agitation was a roommate whose television was too loud. The BCBA arranged for a test of this hypothesis by switching Sondra's roommate on four separate nights over the next month. In no case was the hair pulling observed.

Is an experimental functional analysis necessary in this case?

• • • • • • •

EXPLAINING ASSESSMENT RESULTS (3.03)

Unless the nature of the relationship is clearly explained to the person being assessed in advance and precludes provision of an explanation of results (such as in some organizational consulta- tion, some screenings, and forensic evaluations), behavior ana- lysts ensure that an explanation of the results is provided using language that is reasonably understandable to the person assessed or to another legally authorized person on behalf of the client. Regardless of whether the interpretation is done by the behavior analyst, by assistants, or others, behavior analysts take reasonable steps to ensure that appropriate explanations of results are given.

Behavior analysts explain the results of the assessment, in plain English or other appropriate language, to the client or the client's representative. This is essential to assure that everyone understands the basis for treatment that is to follow. In behavior analysis we seek transparency with all our methods and want all parties to feel comfortable with what we do.

CONSENT—CLIENT RECORDS (3.04)

The behavior analyst obtains the written consent of the client or client-surrogate before obtaining or disclosing client records from or to other sources, including clinical supervisors.

It is occasionally necessary for a behavior analyst to share information about a case with a supervisor, another professional, or an agency. In those cases, the behavior analyst obtains written permission from the client to do so including the supervisor of the behavior analyst in charge of the case.

• • • • • • •

CASE 3.04: HELP WANTED

Dr. Stuart W., a Doctoral-level BCBA (BCBA-D), has been working on Tom's behavioral issues for 2 years. Tom lives in a supported living apartment in the community, and he works at a job with supervision from vocational rehabilitation. Dr. W.'s data shows that Tom frequently arrives late or completely misses work. Tom would rather stay home and sleep; a variety of incentive programs have been ineffective. Dr. W. is wondering if Tom would benefit from counseling. He has a friend and colleague who is a counselor; his plan is to invite his colleague to lunch and tell him about Tom.

Can Dr. W. ethically talk to another professional about Tom to determine if the person would consider taking Tom as a client?

• • • • • • •

DESCRIBING PROGRAM OBJECTIVES (3.05)

The behavior analyst describes, in writing, the objectives of the behavior change program to the client or client-surrogate before attempting to implement the program. And to the extent possible, a risk-benefit analysis should be conducted on the procedures to be implemented to reach the objective.

It is considered standard practice for behavior analysts to specify in writing the objectives of all behavior programs. This statement of objectives should be shared with the client or the client's representative. A new requirement is for behavior analysts to conduct a risk–benefit analysis, which is explained in detail in Chapter 16, "Conducting a Risk–Benefit Analysis."

• • • • • • • •

CASE 3.05: BEGGING FOR A RIDE

Susan is a 52-year-old woman with developmental disabilities. She lives at home with her mother, who is her legal guardian, and she attends a vocational training program. Susan is a client of developmental services, and she receives behavioral programming as needed. Angie is a BCBA who works with clients at the vocational program. Angie has been asked to provide behavioral services for Susan. It seems that Susan has been spending all of her money on junk food. Then, so that she has money, she has been asking staff to give her loans or pay her for small favors. This behavior has escalated to the point that Susan has no money for bus transportation and is making everyone uncomfortable with her begging. Because begging is not really an appropriate behavior, Angie feels that it would be okay to instruct the staff to immediately begin treating begging with social disapproval.

At what point does Angie need to get approval from Susan's mother?

• • • • • • • •

RESPONSES TO CASES

CASE 3.0C: BACK TO BASICS

IQ tests are not a good behavioral measure of a person's ability. They are particularly not the best method of measuring the abilities of a person with profound mental retardation. Theresa needs to have Charlie quickly evaluated using an assessment tool that measures adaptive behaviors and functional skills. Theresa can tell the administrator that behavior analysts are bound by the Guidelines to provide appropriate assessments.

CASE 3.0D: PROCEED WITH CAUTION

Theresa needs to administer the functional assessment and take the baseline data on Charlie's behavior problems again. She needs to do this in order to have an assessment in the new setting. She also needs to do this because, although the BCaBA was doing her best, her work should have been supervised and signed off on by a BCBA.

CASE 3.02B: NOW WHAT?

Florence would not need to carry out an experimental functional assessment if the information she got from the informal analysis was adequate to develop an effective intervention.

CASE 3.04: HELP WANTED

Dr. W. must obtain the written consent of the client (Tom) or his guardian before disclosing Tom's records or giving information such as his name or behavioral specifics to another professional, regardless of the purpose.

CASE 3.05: BEGGING FOR A RIDE

Before implementing any procedures to change Susan's behavior, Angie needs to outline the objectives of the behavior plan in writing for Susan's mother (her legal guardian). It could be that the mother feels Susan has the right to spend her money on snacks as long as she goes to work. The intervention for this problem may well be something for which the mother wishes to have some input.

9

The Behavior Analyst and the Individual Behavior Change Program (Guideline 4)

As alluded to in Chapter 4, in the early evolution of the field, behavior analysts had a modus operandi of carrying out behavior change programs that could be described positively by supporters as "fluid" and by detractors as "making it up as they went along." In the beginning, behavior programs were just extensions of laboratory procedures with adaptations for humans and the settings they occupied. Nothing was written down, and there was no approval process per se. Data were always collected, usually with precision and consistency, and the results were so novel and amazing that all of those involved would marvel at the effects they were seeing with these primitive procedures. With success came recognition of the seriousness of the mission these early leaders had undertaken. The pioneers of behavior analysis quickly realized that these were not just experiments in behavior change but rather a totally new form of therapy—data based to be sure but therapy nonetheless. And

> The pioneers of behavior analysis quickly realized that these were not just experiments in behavior change but rather a totally new form of therapy.

therapy required a new level of care, consideration, thoughtfulness, and responsibility. It became clear that better record keeping would be required. By the mid-1980s, behavior analysis practitioners were fully in compliance with standards of the time, which required that the client, or a surrogate, actually approve the program in writing before it was implemented.

This increased responsibility and accountability also meant that other protocols must be followed as well, such as using least restrictive procedures,* avoiding harmful consequences (including both reinforcers and punishers), and involving the client in any modifications to programs that might be made along the way. Skinner (1953) had always been against the use of punishers, but it took the field of behavior analysis quite a while to codify some statement on this. It was the vetting of these Guidelines that finally resulted in a concise and cohesive position: "The behavior analyst recommends reinforcement rather than punishment whenever possible." The essence of this aspect of the Guidelines is to inform consumers and to remind behavior analysts that, as a field, we are primarily interested in developing behavior

> As a field, we are primarily interested in developing behavior change programs that teach new, appropriate, adaptive behaviors using nonharmful reinforcers whenever possible.

---

* The term least restrictive does not always make sense when applied to procedures as opposed to environments. In the original *Wyatt v. Stickney* (1971) case, a patient kept in an institution (clearly restrictive with locked wards and seclusion rooms) who could be treated in the community (clearly less restrictive by comparison) was entitled to be treated in "the least restrictive environment." When applied to treatments, "least restrictive" suggests that some procedures like time-out are probably more restrictive than Differential Reinforcement of Other Behaviors (DRO), for example. A physical or mechanical restraint is likewise more restrictive than time-out. Or is it? Time-out requires that the person be removed from the environment, perhaps to a place where he or she cannot see others. Is this more or less restrictive? And what about punishment? Is a sharp "No!" contingent on behavior "restrictive"? Other aversive stimuli such as water mist or lemon juice would also be included in this category.

change programs that teach new, appropriate, adaptive behaviors using nonharmful reinforcers whenever possible.

One interesting feature of Guideline 4.0 is that we make it explicit that our form of therapy involves "ongoing data collection." When compared with other forms of treatment, this presents one of the most unique and valuable features. Ongoing, objective data collection helps the behavior analyst understand the effect of treatment, and the consumer is able to make an ongoing evaluation of the worth of the treatment as well.

At the onset of a behavior change program, most of the focus is on finding just the right treatment and implementing it correctly, under safe conditions. One additional requirement for behavior analysts is that some consideration be given to the termination criteria. Basically, we need to ask, "When will we stop treatment?" It is presumed that termination comes when the consumer's behavior has been sufficiently changed to warrant cessation, but what is the criterion? There is a great deal of "clinical judgment" involved in this decision, and of course the client or his or her surrogate must also be involved. By requiring that some thought be given to what level of behavior change is desired, the Guidelines prevent open-ended treatment that goes on and on.

If the behavior analyst is treating self-injurious behavior (SIB), for example, he or she must indicate, and get approval for, some level of acceptable behavior change. "Zero SIB for 2 weeks" might be one such goal. Or, if the behav-

> A great deal of "clinical judgment" goes into the decision of when to stop treatment.

ior change program involves an adaptive behavior, the goal might state, "Carl will be able to completely dress himself, without any assistance, for 3 consecutive days." As often happens, the client or the client's surrogate might at that point decide to terminate treatment, or, as often happens, another goal might be set such as, "Carl will be able to ride the bus independently for 1 week" or

"Carl will be able to complete a full work day with no SIB or inappropriate behavior."

THE BEHAVIOR ANALYST AND THE INDIVIDUAL BEHAVIOR CHANGE PROGRAM (4.0)

The behavior analyst (a) designs programs that are based on behavior analytic principles, including assessments of effects of other intervention methods, (b) involves the client or the client-surrogate in the planning of such programs, (c) obtains the consent of the client, and (d) respects the right of the client to terminate services at any time.

Behavior analysts base their programs on basic principles of behavior, use behavioral methods to evaluate their programs, and involve clients or their legal representatives in the planning of those programs. See also 2.09c for a further discussion of the evaluation of "other" intervention models. Behavior analysts inform clients of their right to end services at any time.

• • • • • • •

CASE 4.0: MASSAGE MESSAGE

Jerry was a Board Certified assistant Behavior Analyst (BCaBA) who had previously worked for years as a massage therapist. One of the first cases he received in a group home for developmentally disabled adults involved a female client who would apparently "out of the blue" run down the hall and hit another client in the back. She would laugh and then go in her room and sit on her bed. Jerry felt that she was tense and that this was the cause of her bursts of unpredictable aggression. He wrote an informal program that involved shoulder rubs for this client following any such incident.

As Jerry's supervisor, how would you handle this situation?

• • • • • • •

DESCRIBING CONDITIONS FOR PROGRAM SUCCESS (4.01)

The behavior analyst describes to the client or client-surrogate the environmental conditions that are necessary for the program to be effective.

Prior to the implementation of a program, the behavior analyst describes to the client or the client's representative the conditions believed necessary for the program to work effectively. This can actually be a rather complex matter because it has to be stated as a series of contingency statements. It is almost always necessary to find the function of the behavior and then to find some way to gain control over the key maintaining variables. If this includes reinforcement, some way of making it contingent on appropriate behavior has to be arranged on a consistent basis without causing satiation. And the program has to be designed in such a way that the client does not suddenly engage in escape behavior.

ENVIRONMENTAL CONDITIONS THAT PRECLUDE IMPLEMENTATION (4.02)

If environmental conditions preclude implementation of a behavior analytic program, the behavior analyst recommends that other professional assistance (i.e., assessment, consultation, or therapeutic intervention by other professionals) be sought.

In most circumstances a behavior analyst, having conducted a behavioral assessment, is going to recommend some sort of behavioral treatment. However, if no BCaBA or Board Certified Behavior Analyst (BCBA) is available to implement the treatment, or if there are no resources available to fund a behavioral treatment, the behavior analyst will refer the case to another professional. One key condition is the cooperation of the major parties involved in the case. For in-home services, it is essential that both parents be on board with the treatment; if one is not and sabotages the intervention, obviously there can be no progress.

ENVIRONMENTAL CONDITIONS THAT HAMPER IMPLEMENTATION (4.03)

If environmental conditions hamper implementation of the behavior analytic program, the behavior analyst seeks to eliminate the environmental constraints, or identifies in writing the obstacles to doing so.

Behavior programs require certain minimum conditions (e.g., a stable environment, some control over reinforcers, consistency in the delivery of consequences, cooperation of key parties) to be effective. The behavior analyst will identify these "environmental constraints" and will attempt to modify or eliminate them prior to implementing a behavior program. If this is not possible, then the behavior analyst will put in writing a description of these conditions and attempt to resolve them.

• • • • • • •

CASE 4.03: COMPETING AGENDA

Dr. Patti S., a Doctoral-level BCBA (BCBA-D), was providing behavioral services to a large inner city preschool program for children with disabilities. The program did a good job with regard to providing the support necessary for behavioral programming to be effective. However, a new early childhood administrator came to the district and decided that prekindergarten staff would be intensively trained off-site in the High Scope (developmental) curriculum model. This newly required intensive training for staff resulted in classes being short-staffed nearly every day. The staff members who remained at the facility were scrambling to meet the basic needs of the children and no longer had time to, for example, take data or to implement interventions.
What is Dr. S.'s first step in handling this situation?

• • • • • • •

APPROVING INTERVENTIONS (4.04)

The behavior analyst must obtain the client's or client-surrogate's approval in writing of the behavior intervention procedures before implementing them.

It is an obligation of the behavior analyst to gain the client's approval, in writing, before a program is begun.

•••••••

CASE 4.04: MAKING ASSUMPTIONS

Juan, a newly certified BCBA, had just started working in a privately owned school for children with autism. He had been asked to work with Carl, a child who has been shrieking and slapping himself in the face. Juan arrived at the school after the previous BCBA resigned. She left behind a functional analysis and a note that said a treatment plan was needed. Due to the self-injurious nature of the behavior, Juan wanted to begin treatment immediately. He told the teacher he assumed the parents would be fine with this because they knew a functional assessment had been conducted by the previous BCBA.

Since the functional assessment had been completed, can Juan begin the treatment?

•••••••

REINFORCEMENT AND PUNISHMENT (4.05)

The behavior analyst recommends reinforcement rather than punishment whenever possible. If punishment procedures are necessary, the behavior analyst always includes reinforcement procedures for alternative behavior in the program.

Behavior analysts have a bias in favor of the use of reinforcers in behavior change programs and against the use of punishment. In some cases, where punishment is the only alternative, reinforcers for other behaviors should always be included as part of the program.

•••••••

CASE 4.05: UNNATURAL CONSEQUENCES

From Case 4.04, Juan decided that Carl's face slapping is maintained by self-reinforcement and is serious enough to warrant a punishment procedure as an intervention. When Carl slapped his face, Juan wanted Carl's hands to be firmly pulled away from his face and for the therapist to say in a loud voice, "No!"

What else does Juan need to do before submitting this program for approval?

• • • • • • •

AVOIDING HARMFUL REINFORCERS (4.06)

The behavior analyst minimizes the use of items as potential reinforcers that may be harmful to the long-term health of the client or participant (e.g., cigarettes, or sugar or fat-laden food), or that may require undesirably marked deprivation procedures as motivating operations.

Although some reinforcers may be quite effective for some clients, if those reinforcers could be harmful in the long-term they should be avoided if at all possible. Behavior analysts should avoid the use of establishing (motivating) operations that involve significant degrees of deprivation.

• • • • • • •

CASE 4.06: STAY SWEET

Mark was the BCaBA assigned to one house in a residential facility for verbal, ambulatory adults with moderate to severe mental retardation. He was supervised by a BCBA who came to the facility for only an hour or so each week. Because of this, Mark was called on to draft most of the behavior programs and to plan interventions. Eddie was an extremely active client who was constantly leaving whichever activity in which he was supposed to be involved. If he was scheduled to be in the house, he would leave and wander around the grounds. If Eddie was scheduled to be in the education building, he would often leave and go to his bedroom. Mark decided that because Eddie liked sweets a good intervention would be to start reinforcing Eddie with candy or a small glass of Coke every 10 minutes through- out the day if Eddie was where he was supposed to be.

Are there any special considerations for this reinforcement schedule that is so rich with unhealthy food?

• • • • • • •

ONGOING DATA COLLECTION (4.07)

The behavior analyst collects data, or asks the client, client-surrogate, or designated others to collect data needed to assess progress within the program.

Behavior analysts always collect data and continue data collection to evaluate a program's effectiveness. The behavior analyst or some other designated person involved with the behavior program might do this.

• • • • • • •

CASE 4.07: ESCALATION PLAN

Michelle, a BCBA, was working with Doug, a 14-year-old who was in a special education class for teenagers with emotional disorders. At home, Doug engaged in mild aggressive behaviors toward his younger brother, which included pushing him or hitting him with a light slap. Doug's brother would yell and start to fight back. Doug's mother told Michelle that the behaviors were not severe enough to really hurt anyone; however, she was concerned that the intensity of the aggression could escalate if it wasn't stopped now. Michelle planned an intervention and sent detailed notes to Doug's mother about how to handle aggressive outbursts. Michelle told the mother she would call every week or so to see how things were going.

Is there anything else Michelle should have done?

• • • • • • •

PROGRAM MODIFICATIONS (4.08)

The behavior analyst modifies the program on the basis of data.

Behavior analysts are "online" with the programs they implement, which means that they continue to look at the data to determine if the program is working and, if necessary, make changes to the program to ensure success.

• • • • • • •

CASE 4.08: PATIENCE

In Case 4.07, Michelle was eventually prompted by her supervisor to implement treatment for the aggression in Doug's home. After 2 weeks of data collection, although Michelle was sure her intervention would be effective, the data showed that Doug's behavior was not improving.

The behavior program for aggression had been highly effective with other students.

Should Michelle just keep trying with this program? How long should she try before she changes to another approach?

• • • • • • •

PROGRAM MODIFICATIONS CONSENT (4.09)

The behavior analyst explains the program modifications and the reasons for the modifications to the client or client-surrogate and obtains consent to implement the modifications.

If it is necessary to make changes to the behavior program, the behavior analyst explains the reasons for the changes to the client or his or her legal representative and receives consent for the changes.

• • • • • • •

CASE 4.09: SLIGHT MODIFICATION

Shakira is a BCBA working in a special education classroom. Students spend part of the school day in the classroom, and they are mainstreamed the remainder of the day. Tawana is a tall, lanky 12-year-old who swears and becomes disruptive in class. She is on a behavior program that worked well until recently when the program became ineffective. Knowing her clients very well, Shakira quickly figured out that Tawana was bored with the reinforcers. Shakira planned some changes in the intervention, including changing the reinforcers, reinforcement schedule, and adding consequences for misbehavior.

Because the behavior plan was already in effect, Shakira was certain that all of the permission forms that were previously signed would cover the new version of the program. Was she correct in assuming this?

· · · · · · ·

LEAST RESTRICTIVE PROCEDURES (4.10)

The behavior analyst reviews and appraises the restrictiveness of alternative interventions and always recommends the least restrictive procedures likely to be effective in dealing with a behavior problem.

In determining alternatives in behavior programs, the behavior analyst will always try to use the least restrictive method, which is, at the same time, still likely to be effective.

· · · · · · ·

CASE 4.10: SIT AND WATCH

Jason, a 10-year-old with learning disabilities and social acting out, was mainstreamed into an elementary school physical education class. Jason would frequently disrupt the whole class with his antics. He would squeal loudly if he missed the ball, and he would make every attempt to run in a humorous manner so that other students would laugh. The coach was frustrated and was ready to implement his own behavioral intervention that was to have Jason run around the track each time he misbehaved. The school principal sent Dr. David K., a BCBA-D, to meet with the coach and discuss alternatives. Dr. K. suggested that the first intervention simply be that when Jason acted out he would be sent to the bench to sit and watch. Dr. K. explained to the coach that this was a procedure that was research based and known to be effective.

For what other reasons was "sit-and-watch" preferable to running around the track?

• • • • • • •

TERMINATION CRITERIA (4.11)

The behavior analyst establishes understandable and objective (i.e., measurable) criteria for the termination of the program and describes them to the client or client-surrogate.

At the onset of behavior programming, the behavior analyst will specify some criterion for determining when to end the program: for example, if the goal was to treat head banging, the criterion might be zero incidents in a 2-week period.

• • • • • • •

CASE 4.11: WHEN TO TELL

Dr. N. was consulting with clients who were senior citizens living in a residential facility. Mrs. Baker refused to walk anywhere. She sat in a wheelchair day after day, and within a short period of time she no longer had the strength to walk to the dining room or down the hall. The medical staff identified walking as the number one goal for Mrs. Baker. Dr. N. knew that behavioral services for this activity would probably be needed only for a few weeks.

Should Dr. N. tell Mrs. Baker he will be working with her until she improves, or should he wait until he is ready to terminate her services?

• • • • • • •

TERMINATING CLIENTS (4.12)

The behavior analyst terminates the relationship with the client when the established criteria for termination are attained, as in when a series of planned or revised intervention goals has been completed.

When the previously established goal has been met, the behavior analyst will inform the client that behavioral services are no longer required and will close the case.

• • • • • • •

CASE 4.12: EXTENDING TREATMENT

In Case 4.11, Dr. N. was exactly correct when he told the facility administrator he would have Mrs. Baker out of the wheelchair and walking again in record time. Dr. N. used very systematic shaping to add some distance to each day's walk. By the end of 2 months, Mrs. Baker could walk to the dining room using a cane. Dr. N. told Mrs. Baker she was ready to "graduate" and walk on her own. She began to say she didn't want Dr. N. to leave the facility. The more he thought about it, Dr. N. decided he could expand and extend Mrs. Baker's walking program. He could try to get her to walk without the cane or to walk a greater distance, such as to the yard outside.

When a client is doing extremely well, is it a good idea to extend programming?

• • • • • • •

RESPONSES TO CASES

CASE 4.0: MASSAGE MESSAGE

As Jerry's supervisor, you would first need to remind him that he is now a behavior analyst and that it is time to leave massage therapy behind and begin thinking in terms of contingencies of reinforcement. It would appear that Jerry needs some on-the-job training on how to analyze cases like this one, including data collection. He will also need to be trained on the importance of working with the legal representatives of the clients, including their right to terminate services.

CASE 4.03: COMPETING AGENDA

Dr. S. needs to identify in writing for the principal and school's prekindergarten district administrator the environmental (staffing) problems that are hampering the implementation of behavioral programs.

CASE 4.04: MAKING ASSUMPTIONS

According to the Guidelines, Juan needs to obtain the client's or client-surrogate's (in this case, the parents) permission for the intervention procedures and could use this as an occasion to meet the parents.

CASE 4.05: UNNATURAL CONSEQUENCES

Because behavior analysts should recommend reinforcement rather than punishment whenever possible, Carl's program needs to have some reinforcement procedures for alternative behaviors, such as holding and playing with a toy, raising his hand to get the teacher's attention, or using a musical instrument or art materials.

CASE 4.06: STAY SWEET

The Guidelines state that behavior analysts should minimize reinforcers that may be harmful to the health of the client. It is possible that this much sugar could have a negative effect on Eddie's blood sugar level. If Eddie was responsive to very small amounts of these reinforcers, such that at the end of the day, he had received only one-half Coke and one-half bag of candy, this might be acceptable. Any food reinforcers would, of course, have to be approved by the medical staff and dietician. And, if this program was successful, Mark would want to stretch the schedule to 15 minutes, then 20 minutes, and so on, so that the total amount of sugar per day was not excessive.

CASE 4.07: ESCALATION PLAN

Whenever an intervention is implemented, data should be collected to evaluate the results of the intervention. It is appropriate for behavior analysts to train clients, professionals, and client-surrogates (in this case, parents) to take data. Because Doug is aggressive in the home setting, the parents need to be taking data at home. The behavior analyst should design a data collection system and train the parents.

CASE 4.08: PATIENCE

Behavior analysts must modify behavior programs on the basis of data, but what is not known, and which must be decided in each case, is how much data. When do you know when it is time to quit a procedure and try something different? This is a difficult question that certainly requires careful thought and input from experienced behavior analysts who understand the client and the setting where the behavior occurs. In this case, because the program has been successful with other students, we need to know more about those cases and the circumstances surrounding the assessment of effectiveness.

CASE 4.09: SLIGHT MODIFICATION

When a behavior program is modified, the behavior analyst needs to explain the modifications and to obtain consent again. In this case, consent would come from the parents. The changes should also be explained to Tawana.

CASE 4.10: SIT AND WATCH

Because this is the first attempt at a behavior plan for Jason, the behavior analyst needs to start with the least restrictive procedures. "Sit-and-watch," which is a brief time-out, is a better starting point than the physically grueling, and potentially dangerous, task of running around a track in the hot sun.

CASE 4.11: WHEN TO TELL

Dr. N. needs to establish criteria for the walking program and explain the criteria to the facility administrator. He also needs to explain to Mrs. Baker, in terms she can understand, that as soon she can walk a certain distance she will "graduate" from her walking program. If she has family members, they should also be consulted on this matter.

CASE 4.12: EXTENDING TREATMENT

In general, the behavior analyst needs to terminate the relationship when the established criteria are obtained. In this case, if the administrator and Mrs. Baker's family wished to further extend her goals, having Dr. N. stay on the case a while longer would be appropriate.

10

The Behavior Analyst as Teacher or Supervisor (Guideline 5)

The majority of Board Certified Behavior Analysts (BCBAs) become supervisors within a short time after completing their graduate training. Training others to carry out behavioral procedures is an essential part of behavior analysis treatment because in most cases the treatment occurs in the client's natural environment where these "significant others" are a large part of the client's life. A student who is referred for classroom behavior problems usually cannot be treated successfully in an off-campus counseling session that occurs after school. An effective treatment will involve observation in the classroom to determine controlling variables, and the teacher will most likely be

> Behavior problems cannot be treated successfully in an off-campus counseling session that occurs after school.

involved in the behavior change program. The behavior analyst might observe that little Jenny is off-task during certain activities, that the other children reinforce it, and that the teacher contributes to the problem by providing unintentional intermittent attention. In this case, the behavior analyst's job consists of training the teacher how to increase the likelihood that Jenny will stay on task (perhaps by changing her class seating arrangement and her academic instruction level) and then additionally training the teacher to respond more systematically to the on-task, off-task behavior (Guideline 5.01). Basically, the teacher will be trained to be much better skilled in ignoring off-task behavior and watching for on-task behavior and immediately reinforcing it. It is entirely appropriate for the behavior analyst to train the teacher in this way because there is no "specialized training" involved. The teacher will have all the prerequisite skills and will have the appropriate "scope of practice" for such an intervention.

> An underlying principle is that behavior analysts do not train others to use behavioral procedures if there is any chance the procedures will be used inappropriately.

It would not be appropriate for the behavior analyst to try to train playground aides in this same use of extinction and reinforcement (Guideline 5.02). Such personnel do not usually have a college degree and are not certified teachers. The underlying principle involved here is that behavior analysts do not train others to use behavioral procedures if there is some chance that they will be used inappropriately. A playground aide might be appropriately trained to take data on the effects of an intervention, but the actual program would need to be carried out by a certified teacher. A similar consideration has to be made in the case of behavioral treatments in residential facilities for individuals with developmental disabilities. The majority of staff members in these facilities have a high school degree and no advanced training. Our Guidelines are clear that training such staff in sophisticated behavioral procedures is inappropriate. These Guidelines are also clear that the behavior analyst is responsible for carrying out the training in the proper way and that proper follow-up supervision is also required.

For BCBAs who become teachers or instructors, the Guidelines set a high standard as well. The behavior analyst is obligated to make clear what the course objectives, requirements, and evaluation procedures (Guidelines 5.03, 5.04, 5.05) are and, further, to employ behavior analysis principles in teaching (Guideline 5.09). In addition, the behavior analyst must know at the outset whether the student (or supervisee) has the prerequisite skills for the course, and, if not, he or she should be referred for remedial skill training (Guideline 5.02). There is a great deal of research on the use of behavioral procedures in teaching; we basically know how to design and execute very effective training for a wide variety of topic areas from preschool through graduate school. The BACB Guidelines insist that these principles be employed with students and supervisees anywhere that "academic policies allow." This is good news for students because our research shows that the use of study objectives, frequent testing, prompt feedback, and active responding are all much preferred by students over traditional teaching methods that involve lectures followed by multiple choice midterm and final exams.

THE BEHAVIOR ANALYST AS TEACHER OR SUPERVISOR (5.0)

Behavior analysts delegate to their employees, supervisees, and research assistants only those responsibilities that such persons can reasonably be expected to perform competently.

Behavior analysts must use good judgment when deciding whether they can pass on certain tasks to their employees or assistants. It certainly makes life easier to hand off certain, perhaps onerous or routine chores to others, but unless you know that the delegated person actually has the skills to accept these responsibilities it is a risky decision. As a general rule, you would want to have actually seen the person perform the task on more than one occasion with close supervision before actually delegating certain responsibilities to him or her.

• • • • • • •

CASE 5.0: THIN AIR

Taking baseline data from videotapes seemed like such an easy task that Dr. Z. had no trouble making the decision to let his student Jessica take over this routine chore. He gave her a set of written definitions of the key behaviors, showed her the equipment, and let her begin working independently. About once a week, he would ask Jessica how it was going, and she seemed enthused about her progress. Dr. Z. was on a plane on his way to a behavioral conference to present the data that Jessica had transcribed: He noticed something funny about the data. After a few minutes it dawned on him—she did not know the difference between whole interval and partial interval recording and would sometimes use one and sometimes the other.

Dr. Z. realized he should have been checking in on Jessica. What should he do about the conference presentation?

• • • • • • •

DESIGNING COMPETENT TRAINING PROGRAMS (5.01)

Behavior analysts who are responsible for education and training programs and supervisory activities seek to ensure that the programs and supervisory activities:

- Are competently designed
- Provide the proper experiences
- Meet the requirements for licensure, certification, or other goals for which claims are made by the program or supervisor.

It is the responsibility of the behavior analyst who is involved in education and training to make sure that courses are properly designed. Because we have a legacy from Skinner in the form of programmed instruction (Holland & Skinner, 1961), care in course design should be of utmost importance. Courses should provide the experiences necessary for teaching behavioral skills, not just lecturing to people, and they should meet licensure and certification requirements per course descriptions.

LIMITATIONS ON TRAINING (5.02)

Behavior analysts do not teach the use of techniques or procedures that require specialized training, licensure, or expertise in other disciplines to individuals who lack the prerequisite training, legal scope of practice, or expertise, except as these techniques may be used in behavioral evaluation of the effects of various treatments, interventions, therapies, or educational methods.

We do not train assistants or paraprofessionals on behavioral procedures unless they have the necessary prerequisites; one exception is training assistants or others in data collection to help a qualified BCBA evaluate the effects of treatment—this is allowed.

• • • • • • •

CASE 5.02: DELEGATE

Dr. S. was a doctoral-level BCBA (BCBA-D) who worked for a company that owned seven group homes. Dr. S. was responsible for the behavior programming of all of the clients in the group homes, but he had Board Certified assistant Behavior Analysts (BCaBAs) and behavioral assistants to help him. Dr. S. was also responsible for arranging or providing training for all staff members who were BCBAs and BCaBAs. Dr. S.'s supervisor, the company president, wanted to make sure all staff had the continuing education units (CEUs) needed for recertification. She instructed Dr. S. to provide some CEU training. Because he was overloaded with work, Dr. S. arranged for the company's master's-level psychometrist to do a daylong workshop on testing instead.
Are there any problems with this plan?

• • • • • • •

PROVIDING COURSE OR SUPERVISION OBJECTIVES (5.03)

The behavior analyst provides a clear description of the objectives of a course or supervision, preferably in writing, at the beginning of the course or supervisory relationship.

Behavior analysts involved in teaching should provide a set of written objectives for the courses they teach. These will generally be quite specific as to exactly what behaviors the students have to engage in to earn a passing grade. Supervisors are also required to specify for new supervisees the objectives for the experience in writing.

• • • • • • •

CASE 5.03: TOUGH ASSIGNMENT

Being accepted for a practicum at Center for Autism Services and Education (CASE) school was considered a major coup. Only two graduate students were accepted each semester, and it was known to be a tough but rewarding assignment. Students got to work with a famous behavior analyst, to sit in on case meetings with teachers and families, and to try their hand at writing behavior programs and taking data to determine if the programs were effective. The drawback was that at the beginning of the assignment the students were not explicitly told what they would be doing. "The program is constantly evolving; every day is a new day," is all that they were told. "You'll learn it as you live it," seemed to be the mantra they reported most often.

What does the "famous behavior analyst" need to do next if she wants to keep getting practicum students to work with her at CASE?

• • • • • • •

DESCRIBING COURSE REQUIREMENTS (5.04)

The behavior analyst provides a clear description of the demands of the supervisory relationship or course (e.g., papers, exams, projects, reports, intervention plans, graphic displays and face to face meetings) preferably in writing at the beginning of the supervisory relationship or course.

Behavior analysts involved in teaching as well as supervision should also provide a clear list of all course requirements at the onset of the course or the supervisory experience. The goal of providing objectives is to allow students to determine if they are ready to take the class and to help them understand what will be expected.

• • • • • • •

CASE 5.04: MORE THAN EXPECTED

Dr. P. was a university professor who taught a course in behavior analysis. Gretchen registered for Dr. P's class. Gretchen was a master's degree student who was interested in eventually getting certified as a BCBA. She was also a single mother with a 2-year-old son. She worked part time as a behavior assistant in an elementary school, and she was taking two university classes each semester. Dr. P. handed out the objectives for the course the first night of class. After reviewing the objectives, Gretchen clearly thought the class would be very beneficial. In the fourth week of classes, Gretchen felt as if she were drowning. There was a quiz in the class every week, and she never dreamed so much study time would be required for this one class. In addition to the quizzes, the students had to write three papers and observe at least two therapy sessions. Gretchen went to see Dr. P. and told her she had never done poorly in a class but that her quiz grades were sinking and she had no idea this was going to be so much work. Dr. P. was unsympathetic, pointing out that she had handed out the objectives on the first night.

What should have been done differently in this case?

• • • • • • •

DESCRIBING EVALUATION REQUIREMENTS (5.05)

The behavior analyst provides a clear description of the requirements for the evaluation of student/supervisee performance at the beginning of the supervisory relationship or course.

The behavior analyst who is involved in teaching should make clear to the students at the beginning of the course how they will be evaluated.

• • • • • • •

CASE 5.05: A FOR EFFORT BUT C FOR THE COURSE

In Case 5.04, Gretchen somehow managed to struggle through the class. She wrote the papers, took the quizzes every week, and went to visit four therapy sessions rather than the required two sessions. Gretchen stayed up late and studied hard for the quizzes, and she obtained near-perfect scores on the remaining exams. Gretchen put extra effort into her papers, finding additional references that were not required, and she took great care when documenting her therapy visits for Dr. P. By going beyond the call of duty, Gretchen was hoping for an A in the course. Gretchen was trying to get some financial assistance for graduate school, and her grade point average was very important to her. Imagine her shock when she checked her grades online, only to discover that she was given a C in the course. Gretchen immediately went to see Dr. P. and tearfully explained that she had never received a C in her life.

Once again, Dr. P. was unmoved and said that the quizzes had accounted for 70% of the grade.

• • • • • • •

PROVIDING FEEDBACK TO STUDENTS/SUPERVISEES (5.06)

The behavior analyst provides feedback regarding the performance of a student or supervisee at least once per two weeks or consistent with BACB requirements.

Because research has shown that frequent feedback can improve motivation, learning, and performance, behavior analyst teachers should strive to provide their students feedback as often as possible. Generally speaking, this feedback should closely follow the performance. If students take an exam every two weeks, they should receive feedback as soon as the exams are passed back, for example. Behavior analysts who are supervisors need to comply with the BACB requirements for feedback (i.e., at least every 2 weeks).

• • • • • • •

CASE 5.06: LOSING TRACK OF TIME

Dr. Andy M., a BCBA-D who taught at the university and did private consulting, was supervising Tara, a graduate student in psychology. Tara, a BCaBA, was assigned to two middle school classrooms where she worked with adolescents who had behavior problems. After not seeing Dr. M. for at least 3 months, Tara received a phone call from him. He told Tara the teachers were not happy with her work and he was very sorry to tell her that she would probably lose her placement at the school.

What is the most ethical response for Dr. M. in this case? What should Tara have done before and after she got the phone call?

• • • • • • •

FEEDBACK TO STUDENTS/SUPERVISEES (5.07)

The behavior analyst provides feedback to the student/supervisee in a way that increases the probability that the student/supervisee will benefit from the feedback.

The ethical behavior analyst who is involved in teaching or supervision should take advantage of the behavior analysis literature related to the effects of feedback on performance. Feedback that is individualized, immediate, descriptive, paired with positive reinforcement, and presented graphically has a greater impact than when it is provided just matter of factly.

• • • • • • •

CASE 5.07: HOW AM I DOING?

Dr. Lora Y. is a BCBA-D who supervises master's students in their practicum at some of the schools where she consults. Dr. Y. is "old school" when it comes to feedback and feels that natural consequences of behavior should be the primary

*shaping tool for graduate students—that is the way it was
in her day. Lois, one of Dr. Y.'s students, is a "new school"
behavior analyst; she loves the field and thrives on feedback.
She will often seek feedback from Dr. Y. immediately following
a day at the school. "You're doing fine," is the extent of Dr. Y.'s
feedback to Lois. Lois isn't seeking reassurance or comfort; she
wants specific feedback so she can improve.*

If you were Lois, what would you do?

• • • • • • •

REINFORCING STUDENT/SUPERVISEE BEHAVIOR (5.08)

The behavior analyst uses positive reinforcement as frequently
as the behavior of the student/supervisee and the environmental
conditions allow.

The positive reinforcement referred to in Guideline 5.08 is most
often going to be in the form of positive comments and kind
words, although a supervisor might also use additional reinforcers such as the choice of where to work. Some supervisors
show their supervisees approval by giving them cases that are
more challenging.

USING BEHAVIOR ANALYSIS PRINCIPLES
IN TEACHING (5.09)

The behavior analyst utilizes as many principles of behavior analysis in teaching a course as the material, conditions, and academic
policies allow.

With applied research stretching back nearly 40 years, we now
have a powerful set of behaviorally based, empirically validated
teaching methods based on basic principles of behavior. Some of
these methods include the use of study objectives, frequent quizzes,
and immediate feedback. By now, the days of long, boring lectures
should be gone and replaced with interactive teaching strategies
and computer-assisted learning modules that guide learning and

provide automatic feedback. Not every academic program is set up to support all these advances, but Guideline 5.09 encourages behavior analysts who are teachers to avail themselves of as many techniques based on behavioral principles as possible.

REQUIREMENTS OF SUPERVISEES (5.10)

The behavior analyst's behavioral requirements of a supervisee must be in the behavioral repertoire of the supervisee. If the behavior required is not in the supervisee's repertoire, the behavior analyst attempts to provide the conditions for the acquisition of the required behavior, and refers the supervisee for remedial skill development services, or provides them with such services, permitting them to meet at least minimal behavioral performance requirements.

This guideline puts both the supervisor and supervisee on notice that they need to be aware of what is expected in practicum experiences. The supervisor needs to make very clear to supervisees exactly what is expected, and supervisees need to accurately describe their current skill sets. If there is not a good match, some remediation will be needed. There is an underlying assumption in Guideline 5.10 that we do not want supervisees to fail; we want them gain skills and improve their confidence in the use of behavioral procedures.

TRAINING, SUPERVISION, AND SAFETY (5.11)

Behavior analysts provide proper training, supervision, and safety precautions to their employees or supervisees and take reasonable steps to see that such persons perform services responsibly, competently, and ethically. If institutional policies, procedures, or practices prevent fulfillment of this obligation, behavior analysts attempt to modify their role or to correct the situation to the extent feasible.

As outlined in earlier guidelines, the behavior analyst supervisor is responsible for designing training opportunities that will lead to successfully acquired behavioral skills. In the process, supervisors must also make sure that supervisees are not put in harm's way. For example, female students, if small in stature, could be harmed if required to implement time-out with large, aggressive adolescent males.

· · · · · · ·

CASE 5.11: HOUSE OF ILL REPUTE

Danielle, a BCaBA who was working on her master's degree in applied behavior analysis, worked part time for a company that did in-home training with children with autism spectrum disorder. Excited about her first assignment with a special needs child, Danielle arrived at the child's home a little early for her 4 p.m. appointment. She knocked on the door and was met by a young woman who seemed very nervous. Danielle started working with the child, Niko, at the kitchen table and before long, she heard raised voices and yelling coming from the bedroom down the hall. The door opened and a bedraggled, young man in his 20s blurted out, "Don't tell me what to do, b**ch!" He promptly left the house, slamming the door behind him. Over several subsequent visits, Danielle was sure she saw drug paraphernalia lying around and other strange men coming and going. One took a long look at her as he was leaving. He licked his lips and gave her a menacing grin.

After several visits, Danielle reported these circumstances to her supervisor, whose reply was, "Well, we have to deal with all kinds these days. We don't judge people. We are there to help Niko. He needs us and our services."

What would a good, ethical behavior analyst supervisor do?

· · · · · · ·

RESPONSES TO CASES

CASE 5.0: THIN AIR

Dr. Z. paid severely for his misjudgment about Jessica. He had to apologize about having no data to present and did not even try to explain to

*his colleagues how this happened. This situation was sufficiently embar-
rassing that Dr. Z. is unlikely to make this mistake again.*

CASE 5.02: DELEGATE

*For BCBAs and BCaBAs, training needs to be done by a person who is a
BCBA; the psychologist was not qualified to do CEU training for behavior
analysts. Further, testing is an area that requires specialized training and
supervision. The only exception to this would be a workshop that was
designed to simply familiarize participants with testing procedures. Six
hours of "familiarization" would probably be excessive, and in the case
of these BCBAs and BCaBAs they would be better off earning CEUs. If
Dr. S. cannot do the training, he should find another BCBA.*

CASE 5.03: TOUGH ASSIGNMENT

*Our famous behavior analyst will need to work with her staff to come
up with some clear objectives for the practicum experience. They do not
need to be complete or perfect but good enough so that new students have
a good idea of what they will be expected to do and the skills they will
acquire in the practicum. This might help some students make the decision to wait a semester and try a practicum that is not so challenging.*

CASE 5.04: MORE THAN EXPECTED

*Handing out course objectives is not enough. Dr. P. should have also pro-
vided the students with a clear description of all the requirements of the
course. When not provided with course requirements, Gretchen should
have asked for them. If Gretchen had known the amount of work that was
involved, she would probably have chosen to take the class at a later time.*

CASE 5.05: A FOR EFFORT BUT C FOR THE COURSE

*The Guidelines state that behavior analysts who teach or supervise others
should provide a clear description for evaluating student performance at
the beginning of the course. On the first night of class, the students should
have received a written point system or another method of explaining not
only what the course requirements were but also how much weight would
be given to each. After some soul searching, Gretchen went to the department chair to complain.*

CASE 5.06: LOSING TRACK OF TIME

Behavior analysts who accept the responsibility of supervising others need to provide the student (or supervisee) with feedback. To do this effectively, Dr. M. cannot go 3 months or more without observing or meeting with Tara and shaping her performance. In fact, Dr. M. should be meeting with Tara at least 1 hour per week to provide her with feedback and training as necessary, including giving feedback from the teachers. If this had been done, Tara most likely would have made the necessary adjustments to her behavior so that the teachers were satisfied with her performance.

CASE 5.07: HOW AM I DOING?

Lois is entitled to frequent feedback of a descriptive nature, descriptive enough so that she can improve her performance. "You are doing fine" simply does not meet the standard. Lois is in a somewhat touchy position. She really needs to give her supervisor some feedback, as in, "I need more details please." Lois could ask a very direct question such as, "Thank you for observing me this morning when I was debriefing Ms. Marshall on her classroom management system. Is there anything I could do differently?" If this doesn't work, Lois may have to ask for a meeting with Dr. Y.'s supervisor.

CASE 5.11: HOUSE OF ILL REPUTE

Danielle's supervisor is ignoring Guideline 5.11 (which includes a provision pertaining to safety) and does so at her peril. Danielle should have voiced concerns to the supervisor after the very first observation of possibly illegal behavior (i.e., prostitution and drugs). If the supervisor agrees to pull Danielle from the home but indicates that she will assign another consultant in the home to replace her, the red flag goes up. While Niko clearly deserves behavioral services, it would appear that he too is in a potentially dangerous environment. The right call here would be that the supervisor would contact the Department of Protective Services (DPS) to report the situation. Danielle will be interviewed by DPS and will need to supply the details since she was the witness and has firsthand knowledge of the situation.

11

The Behavior Analyst and the Workplace (Guideline 6)

Behavior analysts have been active in the workplace since the early 1970s. Behavior analysis in business and industry is known as organizational behavior management (OBM) or performance management (PM). This special field has demonstrated that basic principles of behavior can be applied successfully in the business arena to produce happier, more productive employees (Daniels, 2000; Daniels & Daniels, 2004; Frederiksen, 1982; O'Brien, Dickinson, & Rosow, 1982). Guideline 6.0 requires the behavior analyst working in business and industry to be "adequately prepared" to consult in these organizations (Guideline 6.03). This means that consultants in business and industry must have had the necessary coursework and practicum supervision before offering their services in settings where the bottom line is important. As in any setting, the principles of behavior could be misused, probably to the disadvantage of workers rather than management, because management hires most consultants. Our guidelines require behavior analysts to develop

> Our guidelines require behavior analysts to develop interventions that will "enhance the well-being of employees."

interventions that (1) are well thought out (Guideline 6.02), (2) benefit both employees as well as management (Guideline 6.04), and (3) "enhance the well-being of employees." This latter condition shows an awareness that it would be quite easy to put employees at risk. For example, an unethical consultant could develop new schedules of reinforcement that would dramatically boost efficiency. Under some circumstances, much higher rates of performance could result in increased stress or injuries. In addition, there is warranted concern that the misuse of behavioral procedures could cause a backlash by employees and leave a bad taste in the mouth of management about behavior analysis.

Another feature of this guideline is that it stresses a more common ethical standard about employment in general. That is, behavior analysts, like other professionals, have an obligation to adhere to job commitments (Guideline 6.01). If you sign a 2-year contract with an organization, you are expected to stay with that company for the full 2-year period. Or if your contract includes a "noncompete clause," it is ethical only for you to abide by this restriction should you leave the firm. To break your contract and go into competition with your former employer is doubly unethical and likely to result in censure from your colleagues and a potential lawsuit as well.

> **Behavior analysts, like other professionals, have an obligation to adhere to job commitments.**

One final ethical issue is covered in this guideline. This has to do with a potential conflict between your commitment to these Behavior Analysis Certification Board (BACB) Guidelines and your employer. The most likely problem is that someone in your organization will ask you to do something "unethical" according to our standards. This might involve an apparently innocuous act of signing some paperwork indicating that you approve a behavior program when you do not or to indicate that you have carried out some training for which you were not involved. Organizations, particularly in human services, come under periodic review from state or federal agencies and discover, on short notice, that they are deficient on certain critical standards. Many of these involve documentation of client records indicating that clients have been assessed, that treatments have been provided, or that certain goals have been met. All of this usually requires the signature of the Board Certified Behavior Analyst (BCBA), which attests to these facts—or not. Pressure on you to "cooperate" could be intense, but to comply would clearly be a violation of our ethical standards. Guideline 6.06 urges you to seek resolution of such conflicts without violating your adherence to the ethical principles of our field.

THE BEHAVIOR ANALYST AND THE WORKPLACE (6.0)

The behavior analyst adheres to job commitments, assesses employee interactions before intervention, works within his/her scope of training, develops interventions that benefit employees, and resolves conflicts within these Guidelines.

JOB COMMITMENTS (6.01)

The behavior analyst adheres to job commitments made to the employing organization.

Behavior analysts are not different from other professionals when it comes to job commitments: the rule is that you follow through with your agreements.

• • • • • • •

CASE 6.01: GOOD FAITH?

Faith was a PhD-level BCBA who accepted a new job working for a large behavioral consulting firm. Faith signed an employment contract stating that she would stay with the company at least 2 years and that she would work a minimum of 20 billable hours per week. The consulting firm spent 2 months training Faith; she began work and quickly decided she did not want to work 20 hours each week. Without telling anyone, she dropped her caseload so that she was working 12 to 15 hours weekly. Then, after only 6 months on the job, Faith accepted an offer for more money with a competing company.

What are the Guidelines violations here?

• • • • • • •

ASSESSING EMPLOYEE INTERACTIONS (6.02)

The behavior analyst assesses the behavior–environment inter-actions of the employees before designing behavior analytic programs.

Behavior analysts consulting in business settings are often asked to find ways of improving performance. The most direct way may be through changes in the way that employees are paid or in the use of disincentives for poor performance. However, we should not lose sight of the fact that some consistently less-than-stellar behavior may be due to the physical environment itself. Employees who work in settings where the equipment is in need of repair, where it is loud and noisy, or where there are safety issues should not be faulted for their performance. The ethical behavior analyst always takes these environmental factors into account and brings these issues to the attention of management for correction before proposing solutions involving contingencies of reinforcement.

• • • • • • •

CASE 6.02: ENVIRONMENTAL DESIGN

Dr. Bill R., a Doctoral-level BCBA (BCBA-D), was assigned to work in four 16-bed houses in a residential facility. Dr. R. started this new placement by going to the houses, reviewing client folders, and taking the clients who needed behavior pro-grams to a training room so he could get to know them. Dr. R. figured he would spend the first few weeks getting programs written, data sheets designed, and any assessments that needed to be done completed. Two weeks later, he showed up at one house to train the staff on a behavior program. While he waited for a shift supervisor to gather staff members together, Dr. R. asked one staff person if she had worked on any behavior programs with clients. She said, "Well, that other fella who was here asked us to take data all day long. I'm telling you, we don't have time for all that garbage!" Dr. R. continued to wait because some staff members had not returned from lunch on time. Every so often, one particular staff member would go to a client who needed to do an activity that was scheduled. In a very loud, threatening, and negative voice, this staff member would bark out an order such as, "Richard, I told you it was time to get ready. You better get up outta here and get dressed before that bus gets here. I'm not tellin' you again."

Do the Guidelines offer any advice that could have helped Dr. R.?

• • • • • • •

PREPARING FOR CONSULTATION (6.03)

The behavior analyst implements or consults on behavior management programs for which the behavior analyst has been adequately prepared.

It would simply be unethical for a behavior analyst to consult in any business setting unless he or she was properly trained for the task. There are enough differences between business or industrial settings and typical human services settings that special preparation is necessary.

• • • • • •

CASE 6.03: FREE ADVICE

Frederick's next-door neighbor was the general manager of a hardware store that was part of a nationally recognized chain. Frederick, a BCBA, specialized in the design of sheltered workshops for the physically handicapped. One day at a community barbecue, the neighbor began telling Frederick about some performance problems of his employees. He said the employees came to work late and showed no initiative, and their customer service skills left much to be desired. Because Frederick encountered these same problems in his workshops, he began offering suggestions.

What might be a more appropriate response from Frederick?

• • • • • • •

EMPLOYEES INTERVENTIONS (6.04)

The behavior analyst develops interventions that benefit the employees as well as management.

Consultants in business settings are almost always hired by management to solve performance problems that affect the bottom line of the company. As a behavior analyst, you should at the same time make sure that any interventions you propose will also work to the advantage of the employees.

• • • • • • •

CASE 6.04: BONUS

Sharon P. felt she was very lucky to be working for one of the largest business-consulting firms in the country. Although it was not exactly behaviorally oriented, she was allowed to work on special projects that involved company mergers. The opportunities for using behavioral solutions were enormous, and Sharon felt good about the contribution she was making until the day that she was assigned to an oil rig in the Gulf of Mexico. She would work 2 weeks straight, living in a nicely appointed cubicle on the rig, and then get a week off. Her assignment was to figure out how to increase the productivity of the 153 workers by 9% to at least 1.9 million barrels a day of crude oil. Currently they were rated the lowest of any of the southern-sector platforms with a score of 85% efficiency. Each 1% deficit was costing the company $2.5 million per year, and Sharon was under intense pressure from the company president to find a solution. After 3 months, she came up with a plan that involved *an intermittent schedule of reinforcement, which would increase the efficiency of the "roughnecks" and "roustabouts" (roughnecks and roustabouts are the names for specific oil rig jobs; these are not intended to be derogatory terms for workers). Basically, she was proposing to have them earn daily and weekly bonuses for increased production without risking accidents. If they could meet the goals, they would increase their daily salaries from $300 to $350 per day, which Sharon deemed the minimum necessary to get this boost in productivity.*

The company president liked Sharon's plan but said that $50 per day was ridiculous. Should she go back to the drawing board for a new plan?

• • • • • • • •

EMPLOYEE HEALTH AND WELL-BEING (6.05)

The behavior analyst develops interventions that enhance the health and well-being of the employees.

It is not difficult to devise ingenious schedules of reinforcement that will motivate employees to be more productive; the concern is that this might, at the same time, put them at risk for illness or injury. Working faster could easily lead to taking shortcuts or ignoring safety standards that are designed to prevent employees from injuring themselves.

• • • • • • •

CASE 6.05: ENHANCE THIS

Peter B. received his PhD in industrial and organizational psychology and was quickly hired by a large online retailer to improve productivity in the shipping department. After making informal observations over a 3-week period, Peter recommended that the company institute a work enhancement system that would encourage employees to pick up the pace of packing boxes or be fired. His estimate was that overall output could be increased by at least 15% with this "enhancement" *and that this would increase the bottom line by nearly $1 million a year. A BCBA working in the human resources department got wind of this proposal and asked to review it before it was put in place.*

Why might the BCBA be interested?

• • • • • • •

CONFLICTS WITH ORGANIZATIONS (6.06)

If the demands of an organization with which behavior analysts are affiliated conflict with these Guidelines, behavior analysts clarify the nature of the conflict, make known their commitment to these Guidelines, and to the extent feasible, seek to resolve the conflict in a way that permits the fullest adherence to these Guidelines.

It should be apparent from this guideline that behavior analysts take their ethics seriously, even to the point of letting others know of our high standards and that we feel the need to resolve any conflict between these Guidelines and other work-related demands.

• • • • • • •

CASE 6.06: PANIC ENSUES

A company owning several residential facilities and group homes was getting ready to undergo a federal review. As soon as the administrators heard that the review team was coming, they went into their hysterical mode. Heather was a BCBA who worked in the facilities. In preparation for the review, Heather was instructed by one administrator to "… get over there to those houses, get some assessments written up, write some behavior programs, and make sure there is some data. You may have to backdate some of it if necessary." Heather was nervous about this because she was an honest person and she had not been given the opportunity to spend time with these clients.

Assuming that she wishes to use professional language, what should Heather say to the administrator?

• • • • • • •

RESPONSES TO CASES

CASE 6.01: GOOD FAITH?

Faith agreed to stay with the company for 2 years, and she left after 6 months. She signed a contract and clearly is in violation of the Guidelines and her contract. The Guidelines say that behavior analysts adhere to their job commitments. Faith should have worked the promised 20 hours per week unless a schedule change was mutually agreed on by the consulting firm. Sometimes, things happen in life so that one cannot honor a commitment (e.g., a behavior analyst feels the need to relocate to be with a dying parent). In these cases, the behavior analyst should make every attempt to work with the employer to arrange a smooth transition.

CASE 6.02: ENVIRONMENTAL DESIGN

The Guidelines state that behavior analysts should assess the behavior–environment interactions of the employees before designing behavior analytic programs. Dr. R. would have a smoother start if he knew what he was dealing with in terms of staff attitudes and behavior before trying to implement detailed or sophisticated programs.

CASE 6.03: FREE ADVICE

As exciting as it might be to expand his consulting from sheltered workshops to big-time businesses, Frederick needs to reflect on his lack of experience and training in this area and recommend that his neighbor contact a person trained in PM or perhaps direct him to a consulting firm that does this sort of work routinely.

CASE 6.04: BONUS

According to the Guidelines, Sharon did the right thing in proposing a pay-for-performance system that would benefit management (they stood to make millions) and the oil rig workers as well. She now has an ethical dilemma that may result in her refusing to work on the oil rig contract for her consulting firm. Her position was that it was unethical for her to design a system that got the roughnecks and roustabouts to work harder without their earning any increased compensation for such difficult and dangerous work.

CASE 6.05: ENHANCE THIS

BCBAs are required to follow these Guidelines, but in this case the industrial psychologist would not need to adhere to them. Certainly any time there is an increase in productivity, there is some chance that this involves employees working faster or possibly cutting corners to avoid being fired. Both situations might put them at some risk for injury, and someone needs to ask questions about the safety and well-being of the employees. The BCBA was correct in raising questions in this case, and, if he had some expertise in PM, he might recommend the use of a pay-for-performance system instead of the "work-or-get-fired" approach.

CASE 6.06: PANIC ENSUES

The administrator is engaging in serious unethical conduct. Heather needs to show her the Guidelines and tell her she will do her best to assess the situation and work within the Guidelines to make any program improvements she can before the review team arrives. If the administrator persists, Heather should reply with the following: "Please don't ask me to violate my professional ethics." Should the administrator not back down, Heather may need to consider employment with a more ethical organization.

12

The Behavior Analyst's Ethical Responsibility to the Field of Behavior Analysis (Guideline 7)

Behavior analysis, although growing rapidly as a profession (G. L. Shook, personal communication, May 30, 2004), is still a very small field when compared with other related areas such as social work or clinical psychology. For the most part, we are not yet on the radar screens of most Americans, and, based on our past experience, we know that unethical conduct by a small number of persons can reflect badly on our whole field. If we are to gain the trust of the public, we must set a very high standard of moral and ethical conduct. To be an ethical behavior analyst means not only upholding these Guidelines for your protection and the protection of your clients but also preserving and enhancing the reputation of behavior analysis in general. Guideline 7.0 makes it clear that each of us should "support the values of the field." This no doubt includes the nine core ethical principles discussed in Chapter 2 as well as those values inherent in a behavioral approach. In addition to honesty, fairness, taking responsibility, and promoting autonomy, behavior analysts also promote the value of objective,

> If we are to gain the trust of the public, we must set a very high standard of moral and ethical conduct.

reliable data in determining treatment effectiveness, in using that data in decision making, and in focusing on individual behavior as our primary focus of study. Behavior analysts value novel assessments, effective nonintrusive interventions, and the production of socially significant changes in behavior that have worth to the individual and to society. We believe in optimizing each individual's worth, dignity, and independence and in developing the repertoires necessary to accomplish these goals. It is sometimes necessary to remind our colleagues of these basic values, and this guideline provides this occasion.

Additionally, Guideline 7.0 is a prompt to all behavior analysts to promote our methodology and findings to the public (Guideline 7.02) and to ourselves to occasionally review the Guidelines so we are well aware of the standards that have been set. A somewhat onerous task involves monitoring other professionals (or paraprofessionals) in our community to make sure that they do not misrepresent themselves as certified when they are not. This vigilance is warranted considering the harm that could be done to clients by practitioners who are not properly trained. The additional harm to the reputation of our field should something happen to a client is also a constant worry to those who work hard to maintain high standards. It is basically unethical to turn a blind eye to those who are misrepresenting themselves as BCBAs when they are

> It is basically unethical to turn a blind eye to those who are misrepresenting themselves as BCBAs when they are not.

not. How one "discourages" these noncertified individuals is not spelled out in the Guidelines, but presumably contacting the Behavior Analysis Certification Board (BACB) would be a first step; another might involve contacting the Association for Behavior Analysis (ABA) or your local state association for advice and assistance.

THE BEHAVIOR ANALYST'S ETHICAL RESPONSIBILITY TO THE FIELD OF BEHAVIOR ANALYSIS (7.0)

The behavior analyst has a responsibility to support the values of the field, to disseminate knowledge to the public, to be familiar with these guidelines, and to discourage misrepresentation by non-certified individuals.

AFFIRMING PRINCIPLES (7.01)

The behavior analyst upholds and advances the values, ethics, principles, and mission of the field of behavior analysis; participation in both state and national or international behavior analysis organizations is strongly encouraged.

Behavior analysts have an obligation to speak out on behalf of the field and to support the values of the field. These include honesty, integrity, fairness, and the continuing search for basic principles of behavior that can be used to improve the human condition. To this end, the ethical behavior analyst attends and participates in the various organizations at the state, national, and international level.

• • • • • • •

CASE 7.01: STAY AT HOME

Dr. Christopher S. is a Board Certified Behavior Analyst (BCBA) who has worked in developmental disabilities (DD) settings for 10 years. Dr. S. attends local chapter meetings to earn the minimum number of continuing education unit (CEU) credits required. Dr. S. has never traveled to a state association meeting or to the Association for Behavior Analysis International conference held in a different city in May of each year. Dr. S. does not have a family, and he has plenty of money to travel. He has been described by some of his colleagues as "lazy" and by others as "indifferent" with regard to staying current with the field.

Does this rise to the level of unethical conduct?

• • • • • • •

DISSEMINATING BEHAVIOR ANALYSIS (7.02)

The behavior analyst assists the profession in making behavior analysis methodology available to the general public.

One area of responsibility to the field of behavior analysis involves helping to educate the general public about our profession. This might involve speaking at local civic groups, writing letters to the editor of the local newspaper to correct some misinformation about behavior analysis, or participating in training workshops for parents, teachers, or other professionals on some aspect of behavior analysis methodology.

• • • • • • •

CASE 7.02: SPREAD THE WORD

Dr. B. is a BCBA who teaches university classes in behavior analysis and as a hobby started training his dog. When he got involved in competitive dog training, he saw that many dog trainers were misusing the principles of operant conditioning. He would occasionally prompt these uninformed trainers about the proper use of operant conditioning and spoke often of his experiences in his behavior analysis classes. One day while reviewing the BACB Guidelines, he noticed that behavior analysts have a "responsibility to the field" to help "educate the general public about our profession." Subsequently, Dr. B. collaborated with a colleague who was writing a book for dog trainers called How Dogs Learn. *The book was based on basic principles of behavior analysis.*

What are some other areas where a creative behavior analyst could take the message of behavior analysis to the general public?

• • • • • • •

BEING FAMILIAR WITH THESE GUIDELINES (7.03)

Behavior analysts have an obligation to be familiar with these Guidelines, other applicable ethics codes, and their application to behavior analysts' work. Lack of awareness or misunderstanding of a conduct standard is not itself a defense to a charge of unethical conduct.

These Guidelines are designed to assist behavior analysts in the conduct of their professional lives. It is imperative that we all are acquainted with them as well as other ethics codes, which may be relevant. Ignorance of the standards is no excuse should you be accused of unethical behavior.

• • • • • • •

CASE 7.03: MATCHMAKER

Darla was a Board Certified assistant Behavior Analyst (BCaBA) who was working for a behavioral services company that owned a residential facility, a sheltered workshop, and some group homes. Darla was a hard worker. She was somewhat shy but was well liked by other employees. Darla's supervisor, Ken, was a happily married BCBA, and, although he did not behave inappropriately around Darla, he often encouraged other staff members who were his good friends to invite Darla on dates, to parties, or to lunch or dinner. He felt like she should have a more active social life. Darla soon picked up on this manipulation and decided to have a talk with Ken. She told him she needed to let him know he was making her feel uncomfortable and possibly violating the behavior analyst's Guidelines for Responsible Conduct Standard 1.07a. Ken took offense at his well-meaning gestures and advised Darla to "lighten up." He said the Guidelines pertained to professional issues and could not be used to "tell me how to live my life."

Did Darla go too far in suggesting that Ken was engaging in unethical conduct?

• • • • • • •

DISCOURAGING MISREPRESENTATION BY NONCERTIFIED INDIVIDUALS (7.04)

Behavior analysts discourage non-certified practitioners from misrepresenting that they are certified.

Should you run into someone who presents himself or herself as a BCBA or BCaBA, you have an obligation to point out the Guidelines and dissuade that person from representing himself or herself as a certified behavior analyst.

• • • • • • •

CASE 7.04: SPEAKING TRUTH TO POWER

Two BCaBAs have accepted positions at a privately owned residential school for children with autism. In the last 6 months, the school fired the director of behavior analysis and the three BCaBAs who were on staff in an attempt to balance the budget. Parents of the children paid more than $50,000 per year to have their children in the program. The well-trained BCaBAs were horrified to find out that behavioral programming was no longer being provided at this school. Under new fiscally conservative management, the program drifted to become a very exclusive babysitting service for children with autism. On all of the printed literature and Web pages describing the school, the advertising clearly offers "behavior analytic treatment" as one of the services.

What should the two BCaBAs do? Taking on the school administration sounds like it could cause a lot of trouble and cost them their jobs.

• • • • • • •

RESPONSES TO CASES

CASE 7.01: STAY AT HOME

Dr. S. has no excuse for not attending conferences for his continuing professional development. Conferences are an opportunity to network with colleagues, to learn about the latest innovative research and the newest leading-edge behavioral treatment techniques, and to become a part of the behavioral community. Conferences give you a chance to meet the leading experts in behavior analysis. You can improve your technical skills by learning about graphing, data collection systems, and so forth.

You might get ideas for how you can provide new services or programs for your clients.

CASE 7.02: SPREAD THE WORD

Behavior analysts can help educate parents by speaking at a Parent–Teacher Organization (PTO) meeting, they can talk to people in the hospitality industry about performance management (PM), and they can use good behavioral procedures informally at their jobs. When the local newspaper runs a story that has behavioral implications, a behavior analyst could write a letter to the editor outlining a good behavioral solution.

CASE 7.03: MATCHMAKER

According to Guideline 7.03, Ken, as a BCBA, is responsible for familiarity with the Guidelines. If he was familiar with the Guidelines, he would know about Section 1.07a, which pertains to "exploitative" relationships with supervisees. Although he does not consider his well-meaning gestures to be unethical, Darla does. He needs to be sensitive to her needs and realize that some people are very sensitive to manipulation and view it as a form of exploitation.

Ken should also know about Section 1.06. This section addresses multiple relationships. If Ken has a supervisory relationship with staff members who are his "good friends," he potentially has some multiple relationship or conflict of interest problems as well. Ken would be well advised to read through the BACB Guidelines carefully to see what else he is missing.

CASE 7.04: SPEAKING TRUTH TO POWER

Problem number one is that these two associates are not supervised by a BCBA. Problem number two is that from this description the program has no integrity and the BCaBAs should rethink their association with the organization. First, they should go to the management and point out their concerns and the ethical issues connected with them. Next, if they get no response, they should consider quitting and reporting the organization to the BACB and to the Association for Behavior Analysis International (ABAI). Finally, depending on what their relationship is with the parents, they may choose to share some of their concerns on their way out.

13

The Behavior Analyst's Ethical Responsibility to Colleagues (Guideline 8)

Behavior analysts have, in their vast catalog of work to be done, a clear set of responsibilities to their colleagues. If you are a practitioner or therapist, you may be concerned about possible ethical violations of other behavior analysts. It should first be understood that attending to a situation like this does not make you a "busybody" or "snitch." Most of us have been culturally conditioned by parents and teachers to "mind your own business," and in your private life this is a pretty good rule to follow. How others conduct their lives really is their own business, unless, of course, it affects your life in some way. This is basically the situation you confront when you believe that a behavioral colleague has violated the Behavior Analyst Certification Board (BACB) Guidelines for Responsible Conduct. It becomes your business by virtue of the fact that an unethical colleague can damage not only their reputation but also yours. It is in this vein that Guideline 8.01 is written to encourage you, despite how uncomfortable it may make you feel, to bring the issue in question to the attention of the person and seek a resolution. Ideally, the

> Unethical colleagues can damage not only their reputation but also yours.

individual will quickly see the error of his or her ways, apologize, and correct the situation with appropriate action. It is not your job to dictate the action but rather to serve as a "trusted colleague" for the person on behalf of the field and possibly the client who may have been involved.* In this role you should seek an ethical solution to the problem and then fade from the picture as quickly as possible. This works most of the time. However, it might happen that the colleague stubbornly resists recognizing the problem or refuses to do anything about it. This will present you with a dilemma that the Guidelines do not cover. If this happens, you may want to check the "Disciplinary Standards, Procedures for Appeals" section of the BACB Web site (BACB, 1998–2010) for further details on what to do next.

THE BEHAVIOR ANALYST'S ETHICAL RESPONSIBILITY TO COLLEAGUES (8.0)

> Behavior analysts have an obligation to bring attention to and resolve ethical violations by colleagues.

In general, people don't like conflict, and behavior analysts are no exception. For this reason, Guideline 8.0 can make even a strong behavior analyst somewhat squeamish. Most of the time, the first reaction to an apparently unethical act is to be incensed especially if the unethical behavior of another professional affected a client's right to treatment, confidentiality, or safety. But when confronted with an ethics violation calm and caution must rule the day. First, you have to be sure

> When behavior analysts become aware of ethical violations, doing nothing to correct the problems can serve no good purpose.

---

* Note that this guideline does not cover any acts that constitute actual illegal behavior. In this case, you would need to contact the proper authorities and let them handle the matter.

that you are operating with firsthand evidence. For example, hearing a rumor about an alleged abuse such as, "She yelled at him and then spit in his face!" is not something you can operate on yourself. If you heard this from a teacher, you should tell the teacher it is his or her duty to report the incident but you cannot. If you see an abuse, you must report it. If you overhear a conversation where a colleague is talking about a client and using the client's name, you are justified in approaching the colleague, not to confront or accuse but to clarify and try to understand what happened. If your observation was correct and the person admits the action, you have an obligation to try to educate the individual about the relevant guidelines.

• • • • • • •

CASE 8.0: WHAT IS THE HARM?

Tanya is an experienced Board Certified Behavior Analyst (BCBA) who is an independent contractor. She provides behavioral services for 4 hours per week with RBC Agency. Dr. T., the owner of the RBC consulting firm, is also a BCBA. Mrs. Wells, one of Tanya's clients, recently reported to Tanya that Dr. T. called her and in a very friendly voice asked if she would be willing to write a letter of support to the school board describing how great RBC's services are. Dr. T. added that if she couldn't collect a lot of letters that she would no longer have a contract with the school district and Mrs. Wells might lose the behavioral services for her child. Tanya was irate since a PhD-level BCBA should know better than to solicit testimonials from clients.

What is Tanya's next step?

• • • • • • •

ETHICAL VIOLATIONS BY BEHAVIORAL AND NONBEHAVIORAL COLLEAGUES (8.01)

When behavior analysts believe that there may have been an ethical violation by another behavior analyst, or non behavioral colleague, they attempt to resolve the issue by bringing it to the attention of that individual if an informal resolution appears appropriate and the intervention does not violate any confidentiality rights that may be involved. If resolution is not obtained, and the behavior analyst believes a client's rights are being violated, the behavior analyst may take additional steps as necessary for the protection of the client.

When you are providing behavior analysis services, there could be circumstances under which you determine that another behavior analyst or nonbehavioral colleague has engaged in what you consider to be unethical conduct. It is your duty to try to resolve the issue by bringing it to the attention of the individual if (1) you believe that the issue can be handled unofficially, and (2) your action will not violate any client's right to confidentiality.

It is best to start the conversation with a casual, not confrontational tone, and simply ask questions to clarify what you believe to be true. You may discover that you are mistaken and that you can back out of the interaction with apologies for taking up the person's time. If the person confirms your observations (remember you cannot operate based on hearsay, you must have firsthand evidence), then you can proceed to point out specific items in the guidelines that are pertinent. You may be able to resolve the issue at this point. In the case of a nonbehavioral colleague, you can repeat this same strategy and point to our Guidelines as an example of a worthy standard for protecting client rights. Keep in mind that other professions have their own Codes of Ethics, and it might be worthwhile for you to review those before having a conversation with a nonbehavioral colleague.

For both behavioral and nonbehavioral colleagues, if you are not able to achieve satisfaction it may be necessary for you to take further steps depending on the severity of the breach of ethical conduct. This might involve contacting the BACB if the person is Board Certified or the appropriate professional association if the professional is not a behavior analyst.

• • • • • • •

CASE 8.01: THE SLEEPY DOCTOR

Miranda routinely went with her client on doctor visits. On a recent trip to see the psychiatrist, Miranda was astonished to discover that 5 minutes into the appointment his head fell forward, and he appeared to be asleep. After a minute or so, the psychiatrist sat up straight and continued the conversation. Then it happened again, and this time he was out for nearly 2 minutes. The client was unaware of what was going on, but Miranda was conflicted. Should she say something? Try to wake him up? Not knowing what was appropriate, she said nothing, and the normal 20-minute appointment took nearly 45 minutes to complete.

What should Miranda do?

• • • • • • •

RESPONSES TO CASES

CASE 8.0: WHAT IS THE HARM?

Although Mrs. Wells was very clear about the conversation and Tanya had every reason to believe her, this was secondhand information. Tanya had no direct knowledge of the conversation. Tanya consulted a trusted colleague who advised her that she could not approach the owner directly but that she could educate Mrs. Wells about our Code of Ethics. Since Mrs. Wells had not yet written the testimonial letter, Tanya told her that writing the letter was certainly not required. Further, Tanya told Mrs. Wells that if Dr. T. contacted her again she should tell Dr. T. that she was aware of the BACB Guidelines and Code Item 9.07.

CASE 8.01: THE SLEEPY DOCTOR

Miranda checked with her supervisor when she got back to the facility and told her about the doctor visit. Her supervisor said, "I can't do anything. I wasn't there; it's up to you." After stewing on the incident for a couple of days, Miranda decided to call the psychiatrist's office and speak to his nurse. She explained what happened, and the nurse apologized profusely. "We normally have one of the nurses sit in on the meetings. They will nudge him if he starts to doze off. He's had this problem for a while, but he is not accepting it at all. We don't know what to do." Miranda dropped the matter for the time being. She felt that (1) she was on record as having reported the problem, and (2) she had reported the problem to someone who might be able to do something if the problem continued.

14

The Behavior Analyst's Ethical Responsibility to Society (Guideline 9)

Behavior analysts, like all good citizens, are interested in promoting the general welfare of our society. With our expertise in analyzing contingencies of reinforcement, we have a particular interest in encouraging the culture to make better use of the knowledge we have gained over the past 60 years about the basic principles of behavior. All around us we see other methods used to deal with problematic behavior. Many of these methods are ineffective or counterproductive. The prison system incarcerates the guilty and calls it "punishment," but there is no real evidence that putting people behind bars is actually functional in reducing future incidents of the targeted behaviors. There is evidence that so-called boot camps for delinquents are ineffective, but they are politically popular and so persist in many communities. Schools operate primarily on the basis of aversive control (e.g., loss of recess, detention, paddling, suspension), although we now have nearly

> Behavior analysts have a particular interest in encouraging the culture to make good use of the knowledge we have gained about the basic principles of behavior.

30 years of data showing how positive reinforcement can be used in the classroom to produce truly extraordinary performance gains. Many children with autism, if given the opportunity for behavioral treatment, can make great strides in their socialization and language skills with a significant number joining the mainstream educational system.

> **Most of the approaches that are used within the community of practitioners are unsupported by empirical evidence.**

However, myths persist about the use of special diets, injections of strange substances, and clearly discredited procedures such as facilitated communication (Singer & Lalich, 1996). In clinical psychology, Beutler (2000, p. 1–2) summarized the recent findings this way: "Accumulating evidence indicates that most of the theories and approaches that are used within the community of practitioners are unsupported by empirical evidence of effects."

For all these reasons and more, the Behavior Analyst Certification Board (BACB) Guidelines prompt behavior analysts to do what they can to promote the application of behavior principles in society as "an alternative approach to treatment and intervention" (Guidelines 9.0 and 9.01). Beyond promoting behavior principles, we encourage consumers to think in terms of empirically based treatments and data-based decision making. We would truly like our culture to become more scientifically oriented when it comes to understanding human behavior. Opportunities to make this point may come up in habilitation team meetings where some decision is about to be made about treatment or in conversation with a client about options that are available. Our ethical guidelines suggest that we look for these opportunities and try to make the best of them without making enemies in the process.

> **Guideline 9.02 inspires behavior analysts to keep the focus on "behavior per se" as a focus of our scientific research and therapy.**

There is a long tradition in psychology of diverting attention from observable behavior to some other level of analysis. A person who smokes is said to have a "need" to smoke, or an employee who is nonproductive might be said to have a "poor attitude." Our Guideline 9.02, in very simple terms, inspires behavior analysts to keep the focus on "behavior per se" as a focus of our scientific research and presumably our therapy as well. As in promoting the application of behavior principles, this guideline suggests that we look for opportunities to bring the discussion back to actual behavior, unvarnished with explanatory theories or pseudo scientific, politically correct "psychobabble." Rather than label a child who is "off-task" a great deal of the time with attention deficit hyperactivity disorder (ADHD) and refer him to a pediatrician for medication to control his behavior, this guideline suggests that the behavior analyst should suggest an analysis of the actual off-task behavior be conducted. The goal would be to determine the functional antecedents, to explore the variations in topography, rate, and function, and to seek a practical environmental intervention that can be implemented in the classroom by a competent teacher.

> Concerns with privacy and confidentiality abound when there is the potential for in-home video to end up on the Internet.

Recent advances in computer technology have completely changed the world. Once only available for limited applications and to companies that could spend in the hundreds of thousands of dollars, computers and electronic equipment are now priced so affordably that they can be used in the average home. One new phenomenon in behavior analysis treatment is the use of interactive videoconferencing by some consultants. Laptop computers and Web cameras placed in the home of a client provide a way for the behavioral professional to provide services to a client who might live several hundred miles away. Some of the advantages of "teleconsulting" are that (1) live support can be provided in the client's home (the child's parents can simply turn on the computer and interact with the behavior analyst), (2) when clients live in geographically remote locations, they can still receive video behavior analysis services even though there are no behavior analysts close by, and (3) there may be substantial cost savings when teleconsulting is compared with a model in which the consultant needs to travel by air and bill for mileage and travel time.

There are clear disadvantages to teleconsulting that raise ethical concerns:

1. Some consultants might use this model as a "quick-and-dirty" solution, not being as thorough as they should be when designing behavior programs and training families.
2. Some behavioral procedures are better demonstrated by actually being present with the client and family (or other professional). This is particularly the case where the skill being taught relies on modeling or physical prompting.
3. Teleconsulting could be so efficient for some behavior analysts that they would try to provide services via this method exclusively, thus never really having face-to-face access with a client.
4. If teleconsulting is adopted as the consultant's main way of work, this could result in the building of a caseload that is too large to do quality behavior analysis consulting.
5. If there are children or teenagers in the home and the equipment is not protected or well supervised, it could be misused or damaged.
6. If a computer goes down on either end or the phone or cable lines are out, the client will not receive services.

Finally, clients must be assured that privacy is protected. In a recent case, computer technicians at a Pennsylvania high school turned on Web cams in school-issued laptops to spy on the students. Practices such as this raise very serious privacy concerns for this new technology.

If you are considering using teleconsulting, remember that as specified in 9.06b, our ethical standards still apply in the Internet age. Concerns with privacy and confidentiality abound whenever there is the potential for in-home video involving a client to end up on the Internet.

Other responsibilities that behavior analysts have to society include being honest in their public statements and advertising and being vigilant in preventing others from misrepresenting behavior analysis practices (Guideline 9.04). We also have an obligation to avoid making false claims about our effectiveness and to ensure that any public statements are factual (Guideline 9.05).

THE BEHAVIOR ANALYST'S ETHICAL RESPONSIBILITY TO SOCIETY (9.0)

> The behavior analyst promotes the general welfare of society through the application of the principles of behavior.

There are many ways the behavior analyst can work to improve our society through the ethical application of basic principles of behavior, and these Guidelines encourage you to do so.

PROMOTION IN SOCIETY (9.01)

> The behavior analyst should promote the application of behavior principles in society by presenting a behavioral alternative to other procedures or methods.

One way of making a difference in society and at the same time promoting the field of behavior analysis is to offer behavioral alternatives to commonly accepted procedures.

• • • • • • •

CASE 9.01: COVERAGE CANCELED

Dr. Judy N. is a Board Certified Behavior Analyst (BCBA) who consults in developmental disabilities (DD) facilities.

> *Dr. N. has been a lifelong dog lover. Dr. N. got a German shep-*
> *herd, a breed she has always loved, and shortly thereafter she*
> *purchased a new house. Dr. N. was very dismayed to have*
> *her homeowner's insurance company tell her certain breeds of*
> *dogs were not insurable by this company and that she would*
> *have to find a new home for her dog. When she asked why, she*
> *was told that the company had a policy of not insuring certain*
> *breeds because of their "aggressive behavior."*
>
> *Are there any behavior analytic solutions that Dr. N. can sug-*
> *gest to her insurance agent and, if necessary, his supervisors?*

• • • • • • •

There are many other examples of how behavior analysts can promote the application of behavioral principles in society. Related to educational settings, one growing trend is to have physically active children placed on prescription drugs by their pediatricians because of their behavior in school. A behavior analyst working in the schools might have an opportunity to ask if the parents had considered a behavioral alternative.

SCIENTIFIC INQUIRY (9.02)

The behavior analyst should promote the analysis of behavior per se as a legitimate field of scientific inquiry.

If you are given an opportunity to speak or write about behavior analysis, you should take that occasion to point out that behavior analysis is a reasonable and valid approach to understanding human behavior.

• • • • • • •

CASE 9.02: STATS AND THE CITY

Dr. Scott J. is a BCBA who is an experienced researcher. Dr. J.
is active in his neighborhood association, and as a neighbor-
hood liaison to local government agencies, he attends city and

county commission meetings. The city commission wants to evaluate the effectiveness of its community programs. City staff members are suggesting survey and statistical research.

In this setting, would it be appropriate for Dr. J. to suggest the use of behavior analysis?

• • • • • • •

PUBLIC STATEMENTS (9.03)

Behavior analysts comply with these Guidelines in public statements relating to their professional services, products, or publications or to the field of behavior analysis.

It is important to remember that these Guidelines are relevant any time you are communicating with the public about your products, services, or the field of behavior analysis; for example, you must uphold high standards of professional behavior (1.0), maintain confidentiality (2.07), not exaggerate your effectiveness (10.0(a), and acknowledge the contribution of others (10.21).

(b) Public statements include but are not limited to paid or unpaid advertising, brochures, printed matter, directory listings, personal resumes or curriculum vitae, interviews or comments for use in media, statements in legal proceedings, lectures and public oral presentations, and published materials.

Public statements are understood to include any form of advertising, listings in professional directories, publication of your vita, or any form of oral presentation whether in a courtroom, public presentation, or in any form of publication.

• • • • • •

CASE 9.03: MIRACLE IN THE MEDIA

Renee was a BCBA who worked in early childhood settings with children born to mothers who were addicted to drugs. A number of the children in the program had also been diagnosed with fetal alcohol syndrome. Renee believed very much in using behavior analysis to help children. When the media called or came to visit the program, they were usually referred to Renee. Renee was an articulate person who had media contacts, and she was "camera friendly." From some past training in marketing and public relations, Renee also knew about putting the spin and hype on a media message to get more coverage. In one television interview, to get a lot of attention for the program and for behavior analysis, Renee was quoted as saying, "For these children, behavior analysis offers a miracle. There is no other method of early childhood education that will do what behavior analysis does for these children—it is a proven fact that this population will be successful adults if they have a behavior analysis prekindergarten program."

For media purposes, was Renee justified in adding some hype to her message?

• • • • • • •

STATEMENTS BY OTHERS (9.04)

(a) Behavior analysts who engage others to create or place public statements that promote their professional practice, products, or activities retain professional responsibility for such statements.

If you hire someone to create public statements, you are responsible for what they generate; that is, you are accountable for errors or misstatements.

(b) Behavior analysts make reasonable efforts to prevent others whom they do not control (such as employers, publishers, sponsors, organizational clients, and representatives of the print or broadcast media) from making deceptive statements concerning behavior analysts' practices or professional or scientific activities.

In your professional life, you may find that others, over whom you have no actual influence, may make misleading or dishonest comments about the field of behavior analysis; should this happen, you are required to make sensible effort to prevent or at least manage these remarks or writings.

· · · · · · ·

CASE 9.04: THE ENTHUSIASTIC JOURNALIST

In Case 9.03, the early childhood program in which Renee worked continued to receive a lot of media attention. An enthusiastic writer for a women's magazine interviewed Renee over the phone. At the end of the interview the writer told her, "I have a great idea for pitching your story. I see the title of the article as being something like, 'Exciting New Program Cures Crack Babies.'"

It is clear to Renee that the program may get donations and funding as a result of media attention, but she isn't so sure about this magazine's angle. Should she say something?

· · · · · · ·

(c) If behavior analysts learn of deceptive statements about their work made by others, behavior analysts make reasonable efforts to correct such statements.

As described in 10.01(f), if you learn of misleading or inaccurate statements made about your work you have an obligation to try and correct them.

(d) A paid advertisement relating to the behavior analyst's activities must be identified as such, unless it is already apparent from the context.

If you develop an ad to place in the newspaper, on the Internet, or on television, you must clearly label it as a paid advertisement (unless it is obvious).

AVOIDANCE OF FALSE OR DECEPTIVE STATEMENTS (9.05)

Behavior analysts do not make public statements that are false, deceptive, misleading, or fraudulent, either because of what they state, convey, or suggest or because of what they omit, concerning their research, practice, or other work activities or those of persons or organizations with which they are affiliated.

Behavior analysts claim as credentials for their behavioral work, only degrees that were primarily or exclusively behavior analytic in content.

Behavior analysts should always tell the truth about their work and about the field. It is inappropriate to cite qualifications other than those in behavior analysis when describing their qualifications in behavior analysis.

• • • • • • •

CASE 9.05: EXPERTISE ILLUSION

Dr. Lily O. was a BCBA who had worked in DD facilities and group homes for 20 years. A company that managed facilities for clients with head injuries was moving to Dr. O.'s state. She knew there would be several jobs available for behavior analysts in these new facilities. Dr. O. started telling people she knew a lot about the behavioral treatment of head injury and that she would be good at these jobs. In some meetings she attended where she said these things, state-level administrators were present. Dr. O. was doing a good sell job for herself, and several well-respected people had agreed to write letters of reference.

Dr. O. did not really lie. She honestly believed she knew a lot about head injury. How do the Guidelines address this?

• • • • • • •

MEDIA PRESENTATIONS AND EMERGING MEDIA-BASED SERVICES (9.06)

(a) When behavior analysts provide advice or comment by means of public lectures, demonstrations, radio or television programs, prerecorded tapes, printed articles, mailed material, or other media, they take reasonable precautions to ensure that (1) the statements are based on appropriate behavior analytic literature and practice, (2) the statements are otherwise consistent with these Guidelines, and (3) the recipients of the information are not encouraged to infer that a relationship has been established with them personally.

When you are asked to speak publicly on behavior analysis, it is imperative that you make your comments consistent with the research literature and all of these Guidelines (not just this section). It is important that you not convey the impression that you have any individual relationship with viewers or listeners when in fact you do not. (Note: this latter point would be relevant in the case of a radio call-in show, for example.)

• • • • • • •

CASE 9.06A: "DOUG, I'M LISTENING..."

Dr. G. was a very well-known behavior analyst with a great "radio voice." He was occasionally asked to handle questions about behavior problems on a local radio call-in show. To make the show lively and interesting, Dr. G. took great pains to remind listeners that what he was suggesting was backed up by empirical research, and he gave examples from his own clinical experience. The show's producer prompted Dr. G. to use the caller's name when giving a reply and to use a "warm tone" to his voice. "Look, all I'm asking you to do is say something like, 'Doug, I know exactly what you are talking about, and I can understand how you feel and here's what I would do in this case...'" Dr. G. preferred a more matter-of-fact approach.
Should he have listened to the producer?

• • • • • • •

(b) When behavior analysts deliver services, teach or conduct research using existing or emerging media (e.g., Internet, e-learning, interactive multi-media), they consider any ethical challenges presented by media-based delivery (e.g., privacy, confidentiality, evidence-based interventions, ongoing data collection and program modifications) and make every effort possible to adhere to the ethical standards described herein.

This standard, added to the Guidelines in 2010, requires that when behavior analysts are using leading-edge technology that the standards developed for standard one-on-one therapy, teaching, and research still apply. Our clients still need to be protected from harm, from exposure, and from nonevidence-based treatments. Behavior analysts delivering services in the home by a high-speed Internet connection need to assure their clients that the feed from the home is secure and cannot be hacked and that any recordings will be secure. And BCBAs venturing into this new territory must maintain their critical thinking about this new mode of treatment delivery. Is there evidence to show that remote consultation is just as good as that delivered face to face? Will clients be given the option? Should teleconsulting be used if it is possible to provide the services in person? How will the service be evaluated by outside agencies?

• • • • • • •

CASE 9.06B: DARCI TRIES THE INTERNET

Darci, an independent contractor and BCBA, was working with a family that lived more than 2 hours away from her office in a major Midwestern city. Although they lived in a remote, rural area, the family had a high-speed connection and router that they used for their in-home business. It occurred to Darci that she could save driving time by setting up a Web cam in the living room where she normally conducted language sessions with the 3-year-old child with autism. Darci planned to continue to make the drive once a month, but she felt it would be a better use of time to simply have the family connect with her on the Internet on the other weeks. The mom had observed Darci's therapy session with her child and was interested in trying the new system, especially once she heard that the hourly fee would be reduced by 30% for these teleconsulting sessions.

What questions should the family ask of Darci? What ethical considerations should Darci think about before starting this new time saving venture?

• • • • • • •

TESTIMONIALS (9.07)

Behavior analysts do not solicit testimonials from current clients or patients or other persons who because of their particular circumstances are vulnerable to undue influence.

It is inappropriate for behavior analysts to ask their current clients to issue quotable statements of support on their behalf for the purpose of advertising. To do so might put clients in an awkward position with regard to their current treatment. For example, they might think that they need make positive public statements for you to keep treating them. You may ask past clients for a statement of satisfaction with your services. If you do this, you will need to tell them the purpose of the request and how the information will be used. (Note: behavior analysts must always bear in mind the requirement of client confidentiality that in most cases would preclude using this type of information. Testimonials also should come with disclaimers indicating that such positive outcomes may not occur in all instances since each case is unique.)

• • • • • • •

CASE 9.07: SCRAPBOOKING KEEPSAKES

Sandy C. was a BCaBA who worked with Medicaid waiver clients. She was a graduate student who was working toward her BCBA certification. In Sandy's free time, she enjoyed the hobby of scrapbooking, in which scrapbook pages are elaborately decorated with photos, sayings, clippings, and artwork. Sandy dearly loved her work with clients and decided that she would make a scrapbook about her clients as a sort of keepsake and something she could show her mother when she visited at Thanksgiving. Sandy asked her present clients and some from the recent past to write comments about how she helped them. Sandy artfully put the comments in a scrapbook along with photos of the clients and some cute clip art that she found online. One day when she was meeting with a case

manager for the first time, she showed the case manager her
treasured scrapbook as an example of her work.
Was there a problem with this?

• • • • • • •

IN-PERSON SOLICITATION (9.08)

Behavior analysts do not engage, directly or through agents, in uninvited in-person solicitation of business from actual or potential users of services who, because of their particular circumstances are vulnerable to undue influence, except that organizational behavior management or performance management services may be marketed to corporate entities regardless of their projected financial position.

Behavior analysts may, in the course of their daily activities, meet people who clearly need their services. These might be neighbors, business acquaintances, relatives, or individuals in a setting where the behavior analyst is currently consulting or providing treatment who are in a crisis situation and need immediate help of some sort. To offer services at this time is to take advantage of their stressful situation and is considered highly inappropriate. If they make a request such as, "I just don't know what to do; can you help me?" it is appropriate to make a referral to an appropriate professional.

• • • • • • •

CASE 9.08: SHOPPING FOR CLIENTS

Roman was a fresh-out-of graduate school BCBA who was just establishing himself in a midsized town not far from where he got his degree. He had some new friends and found himself often explaining what he did professionally. On the day that his new business cards came back from the printer, he happened to be standing in line at the grocery store behind a mother with a screaming toddler. She was trying to ignore the child and looked like she was waiting for a break in the crying to try to reinforce some quiet behavior when the cashier pulled out a piece of candy and gave it to the child. The child immediately quit crying, the cashier looked delighted with his quick thinking, and the mother was dumbfounded. Roman reached in his pocket, pulled out a business card, and handed it to the mother, saying, "Give me a call; I can help you." When he went through the checkout process, he handed another card to the cashier and said, "I'm not sure that what you did with that child was the right thing to do; give me a call sometime."

Was Roman operating ethically in this situation?

• • • • • • •

RESPONSES TO CASES

CASE 9.01: COVERAGE CANCELED

Dr. N. has been a responsible dog owner, and her dog is now well trained, thanks to successful operant conditioning procedures. As a behavior analyst, she could try to influence the insurance company's policy by offering to meet with the insurance agent's supervisors or to give talks at insurance conferences on dog behavior, dog training, and how behavior analysis can be used as a proven training technique by homeowners to prepare their dogs so that they are safe, nonthreatening, good citizens. Dr. N. could also contact the American Kennel Club and ask for its assistance in lobbying for homeowners' insurance for those homeowners who have taken the extra effort to train their dogs and have them tested for the Canine Good Citizen certificate that is issued by the American Kennel Club.

The idea here is that the behavior analyst has recognized a problem that affects many people (i.e., dog owners losing their insurance due to owning a specific breed of dog), and as a person with behavioral skills there is some responsibility to educate relevant professionals about effective behavioral solutions. In other unrelated cases, the behavior analyst could contact the relevant national organization to have an impact.

CASE 9.02: STATS AND THE CITY

Behavior analysts should promote the analysis of behavior as a legitimate field of scientific inquiry. Dr. J. can suggest some ways that behavior analytic research can be done to evaluate the effectiveness of community programs, particularly if they are interested in making socially significant improvements to these programs.

CASE 9.03: MIRACLE IN THE MEDIA

Behavior analysts need to comply with the Guidelines in public statements relating to the field of behavior analysis. Renee should not have promised a miracle cure. The use of the word miracle is entirely inappropriate. She also should have not made claims about the long-term effects of this early childhood program unless the longitudinal research had been done.

CASE 9.04: THE ENTHUSIASTIC JOURNALIST

According to the Guidelines, behavior analysts who are working with others to place public statements about behavior analysis are responsible for those statements. Renee should have some assurance that the article will be written and presented in a manner that she can accept, or she should decline the interview. Note that most writers resist the idea that the source (in this case, Renee) will be able to review the article before it goes to print. It would be a good idea for Renee to tape-record the interview (the magazine writer should, of course, be told of the taping) and then, as soon as the phone call is over, to review the tape and type up the key quotes she made and send them to the writer. All of this extra work ensures that what goes out in print is exactly what Renee said and will prevent her having to try to correct the record after the magazine article has been published.

CASE 9.05: EXPERTISE ILLUSION

Behavior analysts do not make false or deceptive statements. By saying she knows a lot about head injury, Dr. O. is implying she has been trained in the area and has worked with clients with head injury. She needs to be very explicit and say, "I am very interested in this area and would like to learn about it. I am going to see if there is a job that fits with my current skills when the new facility opens."

CASE 9.06A: "DOUG, I'M LISTENING…"

Dr. G. has to find the fine balance between being good at the media (if he's not, he'll be fired and won't be able to get the behavior analysis message out) and being ethical. He can take some of the producer's advice to be a little warmer, but he needs to avoid making any statements that suggest he knows more about the caller than he does.

CASE 9.06B: DARCI TRIES THE INTERNET

The family should think seriously about this option before jumping into it simply because it sounds interesting and might save them some money. For example, do they know for sure that any images that are sent from their living room will not be viewable by their neighbors? They should also ask Darci if she is keeping copies of the video feed and how she plans to store it. Just as any consumer should ask about any type of proposed therapy, the parents should ask if there is any research on remotely delivered behavioral services for the same problems or issues their child has, and, if so, could they have a copy to study.

Darci should consider and present to the family other possible alternatives; for example, if she can't make the visit every week, could she train a qualified assistant (from the local community) to provide services during alternate weeks? Darci should spend some time looking through journal articles related to remote treatment using behavior analysis. She might also want to consult with behavior analysts who offer teleconsulting to make sure she is on firm ground before she proceeds. Darci needs to remember that "Do no harm" and "Right to Effective Treatment" still apply and that confidentiality is a serious concern when video cameras are brought into the home.

CASE 9.07: SCRAPBOOKING KEEPSAKES

The Guidelines state that behavior analysts do not solicit testimonials from clients. Sandy was in violation of the Guidelines for both asking for the letters and showing them to others. Sandy needs to restrict her scrapbooking to topics such as family photos or fun with friends.

CASE 9.08: SHOPPING FOR CLIENTS

Roman was enthusiastic and evangelistic about his work but way out of line in giving the business card to the mother of the screaming toddler. Giving the card to the cashier was just a waste of time. Roman might consider setting up a meeting with the store manager and telling him of his observation with the cashier (without naming names) and suggest that the manager could do training for employees on basic principles of behavior for the retail setting.

15

The Behavior Analyst and Research (Guideline 10)

Conducting research in behavior analysis involves the most complex set of requirements that can be found in these Behavior Analyst Certification Board (BACB) Guidelines. Some are quite broad and include planning your research in such a way that the findings will not be misused by others (Guideline 10.0a) and will be ethically acceptable by other researchers and presumably consumers as well (Guideline 10.0e). Others require the behavior analyst researcher to attend to the fine details of debriefing (Guideline 10.11) and paying participants (Guideline 10.15). In the most general sense, this guideline makes it clear that "Do no harm" is certainly the watchword of the applied behavioral researcher (Guideline 10.01b), whether it involves carefully supervising assistants (Guideline 10.0b), obtaining informed consent (Guideline 10.04), or, later in the process, using the findings for instructive purposes (Guideline 10.02). Of course, the best protection against harming participants is to always seek advance approval of your local Institutional Review Board (IRB; Guideline 10.0e). Also seek guidance via peer consultation when

> Guideline 10.0 makes it clear that "Do no harm" is the watchword of the applied behavioral researcher.

designing your study. It goes without saying that behavioral researchers will comply with state and federal law (Guideline 10.03), will obtain informed consent from participants (Guideline 10.04), and will inform them of how the data will be used (Guideline 10.06). It is in the best interest of the behavior analysis researcher and the field if participants are not only spared any harm but also treated as well as possible while they are involved in any experiment (or therapy). Because most applied behavioral research is conducted in the participant's environment, the researcher has an obligation to avoid interfering as much as possible and to collect only necessary data for the study (Guideline 10.07). Participants should be ensured anonymity (Guideline 10.09), should be informed that they can withdraw at any time (Guideline 10.10), and should be debriefed at the conclusion of the study (Guideline 10.11). Most behavioral research does not involve any deception, but, if it is essential for the conduct of the study and there are no alternatives, it is permissible as long it does not involve any physical risk or adverse emotional experience (Guideline 10.05a–10.05c). Behavior analysts using animals in their research must comply with the Federal Animal Welfare Act (1990) and ensure that the animals are treated humanely (Guideline 10.18).

It is a common courtesy and also a Guideline that once the research is concluded and is being written for publication, the behavioral researcher will acknowledge those who helped with the study (Guideline 10.21) and will pay particular attention to the issue of who receives publication credit (Guideline 10.20, 10.21, 10.22).

THE BEHAVIOR ANALYST AND RESEARCH (10.0)

Behavior analysts design, conduct, and report research in accordance with recognized standards of scientific competence and ethical research. Behavior analysts conduct research with human and nonhuman research participants according to the proposal approved by a local human research committee, and/or Institutional Review Board.

Behavior analysts involved in research must be specially trained to high standards of proficiency and conduct themselves in an ethical fashion. They must have a proposed plan of research, which is then submitted to an IRB or other local human research committee (e.g., educational research must be approved by the local school board research committee). Further, ethical behavior analysts must follow the plan once it is approved.

• • • • • • • •

CASE 10.0: FLEXIBLE RESEARCH

Ron was a graduate student seeking his certificate in Applied Behavior Analysis. As a part of the psychology department's training, Ron had a part-time position to provide behavioral services in two middle schools. This work was closely supervised by a Board Certified Behavior Analyst (BCBA). A real believer in the potential of behavior analysis to make a difference in society, Ron was also interested in behavioral analytic research in a wide variety of areas, including behavioral safety, performance management (PM), and behavioral sports psychology. He wanted to be a researcher and was very eager to get published. Ron played tennis in high school, and he felt that he could help the tennis team increase its frequency of wins. Ron approached the tennis coach and asked if he could do some research to improve the performance of tennis team members. Because this was not an official psychology departmental assignment for Ron, he told the coach he was going to be "flexible to the max, sort of making this up as I go along, you know, rolling with the punches." He hoped the coach understood the need to be flexible. Ron figured that as the weeks progressed the interventions he needed to implement would become more apparent.

The coach did give his permission for Ron to do the research and work with the team. Were any other approvals needed?

• • • • • • •

(a) Behavior analysts plan their research so as to minimize the possibility that results will be misleading.

A great deal of planning goes into research, and one goal is to ensure that when the results are obtained they are truthful.

• • • • • • •

CASE 10.0A: SPIN THE DATA

Using Case 10.0, in this case Ron's major professor heard about this research project. Ron finally got on track writing the proposal, getting approval, and detailing the proposed interventions. Ron was taking data throughout the study, and he had observers taking data when he was unavailable. It came time to write the results. One method of graphing the data showed absolutely no effect of the interventions on the performance of tennis team members. If Ron used certain statistical tests or presented only the data from a few participants, the results appeared to be a little better. Ron felt that he owed it to the coach and players to present the data in the most positive manner possible.

Is there any problem with selecting a method of data presentation that shows the research in the most positive way possible?

• • • • • • •

(b) Behavior analysts conduct research competently and with due concern for the dignity and welfare of the participants. Researchers and assistants are permitted to perform only those tasks for which they are appropriately trained and prepared.

It is expected that behavior analysts will be proficient in carrying out their research and that uppermost in their considerations will be the safety and well-being of the participants.

• • • • • • •

CASE 10.0B: SAFE CROSSING

Several years ago, some research was conducted on teaching safety skills to elementary school children. In this research, the children were taught to cross the street safely after school. As one can imagine, during the baseline phase in a study like this, observers might be watching children who crossed the street without looking both ways or who engaged in other unsafe behaviors.

What rules are necessary during the baseline phase?

• • • • • • •

(c) Behavior analysts are responsible for the ethical conduct of research conducted by them or by others under their supervision or control.

Behavior analysts involved in research must remember that they are responsible for all of those involved on the research team including observers, therapists, or data analysts.

• • • • • • •

CASE 10.0C: WATCH THAT OBSERVER

Dr. Yung-Ha C. was a BCBA who taught in a university psychology program. Dr. C. was conducting research in a school that dealt with the effects of teacher approval and prompts on student behavior. In this study, observers cued teachers when it was time to reinforce children for target behaviors. Dr. C. trained undergraduate students on the observation system. He met with them in his office as a group one time per week to talk about the progress of the study. In addition, a graduate student had trained a teacher aide to take the data and serve as a reliability observer. Several weeks into the study, one of the undergraduate observers complained to Dr. C. about Kirsten, the teacher aide who was taking data. Kirsten apparently did not like one child in the study and was not giving the teacher the cues to reinforce this child. Sometimes, when sitting with a reliability observer at her side, Kirsten would make fun of the teacher's poor teaching, muttering under her breath, "That was just brilliant, just brilliant. Why don't you let that kid run the class?"

If you were Dr. C., what would you do?

• • • • • • •

(d) Behavior analysts conducting applied research conjointly with provision of clinical or human services obtain required external reviews of proposed clinical research and observe requirements for both intervention and research involvement by client-participants.

Behavioral researchers in clinical, educational, or rehabilitative settings will have their research proposals approved by the clinic, school, or hospital where they want to work and also by relevant external review committees (i.e., IRB).

• • • • • • •

CASE 10.0D: RESEARCH APPROVALS

Carl was a graduate student who was working on his master's degree in behavioral psychology. He wanted to do research in a high school that was in a low-income neighborhood. He began volunteering at the school, and he established an excellent working relationship with the principal and some of the teachers. When it came time to start his study, Carl provided each of his committee members with a prospectus. He met with the school and got the approvals to conduct his research. He sent an email to everyone on his committee saying that he had obtained "approvals to start his study."

Was Carl ready to begin his research after obtaining approvals from the school principal and the teachers involved in the study?

• • • • • • •

(e) In planning research, behavior analysts consider its ethical acceptability under these Guidelines. If an ethical issue is unclear, behavior analysts seek to resolve the issue through consultation with institutional review boards, animal care and use committees, peer consultations, or other proper mechanisms.

The Guidelines describe in detail the ethical requirements for behavior analyst researchers. If you have any question about an ethical issue, you should contact the relevant committees or IRB to seek a resolution before the research begins.

• • • • • • •

CASE 10.0E: THE TROUBLE WITH TOYS

Shondra was a BCBA who had all of the necessary approvals to begin her research with young children at a neighborhood community center. Shondra had her committee members sign off on the research, the community center's director had approved the study, and she had IRB approval. To get the IRB and committee approvals, Shondra submitted a detailed prospectus outlining her plans for both the baseline and intervention phases of her study. Shondra's research was designed to evaluate the effectiveness of token reinforcers. Children could earn tokens that could be exchanged for small, inexpensive toys. After beginning her study, Shondra noticed that the toys were the source of some unethical conduct on the part of the teachers. The teachers were very much aware of which children in the program came from low-income homes and which children were middle class. The teachers began systematically discriminating against the children whom they perceived did not need the toys. Shondra's study had gone awry.
What is her next move?

• • • • • • •

SCHOLARSHIP AND RESEARCH (10.01)

(a) The behavior analyst engaged in study and research is guided by the conventions of the science of behavior including the emphasis on the analysis of individual behavior and strives to model appropriate applications in professional life.

Behavior analyst researchers conduct their research in the tradition of Skinner's (1953) model of operant conditioning and emulate this practice in their occupation.

• • • • • • •

CASE 10.01A: BRUCE'S BAND

Bruce was a BCBA and a graduate student who worked in a residential developmental disabilities (DD) facility for ambulatory, verbal adults. He supervised two houses that each had 16 clients. As a hobby, Bruce loved music. He played in a small band, and he listened to many types of music. Bruce decided that as a part of his behavioral programming responsibilities, he would do a research project that evaluated the effects of music therapy on his clients. He would play music in the houses for an hour each day, keeping a record of the type of music played. Then, at the end of the hour, Bruce would ask the clients how the music made them feel.

Bruce was surprised when his behavioral colleagues were not so impressed with this idea. What was the problem?

• • • • • • •

(b) Behavior analysts take reasonable steps to avoid harming their clients, research participants, students, and others with whom they work, and to minimize harm where it is foreseeable and unavoidable. Harm is defined here as negative effects or side effects of behavior analysis that outweigh positive effects in the particular instance, and that are behavioral or physical and directly observable.

Do no harm: Researchers do everything they can to make sure that experimental participants are not injured in any way in the course of a study. Behavior analysts are particularly concerned that any negative effects are in all cases outweighed by the benefits of the study to the participant.

• • • • • • •

CASE 10.01B: WORK FASTER

Dr. Sam H. is a BCBA who consults and conducts research in PM settings. Dr. H. was hired by a medical computer data-entry service to increase productivity. Workers at this company sat

at desks wearing headphones, and they typed patient records
that had been voice-recorded by physicians. To get more work
done faster (and thus more money for the data-entry company),
Dr. H. recommended that data-entry clerks increase their pro-
ductivity by 20%. This would mean that breaks needed to be
shorter or that typing needed to be faster. Dr. H. wanted to pay
incentives to staff members for each additional record that was
typed beyond some specified quota.

The benefit was that workers might be able to make more
money. Were there any risks that Dr. H. should have wor-
ried about?

• • • • • • •

(c) Because behavior analysts' scientific and professional judgments and actions affect the lives of others, they are alert to and
guard against personal, financial, social, organizational, or political factors that might lead to misuse of their influence.

Researchers have a somewhat elevated status in our culture and
are often looked to for advice or recommendations; that being the
case, they need to be careful not to let their opinions be influenced
by factors unrelated to the scientific data that are available.

• • • • • • •

CASE 10.01C: BANDWAGON EFFECT

Dr. X. was a well-known behavior analyst and researcher. He
had been published in many journals and was a recognized
speaker at conferences and seminars. A private company in
another state that offered comprehensive services to people
with DD offered Dr. X. a high-powered, high-paying job. The
company had a residential facility, sheltered workshops, and
a private school. Dr. X. could not resist going to work for this
company as the new director of research. Once he was set-
tled in his new job, Dr. X. realized that the private company
was not so much interested in a sound behavior program and
behavioral research as it was in using his name and reputation
to justify what it wanted to do. In some areas, the company

wanted to jump on the bandwagon of popular trends that had not been substantiated by research.

Dr. X. had to make some choices. What could he do?

• • • • • • •

(d) Behavior analysts do not participate in activities in which it appears likely that others will misuse their skills or data, unless corrective mechanisms, e.g., peer or external professional or independent review, are available.

Behavior analyst researchers must be wary of forums where their experimental work can be used to support a cause or organization that is not supported by the data.

• • • • • • •

CASE 10.01D: RESEARCH AMMUNITION

Dr. A. was a BCBA who had an excellent reputation. He consulted in a number of DD agencies, and he was on the faculty at a university. Dr. A. believed in community service, so he served on the local Human Rights Committee and was on the board of directors of a local parents' group (for parents of DD and children with autism). Dr. A. had published research on teaching social skills to children with developmental disabilities. Some of the more vocal parent activists found out about Dr. A.'s research. Using Dr. A.'s socialization studies as their ammunition, they went to the school their children attended and caused a ruckus, demanding that their children be placed in regular education classrooms. Dr. A. was mortified that this happened. The worst part of this fiasco was that his studies had nothing to do with DD or children with autism being placed in regular classes.

What should Dr. A. do?

• • • • • • •

(e) Behavior analysts do not exaggerate claims for effectiveness of particular procedures or of behavior analysis in general.

It is important for the credibility of our field that behavior analysts "stick to the data" when explaining their results to others. In particular, it is important that the ethical behavior analyst in no way exaggerate the success of his or her procedures or of behavior analysis more generally; to do so lessens the credibility of the field.

• • • • • • •

CASE 10.01E: BIG CLAIMS

Dr. Virginia G. was a researcher who worked with children with autism. Dr. G. conducted one study with two preschool children with autism. In her study, Dr. G. arranged for the children to attend a preschool class with children who had no disabilities. Dr. G. arranged for the children to have a 1:1 behavior specialist and an additional aide throughout the day. The results of the research showed that the children with autism acquired many new skills while in the class and that their behavior problems were easily managed. Dr. G. was thrilled. She wrote up the results of the research, making the bold statement that children with autism do not need special education classes and can all be treated in the context of classes with typical children.

Dr. C. had the data showing that her participants did great. Is there any problem with her conclusions?

• • • • • • •

(f) If behavior analysts learn of misuse or misrepresentation of their individual work products, they take reasonable and feasible steps to correct or minimize the misuse or misrepresentation.

Some important studies in behavior analysis get picked up by the media or advocates, and, in an effort to build support, the actual results may be distorted. If this should happen to something that you have published, you have an obligation to try to correct the record.

• • • • • • •

CASE 10.01F: MIS-REPRESENTIN'

In Case 10.01(e), when the research was completed, Dr. G. had the university's public relations director send press releases about the findings of her study to several magazines. (Although Dr. G. planned on sending the study to a scientific journal, she wanted the results sent to popular press magazines as well.) Dr. G. found out that the public relations director had put the following spin on the press releases: "Dramatic New Advances in Autism: Children With Autism Don't Need Special Education."

What should Dr. G. do?

• • • • • • •

USING CONFIDENTIAL INFORMATION FOR DIDACTIC OR INSTRUCTIVE PURPOSES (10.02)

(a) Behavior analysts do not disclose in their writings, lectures, or other public media, confidential, personally identifiable information concerning their individual or organizational clients, students, research participants, or other recipients of their services that they obtained during the course of their work, unless the person or organization has consented in writing or unless there is other ethical or legal authorization for doing so.

Behavior analysts must always go out of their way to protect the identity of their experimental participants in their publications or presentations. It is wise to seek consent, in writing, if you foresee needing to do otherwise. In some rare instances, you may be required by the legal system to reveal confidential information.

• • • • • • •

CASE 10.02A: REVEALING

Dr. Richard J. was a BCBA who worked in a mental health facility. Dr. J. had known one of the office assistants, Courtney, since she was 15 years old. Dr. J. met Courtney when she was a participant in research he conducted at a drug treatment facility. Now Courtney was 22 years old and had been "clean" since she was 19. She was working part time in the mental health facility's office and was attending community college classes. It finally looked like she had her life under control. Dr. J. was extremely impressed with Courtney's success. On several occasions, Dr. J. told staff members about Courtney's background and how she should be an inspiration to others. Dr. J. also talked about Courtney as a success case when he gave presentations at conferences. Dr. J. knew about issues pertaining to confidentiality, but he thought Courtney could be an inspiration to his colleagues at the facility and professionals at conferences who needed to hear an example of someone whose life was changed as a result of behavioral treatment.

The colleagues to whom Dr. J. spoke to about Courtney were professionals in the field, and he knew they would not talk about her with other people. Considering this, was it acceptable for Dr. J. to tell other people about Courtney?

• • • • • • • •

(b) Ordinarily, in such scientific and professional presentations, behavior analysts disguise confidential information concerning such persons or organizations so that they are not individually identifiable to others and so that discussions do not cause harm to identifiable participants.

If you are publishing information or giving talks about your participants, it is a good idea to use made-up names and other masked references to avoid causing any harm to those who might associate themselves with your study.

• • • • • • •

CASE 10.02B: PROUD PARENT

Dr. George S. was a BCBA who was a university professor. He gave lectures to psychology and special education students and frequently gave presentations and seminars at conferences. In his personal life, Dr. S. and his wife decided to become foster parents to a 7-year-old, Billy. Billy had been neglected by his substance-abusing mother when he was an infant. At 4 years of age, after an incident of sexual abuse (and a suspicion of many more incidents), Billy was removed from the home of his biological parents. From the time he was 4 until he was 7 years old, Billy was in and out of foster homes. He was a very attractive child, but he had severe behavior problems. When he was 7, Billy went to live with Dr. S. and his wife. Over the next 2 years, Billy had a loving home and a very intensive behavior analysis program. His behavior got much better, and Dr. S. and his wife adopted Billy. Dr. S. had never been so proud of anything in his life as he was about Billy. Dr. S. frequently talked about Billy in his classes and at conferences, telling Billy's whole background, including the sexual abuse, information on his diagnoses, and his family history. At the end of one session, someone came up to Dr. S. and said, "You have done a great job with Billy and I know you are well intended, but aren't you violating Billy's right to confidentiality?"

Dr. S. said that Billy was his child and that as the parent he had the authority to disclose the information. Do you think this is correct?

• • • • • • •

CONFORMING WITH LAWS AND REGULATIONS (10.03)

Behavior analysts plan and conduct research in a manner consistent with all applicable laws and regulations, as well as professional standards governing the conduct of research, and particularly those standards governing research with human participants and animal subjects. Behavior analysts also comply with other applicable laws and regulations relating to mandated reporting requirements.

Behavior analysts involved in research need to be aware that some federal and state laws may regulate the manner in which human and animal subjects may be involved, and they need to comply with these and any other regulations pertaining to reporting on their research activities.

INFORMED CONSENT (10.04)

(a) Using language that is reasonably understandable to participants, behavior analysts inform participants of the nature of the research; they inform participants that they are free to participate or to decline to participate or to withdraw from the research; they explain the foreseeable consequences of declining or withdrawing; they inform participants of significant factors that may be expected to influence their willingness to participate (such as risks, discomfort, adverse effects, or limitations on confidentiality, except as provided in Standard 10.05 below); and they explain other aspects about which the prospective participants inquire.

(b) For persons who are legally incapable of giving informed consent, behavior analysts nevertheless (1) provide an appropriate explanation, (2) discontinue research if the person gives clear signs of unwillingness to continue participation, and (3) obtain appropriate permission from a legally authorized person, if such substitute consent is permitted by law.

Behavior analysts, with the intention of protecting their participants from any distress or duress, should inform them that their participation is completely voluntary and that they can drop out at any time. Further, the participants should be informed in writing about any aspects of the study that present any risk of harm, and behavior analysts should answer completely any questions that potential participants might ask.

A significant amount of behavioral research is done with persons who are not really capable of giving consent. In these cases, the ethical behavior analyst will always obtain permission from the legal representative of the individual; further, the behavior analyst should build into his or her protocol some contingency plan for determining if the individual, although not capable of giving consent, nonetheless shows signs of distress and a desire to drop out.

• • • • • • •

CASE 10.04: BASKETBALL BLUES

Karen was a BCBA who was a doctoral student. She was beginning some research in group homes for adult, ambulatory, verbal clients with developmental disabilities. Karen went to the group homes after the clients got back from the sheltered workshop and observed their leisure skills. Karen decided to do her study in one house with four young women. She wanted to focus on arts and crafts, and she purchased a large number of attractive new materials from her local craft store. Several weeks into the intervention (which involved having materials available, prompting usage, and providing social praise), one client, Wanda, decided she no longer wanted to work on crafts. Wanda wanted to spend her time outside shooting baskets. This was a disaster for Karen because her major professor had told her she could have no less than four participants in her study. Karen observed for a few days to make sure Wanda's interest in basketball was not a novelty. Unfortunately, the rainy summer weather had stopped, and athletic Wanda was ready to be outside every day.

Would it be unethical for Karen to add some additional high-powered reinforcers just for Wanda?

• • • • • • •

DECEPTION IN RESEARCH (10.05)

(a) Behavior analysts do not conduct a study involving deception unless they have determined that the use of deceptive techniques is justified by the study's prospective scientific, educational, or applied value and that equally effective alternative procedures that do not use deception are not feasible.

Ordinarily, behavior analysts are not involved in research involving deception, and the requirement that research participants must give informed consent further decreases this form of dishonest conduct. Only in rare cases might some form of pretext be acceptable (e.g., where exact knowledge of a target behavior or type of intervention might affect the behavior adversely).

• • • • • • •

CASE 10.05A: FRANK'S DECEPTION

Frank was a BCBA who was a doctoral student. Frank was preparing to conduct research in a PM setting. He was going to

work with warehouse workers on safety behaviors. The ware-
house had two levels, and workers frequently had to climb
ladders and place boxes on the second level. Management was
concerned because, very frequently, the workers did not cor-
rectly set the "safety feet" on the ladders. There had been two
falls, and when someone falls to concrete from a ladder the
injuries can be severe. So that Frank could get a baseline that
was not affected by his observations, he trained the workers on
proper lifting procedures. This had nothing to do with Frank's
study, and it gave the workers the impression they were being
observed for lifting techniques.

The Guidelines state that behavior analysts will not be
involved in research involving deception. Was Frank in viola-
tion of the Guidelines?

• • • • • • •

(b) Behavior analysts never deceive research participants about significant aspects that would affect their willingness to participate, such
as physical risks, discomfort, or unpleasant emotional experiences.

It is a given that behavior analysts would never trick individuals into
participating if there was any chance that doing so might increase
risk of physical harm or adversely affect their emotional state.

• • • • • • •

CASE 10.05B: CARLOS'S TIMID SUGGESTION

Carlos was a BCBA who worked on a dual-diagnosis (mental
health and mental retardation) unit of a state hospital. He was
doing a research project with two men who were very physi-
cally aggressive, particularly toward women. Carlos wanted
to determine if there would be less aggression if women talked
to the aggressive men using a firm voice and instructions
(rather than showing any signs of being docile). Carlos asked
several female staff members from around the facility if they
would be willing to participate in his study. He did not specifi-
cally tell them that in some of the sessions he would ask them

*to approach the men in a docile, timid manner (and that he
believed this might result in aggression).*

*If Carlos was correct and the study had clear findings, there
would be implications for teaching women to interact with these
clients in a way that would prevent the aggression. Considering
this, was it ethical for Carlos to proceed as planned?*

• • • • • • •

(c) Any other deception that is an integral feature of the design
and conduct of an experiment must be explained to participants
as early as is feasible, preferably at the conclusion of their participation, but no later than at the conclusion of the research.

If the researcher used a "cover story" to disguise some aspect of
his or her study, the participants should be told about this as soon
as their participation is completed and not later than the end of
the research (i.e., they receive a debriefing and have an opportunity to ask questions).

• • • • • • •

CASE 10.05C: DEBRIEFING

*Dr. M. was advising a student at the end of the spring semes-
ter about what courses to take in the fall. In the course of
the conversation, the student began talking about a "dating
study" that she participated in and how disappointed she was
that she did not find an "ideal mate" as she had been promised. When Dr. M. inquired if she had been debriefed at the
end of the study, she said "no" and, further, that the graduate
student who ran the study did not answer phone messages or
emails that she sent.*

*Dr. M. knew about the study and that it did not involve
dating at all but was rather a study on racial stereotyping. As
a behavior analyst, what are his obligations?*

• • • • • • •

INFORMING OF FUTURE USE (10.06)

Behavior analysts inform research participants of their anticipated sharing or further use of personally identifiable research data and of the possibility of unanticipated future uses.

Participants should be told that you plan to share your data with others (e.g., conference presentations, publication). Note that the sharing of "identifiable research data" is problematic with certain kinds of data, given the recent Health Insurance Portability and Accountability Act (HIPAA) of 1996. You should tell clients that you may continue to present the research at future conferences and that you will not reveal any identifying information such as their name and where they live.

MINIMIZING INTERFERENCE (10.07)

In conducting research, behavior analysts interfere with the participants or environment from which data are collected only in a manner that is warranted by an appropriate research design and that is consistent with behavior analysts' roles as scientific investigators.

Because a great deal of applied behavioral research is carried out in the participants' own setting, the behavior analyst must do everything possible to avoid intrusion or disturbance. Further, it is important for behavior analysts to stick to their research protocol and not attempt to collect any data beyond that agreed to initially by the participants and as approved by the IRB.

• • • • • • •

CASE 10.07: HOWARD DECKS THE HALLS

Howard S. was a graduate student who was going to conduct some behavioral research in a nursing home. He had reviewed the literature in the area of behavioral geriatrics, and he wanted to work on ambulation programs for older people. This was an important area of study because people in nursing homes often refuse to walk or exercise. Howard read about one study that was done on the research unit of a geriatric hospital. In this research facility, when the researchers studied increasing walking distances they had participants walk in the long halls of the nursing home unit. They marked the walls with tape to indicate how far participants had walked. When the clients were settled back in their rooms, the researchers went with a measuring tape, measured the distance, and removed the small pieces of masking tape from the walls. After getting his research approved, Howard came up with a different idea about the way to measure distance walked. He decided that he would leave the tape on the walls and would write the dates on each piece of tape so that clients could see their progress from one day to the next. The nursing home administrator did not like this idea. She told Howard that the facility was committed to making the nursing home an attractive, home-like environment and that pieces of tape from multiple clients every day was not a good idea. This seemed like a small issue, but it caused a major problem between Howard and the administrator. Red-faced and raging, Howard told his major professor that the administrator was an idiot and that she did not understand the importance of research.

What do the Guidelines say that would give Howard some direction regarding the tape on the walls?

• • • • • • •

COMMITMENTS TO RESEARCH PARTICIPANTS (10.08)

Behavior analysts take reasonable measures to honor all commitments they have made to research participants.

If you make a promise to your participants (e.g., you have told them they will receive a fee or some service for participating), it is important that you follow through.

ENSURING PARTICIPANT ANONYMITY (10.09)

> In presenting research, the behavior analyst ensures participant anonymity unless specifically waived by the participant or surrogate.

Behavior analysts should guarantee research participants that their names will not be divulged in print or in any future oral presentation; note that if they should waive this offer of anonymity it is acceptable. However, the common protocol for research is that no names are used. Researchers are studying phenomena, not individuals, so names are not really relevant.

INFORMING OF WITHDRAWAL (10.10)

> The behavior analyst informs the participant that withdrawal from the research may occur at any time without penalty except as stipulated in advance, as in fees contingent upon completing a project.

As a behavior analyst researcher you should, at the outset of the study, inform your participants that they may withdraw at any time without adverse consequences (unless, of course, there was some agreed on contingency at the beginning).

DEBRIEFING (10.11)

> The behavior analyst informs the participant that debriefing will occur at the conclusion of the participant's involvement in the research.

Also, at the outset of the study, you should inform your research participants that they would have a debriefing at the end of the study.

ANSWERING RESEARCH QUESTIONS (10.12)

> The behavior analyst answers all questions of the participant about the research that are consistent with being able to conduct the research.

During the debriefing, the behavior analyst answers all questions pertaining to the study.

WRITTEN CONSENT (10.13)

The behavior analyst must obtain the written consent of the participant or surrogate before beginning the research.

Before your research can begin, you must obtain written consent (a form that you prepare in advance that is signed) from each participant or his or her legal representative.

EXTRA CREDIT (10.14)

If the behavior analyst recruits participants from classes and the participants are provided additional credit for participating in the research, nonparticipating students must be provided alternative activities that generate comparable credit.

Behavior analysts who are doing research with students (e.g., college instruction) often offer extra credit for participating; if you do this, you must also offer some way for nonparticipating students to earn similar credits (i.e., they may not be disadvantaged in their grade for the course by not being selected as a research participant).

• • • • • • •

CASE 10.14: DR. ABDUL Z.'S REWARD SYSTEM

Dr. Abdul Z. was teaching a behavior analysis class to undergraduate students. Dr. Z. was also a researcher, and he told students that if they wanted to be observers on one of his research projects they could earn extra credit for their final grade. The extra points were added to class points, and the course was graded on a curve (based on who had the highest number of points). Some of the students who were unavailable to take data felt that this system was very unfair. They complained to Dr. Z., who said that he believed in using behavior analysis principles and that students who showed more initiative should be rewarded.

What do the Guidelines say about this?

• • • • • • •

PAYING PARTICIPANTS (10.15)

The behavior analyst who pays participants for research involvement or uses money as a reinforcer must obtain Institutional Review Board or Human Rights Committee approval of this practice and conform to any special requirements that may be established in the process of approval.

The use of money as a reinforcer for research participation can present special problems; if you are using money you must make sure this is specified in your application to the IRB or Human Rights Committee (HRC).

• • • • • • •

CASE 10.15: GAS HIKE

Beverly was a doctoral student who worked with low-income parents and their children. Beverly was beginning the research for her dissertation, and she decided to work with families who lived in a neighboring county (25 miles away) to prevent working with any clients with whom she had consulted. Beverly's study involved having the parents bring their children to the university child behavior lab and teaching the parents how to use behavioral procedures to teach new language skills. Beverly's research had been approved by her committee, by the agency who referred the parents, and by the IRB. Beverly had approval from the IRB to pay the parents a flat fee for gas reimbursement. After the third session with one family, the mother made a comment to Beverly about how gas prices were going up and coming to these sessions was expensive. Beverly was afraid this family might drop out of the study. She decided to give these parents an incentive for coming to the sessions. She told the mother she would add $5 to the gas money for each session the family attended, plus, she said,

"I'll also throw in $20 so you can take the kids to get ham-burgers on the way home."

Are there any circumstances under which these additional incentives would have been acceptable?

• • • • • • •

WITHHOLDING PAYMENT (10.16)

The behavior analyst who withholds part of the money earned by the participant until the participant has completed their research involvement must inform the participant of this condition prior to beginning the experiment.

If you are using money as a reinforcer and have some contingency that says the participants receive it only if they complete the whole experiment, you must tell them this at the outset of the study.

GRANT REVIEWS (10.17)

The behavior analyst who serves on grant review panels avoids conducting any research described in grant proposals that the behavior analyst reviewed, except as replications fully crediting the prior researchers.

Some professional behavior analyst researchers may be invited by granting agencies to serve on peer-review committees to evaluate research proposals. This gives them access to research ideas from other investigators that are still in the early stages of development. It is considered unethical for behavior analysts who serve on such committees to use those ideas in their own research (except in the case of replications, and here they must give credit to the earlier researchers).

• • • • • • •

CASE 10.17: GRANTSMANSHIP

Dr. Daniel V. was a behavioral researcher at a university. His specialties were learning disabilities and teaching reading. He also taught graduate seminars. Dr. V. was asked to serve on a grant review committee. In his role on the grant review committee, Dr. V. went to Washington, D.C., twice a year. He and other researchers would convene in a large conference room for 3 days and review grant submissions. In one meeting, several proposals had been submitted that addressed the teaching of reading to children with learning disabilities. Dr. V. was amazed to see in this proposal some new strategies for assessing reading skills and teaching reading. He recommended that the grant be funded. As soon as Dr. V. got back to his own lab at the university, he quickly began some pilot research on the same topic, using the procedures he had read in the grant proposal. He felt that the results would be published anyway and that by the time his research was done the other researchers would probably be credited in the literature.

Was Dr. V. correct in his action and his assumptions?

• • • • • • • •

ANIMAL RESEARCH (10.18)

Behavior analysts who conduct research involving animals treat them humanely and are in compliance with the Federal Animal Welfare Act.

Behavior analysts who are involved in animal research treat them with compassion and comply with the U.S. Code, Title 7, Ch. 54, of the Federal Animal Welfare Act and Regulations (1990).

ACCURACY OF DATA (10.19)

Behavior analysts do not fabricate data or falsify results in their publications. If behavior analysts discover significant errors in their published data, they take reasonable steps to correct such errors in a correction, retraction, erratum, or other appropriate publication means.

As a field that lives by its data, we are exceedingly concerned that published data are absolutely true and properly represent the findings of a study. Therefore, behavior analysts are diligent and scrupulous about checking and double-checking their data to make sure that they are correct before they are sent in for publication. Should some error take place in the publication process such that the final manuscripts contains an error, the behavior analyst will take the necessary steps to make sure that the mistake is corrected.

AUTHORSHIP AND FINDINGS (10.20)

Behavior analysts do not present portions or elements of another's work or data as their own, even if the other work or data source is cited occasionally, nor do they omit findings that might alter others' interpretations of their work or behavior analysis in general.

Plagiarism in any form is unacceptable, unethical conduct. This includes not only written text but data and concepts as well. Always give citations for your sources.

• • • • • • •

CASE 10.20: UNCOVERING PLAGIARISM

Brent was a BCBA who liked attending workshops. He wanted to get the required number of continuing education units (CEUs) each year, but he also felt he could stay current with the field of behavior analysis by attending state and national level workshops. Brent attended the same workshop, given by the same presenter, on three different occasions. He was very surprised when the workshop leader began to show slides and data that Brent recognized as being the work of someone else. At the end of the workshop, Brent approached the presenter and said, "Some of the slides and graphs you showed today look like information I have seen somewhere else. Was some of your data from the research that Dr. (name) has done—he presents this in his workshops." The presenter looked annoyed and told Brent it would be very distracting to give citations and references all the way through a 6-hour workshop. He said that

certainly, if he published someone's work, he would give credit but that workshop information can be shared.
   Do the Guidelines cover this situation?

• • • • • • •

ACKNOWLEDGING CONTRIBUTIONS (10.21)

In presenting research, the behavior analyst acknowledges the contributions of others who contributed to the conduct of the research by including them as co-authors or footnoting their contributions.

Behavior analysts who present or publish their work should recognize those who made an important contribution by including them as coauthors or giving them a footnote. Coauthorship is for members of the research team who contributed a substantial amount to the research (e.g., Could you have done it without them? Did they have input into the goals and design of the study? Did they have input regarding methodology?). Footnotes are appropriate for data collectors, research assistants who looked up articles, and so forth.

• • • • • • •

CASE 10.21: WHO'S FIRST?

Laura was a graduate student who completed a master's thesis in a middle school. In the course of conducting her study on classroom behavior, Laura worked with several teachers, teacher aides, and the school guidance counselor on a regular basis. The teachers and aides took data, and the guidance counselor met with Laura four times to provide academic background information on the children. Laura met at least one time per week with her major professor. He guided her as she planned the study and data collection systems. In addition, one night per week, Laura attended a research meeting for graduate students. Each week, she reported on her progress, and the students asked questions and made suggestions for the study. When the study was completed, written, and

ready to submit to a journal, Laura had a hard time decid-
ing who should be listed as authors and the order in which
names should be listed. She listed herself first, then her major
professor, then the teachers in alphabetical order, the aides in
alphabetical order, the guidance counselor, and two students
from the research meeting. There were 10 authors listed on the
manuscript. Laura's major professor told her that some of the
people listed needed to be credited in a footnote.
Who should be moved to the footnote?

• • • • • • •

PRINCIPAL AUTHORSHIP AND OTHER PUBLICATION CREDITS (10.22)

Principal authorship and other publication credits accurately reflect the relative scientific or professional contributions of the individuals involved, regardless of their relative status. Mere possession of an institutional position, such as Department Chair, does not justify authorship credit. Minor contributions to the research or to the writing for publications are appropriately acknowledged, such as in footnotes or in an introductory statement. Further, these Guidelines recognize and support the ethical requirements for authorship and publication practices contained in the ethical code of the American Psychological Association.

Behavior analysts involved in research will need to determine, at the time an article is submitted for review, the names that will be included and what the order will be if several people made important contributions. The general rule is that the person who made the most significant contribution goes in the first position ("first author") and that other names after that reflect lesser degrees of contribution ("coauthors") in rank order. First authors should resist the temptation to include the name of anyone who simply made some small contribution to the research. Those who did help in lesser ways should be acknowledged in a footnote or possibly a statement at the top of the article.

• • • • • • •

CASE 10.22: FOOTNOTES FOR ALL

A large mental health agency provided comprehensive community services that included staff training, behavioral consultation for clients, and consultation on the mental health unit at the local hospital. Periodically, behavioral researchers from the university became involved in agency projects and applied research would be conducted. On more than one project, everything went well until it came time to submit an article based on the research. The faculty member who designed the research and wrote the first draft of the manuscript wanted himself listed as the first author and generously, in his mind, listed everyone else in a footnote. Students who served as data collectors were angry when they found out they would not be listed as coauthors; they had heard from graduate students that getting your name on a publication was a "ticket to graduate school" and now felt like they had no chance of getting in after having spent 6 months on this project.

Looking back, how should this have been handled differently?

• • • • • • •

PUBLISHING DATA (10.23)

Behavior analysts do not publish, as original data, data that have been previously published. This does not preclude republishing data when they are accompanied by proper acknowledgment.

When writing up your research for publication, remember that the original data can be published only once. If you later refer to these data in a subsequent article, you are required to cite your original publication. Under some circumstances, a manuscript may be published in a second journal, but an explanatory note from the editor or author usually accompanies this.

• • • • • • •

CASE 10.23: DUPLICITY

Marguerite, an undergraduate psychology student, was taking a behavior analysis course in which students had to find articles that illustrated specific uses of behavior analysis. Students read the articles they found and wrote a short paper on each article. The professor asked that students attach a copy of the article to the paper in the event there were any questions about methodology or in case the professor thought the student didn't understand a particular concept. Marguerite found an article on a topic she found interesting. She wrote the paper and turned in the article. She was looking for a new article a few weeks later, and the names of the authors of the first article caught her eye. The article was in a different journal, but the data and writing were identical. Marguerite brought a copy of the article to class and asked the professor if this was a common practice.

Do the Guidelines cover this situation?

• • • • • • •

WITHHOLDING DATA (10.24)

After research results are published, behavior analysts do not withhold the data on which their conclusions are based from other competent professionals who seek to verify the substantive claims through reanalysis and who intend to use such data only for that purpose, provided that the confidentiality of the participants can be protected and unless legal rights concerning proprietary data preclude their release.

It is an ethic of behavior analysts that we share our data with others to strengthen the findings through transparency and replication. Should another behavior analyst request to see your raw data, you are obligated to provide it to them for the purpose of reanalysis. It is assumed that should someone request your data you will take the necessary steps to protect the confidentiality of the participants. The only exception to sharing of data is in the case of data that have been trademarked, patented, or are some-how otherwise exclusively held by a company.

• • • • • • •

CASE 10.24: ACADEMIC STONEWALLING

Gordon was a BCBA who was beginning his doctoral research in a university behavior analysis program. Gordon began out-lining his study, and, as a first step, he reviewed all of the litera-ture. He found one published study that was of major interest to him. The researchers had done something very similar to what Gordon planned to do. Gordon believed it would save him a lot of time if he could use a participant assessment tool that the authors of this study reportedly used. Although it was referred to, the assessment was not published in the journal article. With the approval of his major professor, Gordon contacted the first author of the study to inquire about the assessment. Gordon received no response from the first author despite repeated phone and email messages. Then his major professor began trying to contact the authors. He, too, received no response. Finally, Gordon tried calling again, and the first author of the study happened to answer the phone. He told Gordon that he did not wish to share any information that was not published in the article. He said he may want to do future research and that the assessment was not available for Gordon's use.

Do the Guidelines say anything that can help Gordon make his case?

• • • • • • •

RESPONSES TO CASES

CASE 10.0: FLEXIBLE RESEARCH

The coach's permission was not enough for Ron to do this research. He should have followed the protocol for all research that is done with human participants. Ron needed to submit a detailed proposal to the IRB and any other relevant local HRCs. His major professor should have known he was conducting research on another part of campus.

Further, developing the intervention strategy as he "went along" was not in accordance with the Guidelines. The interventions needed to be detailed in the written research proposal and justified based on previous published research.

CASE 10.0A: SPIN THE DATA

According to the Guidelines, the results of research need to be presented in the most truthful, accurate manner possible. Behavior analysts should not present data so that the results are misleading. It was not appropriate to pick and choose the best participants for data presentation. Ron does not appear ready to do applied research and seems not to have a good understanding of the fundamental ethics and procedures involved. He needs both an ethics seminar and a graduate research methods class.

CASE 10.0B: SAFE CROSSING

The Guidelines state that behavior analysts who are doing research will look after the safety and well-being of the participants. In the street-crossing study, observers simply took data during baseline. However, observers were very well trained, and they understood that nothing was more important than the safety of the children. Observers were placed at critical locations nearby, and they were prepared to intervene immediately if it appeared that a child was in harm's way.

CASE 10.0C: WATCH THAT OBSERVER

Dr. C. should be reminded that he is responsible for the ethical conduct of research of anyone on his research team. He needs to pay a visit to the school and work with Kirsten. If she cannot be counted on to follow the protocol or be a reliable observer, she needs to be removed from the research project.

CASE 10.0D: RESEARCH APPROVALS

Carl needed an approval of the IRB before starting any research in the schools. The approval from school personnel was not sufficient.

CASE 10.0E: THE TROUBLE WITH TOYS

Shondra needs to notify her advisor and her committee. Few beginning researchers realize this, but she should also notify the IRB that the circumstances have changed and that a modified proposal may be forthcoming. The IRB is available to give advice and assistance throughout the course of a research project. It is not merely a body that gives a one-time approval at the beginning of a study.

CASE 10.01A: BRUCE'S BAND

As a behavior analyst who was doing research in the context of behavioral programming, Bruce would be expected to do research that follows a behavior analytic model. He could choose to use music as an intervention and take data using standard data collection systems and single subject design. Rather than ask clients how music "made them feel," Bruce could evaluate if music resulted in decreases in specified maladaptive target behaviors or increased prosocial behaviors.

CASE 10.01B: WORK FASTER

When you are pushing people to do more physically, you need to make sure that any negative effects are outweighed by the benefits of the study. In the case of Dr. H., he would want to make sure that staff members take adequate breaks. It is hard to sit and type all day long, and an intervention that decreased break times (where people can stretch muscles by moving around) could result in neck and back problems, carpal tunnel syndrome, and so forth.

CASE 10.01C: BANDWAGON EFFECT

Dr. X. can hope his old job is still open, he can look for a new job, or he can work to convince the company owners or board that they need to have a reputable behavior analysis program. He could bring in outside experts to meet with them, and he could begin getting appropriate recognition for the program by doing behavior analytic research.

CASE 10.01D: RESEARCH AMMUNITION

The Guidelines caution behavior analysts about being a part of forums where their research can be used to support a cause that is not supported by the data. If the parents were generally reasonable and this appeared to be a one-time problem, Dr. A. could calm the waters by contacting the school, explaining that he had no part in this, and educating the parents about why this was a mistake. However, if after some careful thought,

Dr. A. decided that he was in the midst of some radical, hard-to-manage parents, he may be better off to resign from the board. This is a difficult stance to take, but the behavior analyst should not allow another person or group to damage his or her professional reputation.

CASE 10.01E: BIG CLAIMS

Simply put, Dr. G. overstated her case. She worked with only two children, and she cannot generalize to the whole population based on this. She needs to present her data clearly and explain that for some children her treatment may not have worked. The Guidelines warn behavior analysts about exaggerating the effectiveness of their procedures.

CASE 10.01F: MIS-REPRESENTIN'

Dr. G. needs to "stop the presses" on the press releases. Behavior analysts should correct any misrepresentation of their work. This study dealt with only two children, there was a tremendous support system in place such that the children weren't really functioning independently in regular education, and such a claim would be false.

CASE 10.02A: REVEALING

Dr. J. should not have given identifying information about Courtney or talked about her past with his colleagues or conference participants. Behavior analysts do not disclose in their writings personally identifiable information about clients or research participants. By telling his colleagues about Courtney, it could affect the way that people relate to her or interact with her. If Courtney chooses to tell her own story, that is her right, protected by the First Amendment.

CASE 10.02B: PROUD PARENT

At some point, Billy was a foster child, and Dr. S. was talking about those experiences and using Billy's name. According to the Guidelines, behavior analysts should disguise confidential information (i.e., Billy's diagnoses, his family history) and the person's identity. Dr. S. has adopted Billy, so he will be around for years. It might embarrass Billy to have everyone who meets him knowing about his past. Dr. S. could talk about procedures and how his child reacted to them, such as, "When I used intensive toilet training with my son, he resisted the overcorrection." This is a good place for behavior analysts to think of how they would like to be treated. Not many people would want others to know that they had been sexually abused, and so forth.

CASE 10.04: BASKETBALL BLUES

Karen should have had a contingency plan so that participants could make the choice to drop out. She should also have had extra participants so that if someone dropped out it would not affect her study. A researcher should not want a participant involved in the study for the wrong reasons, such as when the participant is there only to get the reinforcers rather than because the participant enjoys the activity. To ensure that participants don't drop out, procedures should be used such as careful screening and participant selection in the beginning and reinforcer sampling. A good reinforcer sampling assessment might have shown Karen that Wanda did not especially like indoor activities that involved sitting and fine motor skills.

CASE 10.05A: FRANK'S DECEPTION

This case could go either way. If Frank told the workers he was specifically looking at lifting techniques but he was actually observing behaviors related to safety on the ladders, he deceived the participants. He should have told the workers he would be looking at a variety of safety behaviors. He could do the training on proper lifting to help the company, and if the workers came to the conclusion he was observing lifting this was their own assumption.

Behavior analysts do not usually get involved in research that is specifically designed to study deception, as in, "How would college students react in a study when they have been lied to?"

Another example of an unethical, deceptive practice in research would be to tell a teacher you were observing child behavior when you were actually taking data on teacher behavior. At a minimum, the teacher should be told you are observing teacher–child interactions.

CASE 10.05B: CARLOS'S TIMID SUGGESTION

Participants should always be informed of any chance of physical harm or discomfort. In this case, if Carlos suspected one way of interacting with the clients prevented aggression, he could have looked at data under those conditions. He should not, however, have a condition where he specifically instructs research participants to behave in a way that he knows will result in the clients becoming physically aggressive toward the women. In the rare cases aggression may be prompted so it can be treated by a specially trained therapy team (not by research participants).

CASE 10.05C: DEBRIEFING

Dr. M. is in a delicate spot because this student is clearly upset and he knows that she was misled about her participation in an experiment conducted by a colleague of his in the psychology department. Because that faculty member is not a behavior analyst, this code does not necessarily apply to him, but Dr. M. knows that a comparable code item in the American Psychological Association (APA) code of ethics does apply (Standards 6.15 and 6.18). Dr. M. is obligated to bring this to the attention of his faculty colleague.

CASE 10.07: HOWARD DECKS THE HALLS

The Guidelines say that behavior analysts do everything possible to avoid intrusion or disturbance. Howard was being intrusive in this facility, not necessarily by requiring a lot of staff but by trying to alter the environment the administrator wished to maintain.

CASE 10.14: DR. ABDUL Z.'S REWARD SYSTEM

According to the Guidelines, if some members of a class are given extra credit, all class members must be given a chance to earn extra credit. Dr. Z. should have provided some alternative extra credit assignments for students who were not observers on his project.

CASE 10.15: GAS HIKE

If Beverly decided to change the incentives for the study, she needed to go back to the IRB and get approval for a gas reimbursement increase and approval for the meal money. It is not ethical for Beverly to pay one family more for gas and to provide a meal if she is not going to do this for everyone. The only way she could have done this differentially would be to pay based on miles door to door, and by doing this some families may get more money for gas.

CASE 10.17: GRANTSMANSHIP

What is legal and what is ethical are often two different things. It is unethical for Dr. V. to use the work that he saw in a confidential grant review committee. Dr. V. took the high road and decided not to use the research ideas belonging to the other research team until the work was published.

CASE 10.20: UNCOVERING PLAGIARISM

According to Section 9.3 of the Guidelines, "behavior analysts do not present portions or elements of another's work as their own." The ethical behavior analyst will give credit to the author of any work that is used, whether it has been published. Remember that what is ethical and what is legal are sometimes two different things. Several years ago, Dr. B. wrote a book on research methods. The book was self-published and was used for years as the curriculum for university students. The book made its way into the hands of someone who recognized that the book was not copyrighted. The person took the material and the Table of Contents and published a nearly identical book with a major publisher. Dr. B.'s original work was not even listed as one of the references. This was clearly unethical.

CASE 10.21: WHO'S FIRST?

Laura should list herself first because she is the primary investigator. Her major professor should be listed second, given the guidance that he provided on this particular research. In some cases, major professors choose to be listed last in all publications, other than those projects they conducted alone. This is a "signature" of the professor. Other professors will determine how much input they had relative to the student and other members of the research team and may ask to be listed third or fourth. This might be the case if two students were basically coresearchers on a project and the professor provided guidance to them. If one or more of the teachers gave critical input for the study, such as designing data sheets or developing methodology, they should be listed as coauthors. Otherwise, everyone else is credited in a footnote.

CASE 10.22: FOOTNOTES FOR ALL

Authorship and publication credits reflect the relative contributions of the individuals involved. Researchers are listed as authors with the name of the primary person listed first. Data collectors, students who look up articles, and people who carry out some of the client interventions are usually given a footnote acknowledgment. The APA provides some guidelines for authorship in the APA manual under "publication practices." Basically, the faculty member or researcher who has clearly been down this road before should have specified in advance the type of credit that each person would receive if the research was successful and ultimately written up and submitted for publication.

CASE 10.23: DUPLICITY

A researcher can publish data that have been previously published if the data are accompanied by a proper acknowledgment. The main issue here is that researchers should not send virtually the same graphs and text to different journals to get additional publications from the same material ("double dipping").

CASE 10.24: ACADEMIC STONEWALLING

The Guidelines say that behavior analysts do not withhold data on which their conclusions are based. This would seem to apply to background material for a study. Ethical researchers will provide the necessary information so that others can easily replicate their work or so that others do not have to reinvent the wheel when trying to start a very similar research project.

Three

Professional Skills for Ethical Behavior Analysts

In Section III, Chapters 16 through 18, we address three important skills for behavior analysts who want to improve their effectiveness in dealing with ethical issues. Chapter 16 presents a model for conducting a risk–benefit analysis that should be incorporated into daily practice. In Chapter 17, we outline some suggestions for delivering the ethics message effectively when the need arises in one-on-one or group setting. In Chapter 18, we present a new tool for BCBAs, the "Declaration of Professional Practices and Procedures for Behavior Analysts." This declaration can help to avoid misunderstandings about how Association for Behavior Analysis (ABA) services are delivered, and it should prevent ethics issues from consuming the time you could spend working with clients.

16

Conducting a Risk–Benefit Analysis

"**B**ehavior Analyst Indicted for Abusing Client" is the worst nightmare of Association for Behavior Analysts (ABA) pro fessors and professionals everywhere. This shocking hypothetical headline means that someone we trained or worked with fell into a horrible situation where events spun out of control, fateful mistakes were made, a client was seriously injured, and, now, one of our own is going on trial with the possible outcome of a conviction and possible jail time. In this nightmare scenario, in addition to the unspeakable harm that has already come to the client, the damage to the reputation and professional life of the behavior analyst and to our field could be devastating. Ripple effects will be with the client's family forever, and the community will never forget that a child with disabilities was harmed in the name of behavioral treatment.

As upstanding, ethical behavior analysts we want to prevent this tragedy at all costs, but how? The most straightforward way is by conducting a careful, thorough, risk–benefit analysis before treatment is implemented. Risk–benefit analysis is the comparison of the risk of a situation to its related benefits.

The "BACB Task List–Third Edition" (BACB.com), Items 1–6, spelled out exactly what is required: "Initiate, continue, modify, or discontinue behavior analysis services only when the risk–benefit ratio of doing so is lower than the risk-benefit ratio for taking alternative actions." And as of June 2010 the Guidelines for Responsible Conduct recommend risk–benefit analysis as a useful tool (3.05a). A review of the current standard texts in ABA reveals little information about risk–benefit. One book, by Van Houten and Axelrod (1993), contains a historically significant chapter that explains risk–benefit analysis in detail. In Chapter 8, "A Decision-Making Model for Selecting Optimal Treatment Procedure" (Axelrod, Spreat, Berry, & Moyer, 1993), the authors present a simple and elegant model for elucidating this rather obscure (for ABA) process. Spreat, the second author, originally presented his formulation as a mathematical model for treatment selection in which the various factors were weighted (Spreat, 1982). Spreat offered four elements to consider:

1. Probability of treatment success
2. The period of time it takes to eliminate a behavior
3. The distress caused by the procedure
4. The distress caused by the behavior

In this chapter, we propose a strategy that involves researching each behavioral procedure that is recommended and determining the risks and benefits (both from the literature and from professional experience). Presenting the risks and benefits to the consumer in this manner allows for frank and honest discussion so that no one is surprised if unexpected side effects of a treatment should occur partway through a session. Spreat's (1982) model was an important pioneering effort; however, considering the evolution of the practice of behavior analysis and risk analysis, we offer a new four-part procedure:

1. Assess the risk factors for each behavioral procedure.
2. Assess the general risk factors for behavioral treatment.
3. Assess the benefits of behavioral treatment.
4. Reconcile the risks and benefits with the key parties involved.

WHAT IS RISK?

Since 2008, when we all discovered overnight that Wall Street bankers took great risks with our money using credit default swaps to make millions of dollars for themselves, *risk* has become an important new term for Americans.

While we are not able to generalize directly from this field of financial risk management (Crouhy, Galai, & Mark, 2006) to behavior analysis, there are some clear parallels to our profession. To prevent a catastrophe such as the hypothetical headline in the beginning of this chapter, we need to think of ourselves in part as risk analysts or risk managers who determine the factors that can cause "volatility" in our treatment processes. *Risk* is exposure to injury, loss, or danger. Most often, when we talk about risk in the behavioral setting, we are referring to the fact that a client could get hurt; however, for

> **We need to think of ourselves in part as risk analysts who determine the factors that can cause "volatility" in our treatment process.**

behavior analysts, the danger or loss can also be related to one's reputation or harm the field. For the Board Certified Behavior Analyst (BCBA), *volatility* is an unpredicted result of a treatment plan. An example of volatility occurs in a behavior plan when, rather than significantly reducing a self-stimulatory behavior such as hand flapping, the target behavior becomes far worse and morphs into face slapping and screaming tantrums. Identifying "risk factors" that would give us some clue as to the likelihood of this occurrence can prevent such unpredictable results.

RISK–BENEFIT ANALYSIS

In the area of public health, risk–benefit analysis is used to determine the risk of death. Risks of lung cancer due to smoking, tractor fatalities for farmers, police officers killed in the line of duty, and frequently flying professors (Wilson & Crouch, 2001) are all examples of health-related situations that are evaluated by public health agencies. Insurance companies calculate risk related to certain hobbies such as skydiving or mountain climbing.

To calculate risk of death from certain occupations or activities, it is necessary to keep verifiable records over time. Since applied behavior analysis is not an activity for which there is a high probability of death, calculating risk using public health and insurance methods does not make sense. What does make sense is to conduct a risk–benefit analysis for the procedures we use on a regular basis. The goal is not to frighten people away from our effective technology of behavior change but to be upfront with

> Behavior analysts need to clarify for practitioners that some procedures can increase the probability of unintended behaviors.

them. We need to clarify for practitioners that some procedures can increase the probability of unintended behaviors; for example, time-out can produce "emotional responses" such as "crying, aggressiveness, and withdrawal" (Cooper, Heron, & Heward, 2007, p. 363). Doing nothing has its risks as well, and when the options are spelled out to consumers they need to be aware of this choice and the possible consequences.

RISK FACTORS AND THE LACK OF RESEARCH

It is difficult to base our determination of risk factors on the research literature because studies or treatments with a great deal of risk indicate a failure of treatment and would not be published. The factors that can predict the failure of a behavioral program are imbedded in the memories of practicing behavior analysts who have learned about risk factors through experience. Some clues about risk factors can be gathered from journal articles where it is clear that the researchers have taken extra effort to ensure treatment protocols were followed to the letter. Further, in the research setting, interventions are often implemented by master's- or PhD-level therapists who have years and years of training and experience. Finally, although experiments in behavior analysis are most often carried out in controlled settings that match experimental labs in their rigor, for the practicing behavior analyst who is working with low-income clients in a rural area it is a different story altogether. To evaluate treatments, with only intermittent backup from the itinerant therapist, parents with less than a high school education might have to be trained on a short time frame to implement somewhat sophisticated procedures.

RISK–BENEFITS FOR EACH BEHAVIORAL PROCEDURE

All behavioral procedures, including those that are benign (such as positive reinforcement), have risk factors associated with them. In some texts these are referred to as "considerations" (Cooper et al., 2007, p. 370). Of course they have benefits as well. To help behavior analysts look at the risks and benefits of specific behavioral procedures, we have developed a series of worksheets. As shown in Figure 16.1, the sample worksheet for response cost, the *considerations* (i.e., risks) include increased aggression, avoidance, and reductions in desirable behavior. The benefits for response cost as shown in the worksheet include moderate-to-rapid decrease in behavior, convenience, and the fact that response cost can be combined with other behavioral procedures. The responsible Board Certified Behavior Analyst (BCBA) will want to research each behavioral procedure that is proposed and prepare a Procedures Worksheet. Care should be taken to ensure that the summary at the bottom of the page is balanced and objective.

Risk–Benefit Worksheet

ABA Procedure: Time-Out

Special Methods: (1) Non-exclusion time-out (planned ignoring, withdrawal of positive reinforcer, contingent observation, time-out ribbon) (2) Exclusion time-out (time-out room, partition time-out, hallway time-out)

Risks	Notes
1. Can produce unexpected results	*This could be a problem but the BA can be in the room for the first few days.*
2. Can produce emotional responses	*Mom is worried about this.*
3. Can stigmatize the client in the setting where it is used	*This has not been a problem with this teacher in the past.*
4. The mediator using time-out may try it on others	*The BA will need to monitor the aide, teacher will also watch for unsanctioned uses.*

Benefits	Notes
1. Ease of application	*This is a plus since we are working with classroom aides*
2. Time-out is widely accepted as an appropriate treatment	*The school administration is okay with time-out as long as it is approved by the parents, they have a time-out room, it is approved safe.*
3. Rapid suppression of behavior	*The teacher would appreciate a quick reduction in the target behavior*
4. Can be combined with other procedures	*We will use teacher administered token economy for appropriate behavior*

Summary Risks vs Benefits: *Overall it would appear that the benefits outweigh the risks for time-out in this setting. It will be necessary for the BA to be present the first week to make sure all goes well. The mother has approved the use of time-out for at least one month to see how it works.*

Figure 16.1 A model risk–benefit worksheet for time-out. One worksheet is filled out for each ABA procedure after reviewing research on the risks and benefits. The summary at the bottom represents a balanced, honest representation to the client of the risks vs. the benefits.

EIGHT GENERAL RISK FACTORS

In an attempt to understand how risk factors can affect the outcome of a treatment plan, we have identified eight risk factors that are very common (Figure 16.2). In all of these risk factors, there is the potential for harm to someone who may include the client, mediator, a by-stander, the BCBA, or, in a broader sense, the profession of behavior analysis.

The Nature of the Behavior Being Treated

As a general rule, the more severe or intense the problem behavior, the greater the risk of failure of the plan. Intense or severe behaviors do not become so overnight. Severe behavior problems almost always have a long incubation period where they developed from some lesser form to the dangerous topographies that result in the client being referred to a behavior analyst. Most students in 2-year master's programs will not have had an opportunity to learn from an expert how to handle all these dangerous behaviors. While they

> As a general rule, the more severe or intense the problem behavior, the greater the risk of failure of the plan.

might have read several dozen studies and understand basic principles, the details, and subtleties of such treatment are hard won by those who specialize in them. Moderately experienced behavior analysts could easily make a mistake in designing a program for severe aggression that could land them, the client, or other caregivers in the emergency room.

Sufficient Personnel to Administer the Program

As behavior analysts, we count on mediators in the client's natural environment to play a significant role in treatment. The BCBA's job is to do a functional assessment, to pinpoint the function correctly, and to then devise just the right program for a specific client such as a Prader–Willi, Angelman syndrome, or cerebral palsy client. Ordinarily, for a program to be effective it needs to be in

General Risk Factors for Behavioral Treatment

Instructions: After completing a Risk–Benefit Worksheet for each proposed procedure fill out this form and review with the relevant parties.

Risk Factors	Notes
1. Nature of the behavior to be treated—is it SIB or dangerous to others?	Target behavior is non-compliance, running away, some threats of aggression against siblings.
2. Are there sufficient personnel or mediators to administer the treatment?	The Mom would be the primary mediator.
3. Are they skilled and able to administer it correctly?	This is her first time at trying to systematically implement a behavior program.
4. Is the setting appropriate for the treatment? Safe, well-lit, clean, temperature-controlled?	The home is clean and safe but there are two other siblings who can be a problem, they are younger and vulnerable and observations indicate that they reinforce some inappropriate behavior.
5. Is the BA experienced in the treatment of this type of case?	Yes, 3-yrs experience with in-home consultation.
6. Is there any risk to others in the setting?	Yes, some risk to the younger siblings if there should be any increase in aggression.
7. Is there buy-in from the key people associated with this case?	Mother is serious, grandma and mother-in-law could undermine the consistency of the program though.
8. Is there any liability to the BA?	BA is experienced, the program is standard, no unusual reinforcers, no restrictive procedures. Supervision is good.

Summary of General Risks: There are some risk factors that need to be considered before this project is undertaken. To be safe we should plan to have an in-home aide help the Mom with this intervention project and the BA needs to be available 24/7 for the first few days to make sure it goes well.

Figure 16.2 A model general risk factors worksheet for behavioral treatment. These eight factors cover most behavioral applications, but others are included as necessary.

place for the better part of the client's waking hours. In a residential facility this means at least two shifts per day. If a BCBA's behavior treatment plan is carried out only some of the time, it will be far less effective than if it is always in play.

Is the Mediator Well Trained?

Having sufficient numbers of staff members is no guarantee of success if they are not trained to a high degree of compliance with the program. Even positive reinforcement programs can fail if the mediator occasionally makes an error and reinforces an inappropriate behavior. In one facility, we found that evening shift personnel were afraid of a large, volatile, teenager with Prader–Willi Syndrome. Rather than follow the prescribed plan, they would bring in snacks and treats on their shift to bribe the client so he would cause them no trouble. One aide on the evening shift decided that he and the client (who had a history of elopement) would walk several blocks to a

> Having sufficient numbers of staff is no guarantee of success if they not trained to a high degree of compliance with the program.

convenience store for the snacks. While the aide was distracted on a cell call to his girlfriend, the unsupervised teen jaywalked across a major highway into the path of an oncoming pickup truck. He died an hour later of severe head injuries. It turned out that these nightly trips were unauthorized and that no risk–benefit analysis had been conducted. The family was horrified at this unnecessary tragedy and sued the facility.

Is the Setting Appropriate for the Proposed Treatment?

It is established in our BACB Guidelines that we work only in settings where behavioral procedures are likely to be effective (3.01, 3.02, 3.08) because unsatisfactory settings put the procedures at risk for failure. In addition, the setting must not put the behavior analyst at risk.

In one case, a behavior analyst was asked to provide in-home behavioral services for a family in which the mother was an animal lover. Pets are fine, but in this case the mother had large tanks of turtles throughout the house, including in the kitchen. The tanks were full of scummy green water, and before long one of the children was diagnosed with salmonella. Recognizing that the behavior analyst was at risk for catching a contagious disease, the supervisor removed the behavior analyst from the home. In another case where in-home treatment was provided, a behavior analyst discovered that a single mother's boyfriend was using drugs in the home. The consultant was reluctant to terminate services because she felt that she should remain in the home to protect the child. Our advice was to contact the proper authorities and to get out of the home immediately.

Is the Behavior Analyst Experienced in the Treatment of This Type of Case?

This can be a hard question especially for newly minted BCBAs or Board Certified assistant Behavior Analysts (BCaBAs) since they may not want to admit that they are in over their heads. Our Guidelines specifically require BCBAs to operate within the boundaries of their competence (1.03), but it is not specifically stated that to operate out of the boundaries of one's competence can present a risk to both the proper implementation of procedures and the safety of clients.

Is There Risk to Others in the Setting?

In-home and school applications as well as those that are implemented in sheltered work settings present subtle risks to the success of behavioral programs. These settings also present possible safety risks to nearby clients and staff when procedures are implemented. For example, one of the "considerations" in the use of time-out is that it can produce emotional responses and unexpected results. Clients who do not want to go to time-out might attempt to escape by hitting, kicking, slapping, or spitting on anyone who is in the area. The risks of behavioral procedures should never be downplayed to gain approval of the process. Instead, they should be discussed frankly with all parties so that everyone is aware

> # The risks of behavioral procedures should never be downplayed to gain approval of the process.

of possible risks. Mitigation planning should also result from the awareness of risk, and extra staff members may need to be present during the first few days of treatment just to make sure everyone is safe.

Is There Buy-In From Key People Associated With This Case?

Buy-in means not only that others agree with your program proposal but also that they will do everything possible to ensure that it is implemented according to the plan. Buy-in will vary from setting to setting.

If you are operating in a school, it is obvious you need buy-in from the parent, teacher, and principal, but don't forget about the teacher's aide. Persons in this position can make or break a procedure by enthusiastically joining in or showing an "I could not care less" attitude. Buy-in should also be obtained from other key professionals such as the school psychologist, school counselor, and social worker to ensure program success. Any of these individuals can sabotage or sink a treatment by spreading rumors and using competing activities to undermine the program's effects. If there are any "anti-ABA" people in the building, the behavior analyst should work to bring them around before the treatment begins.

Personal Liability: Risk to the Board Certified Behavior Analyst

This risk factor is related to Section 5 regarding the question of the competence of the BACB to handle this case. Is there any possible liability directly to the behavior analyst? If a time-out is to be employed and the BACB demonstrates the procedure, there is some chance that the young client could accidentally get hurt in the process. Will the parents want to hold the BACB liable? Is there some way to mitigate this by doing the demonstration with the teacher or aide the day before so that there is no direct physical contact? If so, this would be preferable and would reduce liability.

FIVE BENEFITS OF BEHAVIORAL TREATMENT

In conducting a balanced risk–benefit analysis, it is necessary to review the benefits of treatment as well as the risks. We recommend developing a form such as the one shown in Figure 16.3

Benefits of Behavioral Treatment

Instructions: After completing a Risk–Benefit Worksheet for each proposed procedure fill out this form and review with the relevant parties.

Benefits	Notes
1. Client behavior is greatly improved, comes into contact with many new reinforcers and more choices	*Client becomes compliant with requests, running away eliminated, no aggressive threats.*
2. Client environment is greatly improved because of change in behavior—less stress for caregiver, peers	*There is a calmer environment for the child and everyone else, low stress*
3. Caregivers feel more in-charge, improved morale, eagerness to move forward with the client	*Mom can return to her preferred role of loving, nurturing, and guiding her child.*
4. Peers in the setting may change their behavior toward the client, providing more opportunities for social reinforcers	*Peers are no longer afraid of client, now willing to spend play time with him*
5. Liability to the setting is greatly reduced	*Mom feels responsible and in charge*

Summary of Benefits: *The benefits are great for this client in this setting, this procedure, if effective, could turn him around and greatly improve his quality of life.*

Figure 16.3 Benefits of behavioral treatment. These five factors cover many behavioral situations, but others may be included as necessary.

where the benefits are in writing for discussion with all of the relevant parties.

Client Direct Benefit

As behavior analysts, our profession is primarily concerned that the client benefit directly from proposed interventions. However, in many cases, we are not explicit about what is expected. Spelling this out in terms of change of rates of behavior and the time frame for success are important here. You should discuss each target behavior in this section as shown in the notes (see Figure 16.3).

Indirect Benefits to the Setting

Often overlooked in an assessment of benefits are those related to the "climate" of the treatment setting. A formerly noncompliant, aggressive child, who is now able to listen to requests and follow them quickly and with a smile, can totally change the atmosphere in a home or classroom, and gains such as these should be considered possible indirect benefits.

Benefits to Mediators and Caregivers

Other often neglected benefits of behavioral treatment are those that are provided to the mediator of successful treatments and for other caregivers in the environment. If you properly prepare mediators and caregivers for the interventions they are about to carry out and they are successful, this can produce a sense of confidence and pride in their accomplishments.

> If you properly prepare mediators and caregivers for the interventions they are about to carry out and they are successful, this can produce a sense of confidence and pride in their accomplishments.

Benefits to Peers in the Setting

While we spend most of our time focusing on the client, other individuals in the setting should not be overlooked as indirect beneficiaries of a successful treatment. In the case of a client's peers, especially if they have been targets of aggression or have been ignored, they will appreciate the reduction in fear and anxiety as well as possible additional attention from parents and teachers.

General Liability to the Setting Is Decreased

If a client is being treated in a rehabilitation or educational setting and exhibits dangerous behaviors, there is some liability to the overseeing organization. Parents or surrogates of students or other clients in the setting can sue for damages and can hold the owners or administrators responsible for any harm that might come to their family member. A client who ceases running away, threatening, or harming other clients or staff means one less headache for administrators and fewer calls to the attorneys who have to prepare for possible litigation.

THREE ADDITIONAL BENEFITS FOR THE BCBA AND THE FIELD

While they will probably not appear on a risk–benefit form or enter into the discussion with clients, three additional benefits deserve consideration. First, the BCBA or BCaBA who is able to make significant improvements in target behaviors as well as to improve the quality of life for the client and others will have not only a sense of relief that everything worked according to plan but also increased confidence in his ability to take on similar cases in the future. Being able to show positive effects builds confidence, improves morale, and encourages future participation in the profession. A second benefit is the reduction of liability to the designer of the behavior

> Being able to show positive effects builds confidence, improves morale, and encourages future participation in the profession.

plan. Getting through a case successfully means the dark cloud of uncertainty has disappeared, at least for the present. One last benefit is the possible contribution to the body of knowledge of ABA and good public relations for the field. While we cannot solicit testimonials from clients, clients often tell others that they were satisfied or even overjoyed with the behavior analysis services that improved their lives.

RISK–BENEFIT ANALYSIS IN PRACTICE

Including risk–benefit analysis in our standard operating procedures essentially adds one more important step to the process of providing ethical treatment. After the intake, a functional assessment is performed. Then a review of the literature reveals a list of likely treatments ranked from most to least restrictive.

At this point, a risk–benefit analysis of the proposed procedures is carried out by filling out forms similar to those previously shown, and a meeting is held with the consumer (or surrogate) to review the notes (see Figure 16.4). There may be some give and take with the person if there are questions about certain side effects or possible unpredictable behavioral effects. These should

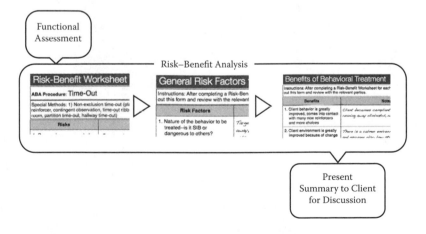

Figure 16.4 Risk–benefit analysis flowchart. The procedure starts with a functional analysis, and after considering the risks and benefits a summary is presented to the client for discussion.

be noted and revisions made as necessary. If after the discussion the consumer does not feel comfortable with a procedure, it may be necessary to withdraw one method in favor of another. It is important to note that it is far better to have this discussion on the front end rather than have some sort of blow-up partway through a course of treatment. At the conclusion of the meeting, all parties should reach consensus on the course of action to be taken. The necessary paperwork will be signed and filed, and treatment can begin with assurance that the risks have been identified and minimized to everyone's satisfaction.

17

Delivering the Ethics Message Effectively

Through in-service training, written materials, continuing education opportunities, and conferences throughout the country, behavior analysts are becoming more sophisticated when it comes to knowing the content of the Guidelines for Responsible Conduct. What behavior analysts are having a hard time with is what to say to another person or exactly how to handle a situation when an ethics problem has been identified. Saying no or giving someone feedback that what they are doing is not appropriate are difficult tasks for many people, and knowing exactly what to say and do when faced with an ethics issue is often far more difficult than identifying the issue and specific code item.

> What behavior analysts are having a hard time with is what to say to another person or exactly how to handle a situation when an ethics problem has been identified.

THE IMPORTANCE OF COMMUNICATIONS SKILLS

Topping off the list of skills for the behavior analyst who wants to make a difference is the ability to be a good communicator. In *25 Essential Skills and Strategies for the Professional Behavior*

Analyst: Expert Tips for Maximizing Consulting Effectiveness (Bailey & Burch, 2010), we presented three chapters on interpersonal communications with colleagues, supervisors, and direct reports. We also described how effective communication or a lack of communication skills affects one's ability to persuade and influence others. When it comes to delivering a message about ethics, you will need to be as much a communicator as you are a behavior analyst.

There will be times when you will need to address an ethics question immediately. This means thinking on your feet and knowing the Guidelines for Responsible Conduct. You might need to refer to the Guidelines for the exact section number and wording, but it is the responsibility of every behavior analyst to know and understand the content that is covered in the Guidelines.

KNOW THE GUIDELINES

Immediate Response Required

A Board Certified Behavior Analyst (BCBA) was working with Ami, a 5-year old girl whose parents were divorced. The child's father was a wealthy businessman who owned a nationally recognized chain of electronics stores. Because he traveled constantly, he saw his little girl only periodically. Ami was basically mute, but over a short period of time the behavior analyst had her saying words and short phrases. Shortly after Ami began speaking in three-word sentences, the dad, on one of his infrequent visits home, observed a session. Tears rolled down his cheeks, and as he was leaving, he said, "You have done such wonderful things for Ami.... I know you are just getting started, and money is probably tight. I would like to give you a little token of appreciation. Maybe you and your roommates could use a new flat-screen TV and a Blu-Ray disc player. Does that sound good?" The behavior analyst had to respond immediately, or a delivery truck would be dropping off a $2,000 high-definition TV to her apartment. Because she had attended an ethics workshop at her state association meeting, she knew that behavior analysts should not accept gifts. Even though she could not cite the guideline number, she had the perfect instant response: "Thank you so much for appreciating the work I've done with your daughter. We behavior analysts have a code of ethics, and I am not allowed to accept gifts. I am delighted you are so pleased with Ami's progress."

Buy Some Time

Unlike the situation where you need to respond immediately, there will be other times when confronted with an ethical issue that you need to buy some time by saying, "Let me get back to you on that. I will call you later this afternoon," or, "I need to check on this; I'll have an answer for you at Tuesday's meeting." Buying time is a good strategy if the ethical issue seems to be in a gray area and you feel the need to review the Guidelines, talk to your supervisor, or consult with a trusted colleague.

> Buying time is a good strategy if the ethical issue seems to be in a gray area.

A behavior analyst who was enrolled in a master's degree program was consulting in the homes of several children. At one visit, a mother said, "You know, there are times when we are busy during the week, and it is hard to fit in these therapy sessions. You don't have classes on the weekends so I was thinking maybe we could change some of our sessions to Saturday mornings. What do you think?" This was a gray area for the young behavior analyst. She needed to recuperate on the weekends, to meet with her study group, and to prepare for exams. Something about this request just didn't feel right. The behavior analyst was acquainted with the Guidelines and was certain there was not one that said, "It is unethical for you to give up your weekends." "I'll have to check with my supervisor and get back to you," was the perfect response. Later that day, the supervisor took her cell call and said a request like this was a mixed professional or ethical issue. The firm had a policy that therapy sessions are run when supervisors are available to handle emergencies (i.e., no weekends).

On the ethical side, the parent agreed at the onset to certain conditions for the therapy (i.e., weekdays only). If the parent was now acting as though she could move sessions around depending on her changing mood or social opportunities, there was a good chance the child's verbal behavior training was not a high priority. The feedback to the mother was straightforward: "I checked with my supervisor about changing our sessions to Saturdays. She says this is against our company policy, which permits us to work only during hours that supervisors are available to handle emergencies. I'm sorry, but we'll have to stick with our regular weekday schedule. If you really want to switch to another day, my supervisor said to just give her a call. Do you need her number?"

There may be times when feedback about an ethical issue needs to be given to a client, parent or family member, another behavior analyst, a nonbehavioral professional, a supervisor or supervisee. In each case, the behavior analyst should think about whether delivering the message is enough. Does a supervisor need to be contacted? Do staff members need to be informed about something a client did? Should an agency be notified about something that has been witnessed?

DELIVERING THE ETHICS MESSAGE TO A CLIENT

The Guidelines identify the client as the individual person along with the family and agency (Code 2.01). In the following case, we are referring to the client as the individual with the target behaviors. In most cases, clients are children, and they won't be involved with ethical misconduct. However, there are situations where behavior analysts work with high-functioning adult clients and they can present some ethical challenges.

Shari was a BCaBA who was assigned to work to a group home for high-functioning male clients. When Dan, one of the clients, started flirting with her, she put his inappropriate comments on extinction. Then he asked, "Shari, why don't you and I go out on

Friday night? You can come and pick me up, and we can go to a movie and out to eat." Clients in the group home had many opportunities for community outings, and this was clearly a request for a "date." Shari knew instantly that dating a client would be a violation of the Guidelines. What should she say?

Here are some things she should not say:

> "Well, okay Dan, and we can work on your social skills. Let
> me think about it."
> "I'm busy on Friday night."
> "Umm, no, Dan I've got a boyfriend."
> "Sorry, I'm just not that into you."

These excuses imply that if she was not busy and did not have a boyfriend Shari would be open to going out with Dan. Accepting the invitation with a plan of training social skills along the way will send a mixed message to Dan. He will think he's just scored a date. Remember the fundamentals of good communication; don't send mixed messages, and don't lie. Shari could say, "Dan, I like you as a friend, but I work here and it is not appropriate for me to go out with a client. Staff members go on outings with the group and some take clients out for training, but we can't go on dates with clients. In my job, I have something called a Code of Ethics—it is a set of rules that says I cannot go out with clients. It just would not be appropriate."

When Shari was telling us her story, we knew what was coming before she said it. She did a good job giving Dan the message as previously presented, and then he said, "I'm getting my very own place in a few weeks. I won't be a client anymore and I have a job lined up at Goodwill. Then can we go out?"

When clients and family members transition to the status of "no longer a client" brings up a special ethical dilemma. Is there any likelihood that they will come back into the system? Does your company have a policy about dating former clients (or their parents)? Shari replied with, "Dan, I like you as a friend but I'm sorry, I'm not interested." Table 17.1 provides some guidelines for knowing what to say when someone asks you to do something unethical.

Table 17.1 Breakdown of Shari's Initial Response to the Date Request

What You Do	What You Say
Use of an autoclitic	"Dan, I like you as a friend…"
State the facts/ situation	"But I work here and it is not appropriate for someone who works here to go out with a client…"
Refer to the Guidelines	"I have something called a Code of Ethics…"
Tell what the Guidelines say	"It says I can't go out with clients…"
Summarize	"It would not be appropriate."

DELIVERING THE ETHICS MESSAGE TO PARENTS AND FAMILY MEMBERS

As much as parents love their children and family members and want to help them, it is astounding how many ethical challenges they can present for behavior analysts. Not taking data, making up stories, not carrying out the program, and crossing the line so their attempts of discipline constitute abuse are just some of the issues reported by behavior analysts.

Erica M. was the mother of Cooper, a 10-year-old boy who was diagnosed with autism. Cooper had very basic expressive language (one to two word sentences such as "Want milk," and "Go outside"). He had frequent tantrums that were set off by noises and not getting what he wanted. He also had a self-stimulatory behavior of licking the area under his bottom lip frequently enough to cause calloused skin the full length of his lower lip. There were two other children in the busy home. The BCBA, Melvin, was becoming increasingly frustrated because Cooper's behaviors were getting worse both at school and home, Mrs. M. was not taking the data needed, and the other children revealed that when Cooper was having a tantrum she gave him a cookie "to get him to calm down."

Melvin went to the home and met with Mrs. M. He told her how the data were important "so we can help Cooper's behavior get better." It seemed as though the heart-to-heart talk worked magic and Mrs. M. had the data sheets ready when Melvin arrived for the next few visits. Before long, Melvin began to notice that something was strange about the data. One day's data was scored for a time period when Melvin knew Cooper was attending an after-school event. Further, the data showed that Cooper was engaging in no self-stimulatory face licking, yet his face was so inflamed there was bleeding at the edges of the calluses. Melvin knew that Mrs. M. was busy making up the data as he pulled into the driveway.

Here's what Melvin should not do or say:

He should not storm into the house and say, "Mrs. M., you have been making up the data. I have been truthful with you and if you are going to lie to me, I quit. I know when the data are not real."

Here's what Melvin should say:

He found a better way to handle this situation so he could get the necessary data. He talked to Mrs. M. at the beginning of the next session:

"Hi, Mrs. M. I noticed your new rose bushes. They look so nice. My mom always had a rose garden when I was growing up." (Mrs. M. talked about her gardening.) Without asking for the data sheet, Melvin said, "Let's talk about Cooper. So, how has it been going?" (Mrs. M. simply said, "Okay.") "Would you say he was having more tantrums or less or about the same? (Mrs. M. said that some days were worse than others). Melvin said, "This has got to be tough for you. You really have your hands full, and I know a 10-year-old with tantrums can be a real challenge." At this point Mrs. M. began to talk about how she was tired and some days she wasn't sure she could do it all. "You're a great mom," he said. "I know your kids mean the world to you. Can we take a look at the data for the last few days?" He reviewed the data sheet and asked, "With all you've got going, how are you feeling about taking data?" Mrs. M. said, "Okay." Then Melvin told her, "You know, these data don't make sense. When I look at the boxes you've checked off—see here and here—it looks like Cooper is never having a tantrum or licking his face. But his lips are dried and chapped. Can you talk to me about that?" Mrs. M. said she had noticed Cooper licking his lips when he watched television and worked on the computer at night. This was the "screen time" he earned as a reinforce, and data weren't collected then. This made sense, and Melvin was able to modify the data collection procedure. Melvin then asked about the data for

Table 17.2 Breakdown of Melvin's Response to Mrs. M. Regarding Falsifying Data

What You Do	What You Say
Establish rapport	"Hi Mrs. M. I noticed your roses…"
Ask questions/listen	"…how has it been going?"
	"…how are you feeling about taking the data?"
Be respectful/understanding of others	"This has gotta be tough for you…"
State the facts/situation	"…this data doesn't make sense…"
Refer to the Guidelines	"In my field, we have a Code of Ethics…"
Summarize—describe what could happen if the Guidelines are not followed	"Cooper could lose his behavioral services."

tantrums. Mrs. M. admitted she was too busy to fill out the forms. She usually did it right before Melvin arrived, and sometimes she forgot what happened a few days earlier. Melvin felt that he'd simply caught Mrs. M. making up data, so he said, "I really need your help getting the data taken properly. In my field, we have a Code of Ethics, and it actually says I am required to have accurate data to provide behavioral treatment for Cooper. If I believed the data were not accurate and we couldn't get it right, Cooper could lose his behavioral services. I would not be able to work with him anymore. Anytime you have questions, just let me know."

Table 17.2 summarizes what Melvin should do and say in this situation.

DELIVERING THE ETHICS MESSAGE TO AGENCIES, SUPERVISORS, OR ADMINISTRATORS

Unfortunately, we've had a number of behavior analysts in our workshops describing situations where an administrator has asked the behavior analyst to do something unethical. Asking the behavior analyst to make up data or assessment results or to say that services for a client were needed when they were not (or vice versa) or asking the consultant to work with a friend's child who was not an official client are some of the administrator-related ethics issues our workshop participants have encountered.

In some cases, the behavior analyst ends the story with, "and so I no longer work there. I could not sleep at night. I found another job." In other cases the behavior analyst said, "I didn't know what to do. I love the clients, and I love the actual job. I was afraid if I told anyone or refused to do what was asked I would get fired. I need my job. I've got two mouths to feed at home."

Wendy was the new BCBA at a residential facility. She had the job of her dreams in her favorite city. After she had been on the job a few months, the administrator called her into the office. "Rumor has it that we are having a review team visit sometime toward the end of the week. I need your help with some behavior programs." She went on to explain that the review team would be checking for assessments and data that were missing for several clients from the last review. She then slid a list across the desk to Wendy. The administrator was asking Wendy to make up assessment results for four clients who had not yet been seen by behavioral services.

Here's what Wendy should not say:

> We always urge restraint in dealing with supervisors. Think before you speak. There is often a lot on the line. Don't ever say, "Are you kidding me?" or "Are you out of your freaking mind? No way am I lying for you," or "Wait until the board hears this."

Here's what Wendy should say:

> "So, what is it you want me to do?" The administrator tells her, "Just fill in the forms" (i.e., essentially make up the assessment results). In a respectful tone, Wendy told the administrator, "I know you really want the facility to pass the review, but I haven't even seen these clients and this would not be right." The administrator's jaw is getting tense. She reminded Wendy that the facility could be in trouble with the state or even lose funding. "Ms. Schultz, I really love working here. I love the program, and I appreciate how much you care about the clients. But, I am a Board Certified Behavior Analyst, and I have a Code of Ethics to uphold. You know I cannot fabricate assessment results. We could get in a lot more trouble for making up data than for not having it. How about this? I will schedule assessment dates for the clients and document those. I can do an initial visit with each client, and I will have notes on my visits when the assessment team comes. How would you feel about this?"

Table 17.3 Breakdown of Wendy's Response to Administrator Request

What You Do	What You Say
Ask questions	"So what is it you want me to do?"
Be respectful and understanding of others	"I know you want the facility to do well on the review..."
Present your point of view	"but I have never assessed the clients and this would not be right."
	"I really love working here, I love the program..."
Reinforce what others are doing right	"and I appreciate how much you care about the clients."
Refer to the Guidelines	"but I have a Code of Ethics to uphold and I can't fabricate assessment results..."
Present a solution	"How about this? I can schedule assessment dates..."

Table 17.3 shows the analysis of Wendy's response.

DELIVERING THE MESSAGE TO NONBEHAVIORAL PROFESSIONALS

One of the most frequently asked ethical questions is: What do I say when other professionals aren't following the Guidelines? The problem is that other professionals do not have to adhere to our Guidelines. They can spend every one of their professional days doing alternative fad treatments that are not scientifically validated. The problem comes when a behavior analyst and these professionals overlap on a case and are treating the same client.

Ian was the BCaBA on a treatment team for Cassie, a kindergarten client with autism. The child was ambulatory, but she had motor problems that resulted in an unusual gait, tripping easily and dropping things. Although she was approaching 6 years of age, Cassie's expressive language was very limited, with only a few words to identify objects. When upset, the little girl would shriek, drop to the floor, curl into a ball, and refuse to get up. The occupational therapist (OT), Debbie, believed that sensory integration therapy was the best course of treatment. "She needs a day full of sensory activities so she can learn to make sense of her environment," the OT said at the treatment team meeting. "You can see she gets on the floor in the fetal position because we are not properly challenging her senses. Rolling on the exercise ball, playing with toys, and jumping on the mini-trampoline are all exercises that will help Cassie's brain develop and her behavior improve."

Here's what Ian should not say at the treatment team meeting:

> In meetings we also urge restraint and firmly believe the advice "Think before you speak" applies here too. Ian should not say, "And just exactly how would this help her brain improve?" or "Are you a big expert on the brain now?" or "No offense, but your field is not scientifically validated."

Here's what should be said to the nonbehavioral professional. Ian has completed his assessment of the child and felt as a behavior analyst, he needed to address the tantrums and refusal to work. He also wanted to get Cassie moving along with language, and his plan was to talk to the speech therapist about discrete trial training. Ian understood that embarrassing other professionals in front of their colleagues is not a good way to win friends. Ideally, Ian would have seen what was coming and been able to meet with the OT before the meeting. He didn't, so the conversation in the treatment team went like this:

> After Debbie, the OT, gave her spiel, Ian said in a calm, friendly voice, "I agree with Debbie that Cassie has some motor problems. She does fall down and Debbie is right—it looks like she does not have good trunk control. I agree that Cassie could benefit from some exercise to strengthen her core and improve her balance. But I want to talk about the behavioral issues. When Cassie screams and drops to the floor, she is having a tantrum. I don't know what sets this of yet, but I would like to have tantrums added to the plan as a target behavior."
>
> The OT said, "If Cassie doesn't have to sit at the table like she is in college and she gets the exercise and play she needs, I am sure she'll be fine." Maintaining a calm and friendly demeanor, Ian told the team, "Tantrums are a behavioral issue. In Cassie's case, we do not know what sets off the tantrums. As a behavior analyst,

Table 17.4 Breakdown of Ian's Response to the Nonbehavioral Professional

What You Do	What You Say
Listen to others	Ian was polite while Debbie (OT) gave her report.
Be respectful of others	"I agree with Debbie that Cassie has motor problems…" etc.
Present your point of view	"I want to talk about the behavioral issues…"
State what you would like to happen	"I would like to have tantrums on the plan as a target behavior…"
Refer to the Guidelines	"I'm bound by a Code of Ethics that says the next step is a functional analysis (FA)"
Present a solution	"We need to put the FA and behavior program with data collection on her plan."

I'm bound by a Code of Ethics that says the next step is to do a functional analysis. This will involve taking data throughout the school day. If I am going to work with Cassie, we need to put the FA and behavior program with data collection on her plan."

Table 17.4 shows the analysis of Ian's verbal reply to the non-behavioral professional.

DELIVERING THE MESSAGE TO ANOTHER BEHAVIOR ANALYST

In some ways dealing with another behavior analyst who is violating the Guidelines is easier than dealing with others because the behavior analyst should know the Guidelines. In other ways, it can be more difficult and awkward to give feedback to a behavioral colleague, especially if that colleague is working for a competing program or consulting firm.

Matt was a BCBA whose students (BCaBAs) told him about another behavior analyst (Dr. X) who was billing for clients she never saw. It seems the BA would talk to staff, then would write a program or send a data sheet, and would bill for the services. Matt felt very uneasy about this, but he decided he should intervene. He called Dr. X and asked if she had a few minutes to talk. Matt began the conversation like this: "We've known each other for a long time, and we're both professional behavior analysts. I've been

Table 17.5 Breakdown of Matt's Response to the Virtual Behavior Analyst

What You Do	What You Say
Be respectful of others	"I know you care about people…"
Ask questions	"Is there any chance you consult via phone?"
Present your point of view	"I don't want to see you get in trouble…"
Refer to the Guidelines	"Have you looked at the Guidelines lately?"
Present a solution	"You could hire BCBAs to work for you."

hearing about a situation that I wanted to ask you about. Is there any chance you consult via phone and don't see the clients?"

Matt's response is shown in the breakdown of Table 17.5.

If Dr. X had said no, this was a misunderstanding, she did this only once when she was sick but immediately got out to see the client when he was well, the conversation could have ended.

Unfortunately, Dr. X said that business was booming and that she was just trying to cover all the bases. When she knows the staff members are reliable, she will consult by phone and email; she can help more clients and meet the demand and improve her cash flow. "I've got boat payments too, you know," was her parting shot. Matt's response was, "I know you care about people and you have always been a responsible professional. I don't want to see you get in trouble or your reputation get trashed. Have you looked at the Guidelines for Responsible Conduct lately? You could hire BCBAs to work for you; then they would sign the assessments and be responsible. My reading of the Guidelines is that you can't sign an assessment for a client you have never seen. I just wanted to let you know I'm concerned as a fellow professional."

SUMMARY

Knowing the ethics code forward and backward does not guarantee that you will be effective in helping others understand it. You will probably have several opportunities each week

> Knowing the ethics code forward and backward does not guarantee that you will be effective in helping others understand it.

to educate someone about our Guidelines and to indicate why they are important as we strive to deliver effective treatment.

The first part of being effective is identifying something that is not quite right; the second part is knowing what to say and how to say it. This can be difficult, especially for new, younger BCBAs who may have to bring the ethics message to someone older with a lot more experience. They should know and should follow the Guidelines, but it is easy to slip into bad habits; being ethical every day is hard work, and people, even good people, will respond to increased response cost with an unethical response now and then. If no one says anything and if nothing bad happens, the behavior is likely to occur again. Supervisors can become overwhelmed with responsibilities, parents are consumed with a goal of trying everything and anything that might work and don't have the time to ask whether there is research to back up a claim. Being ethical is a big responsibility. It's hard, but if being ethical were easy everyone would be ethical. Be strong. Deliver the ethics message every chance you get.

18

Avoiding the "Slippery Slope" of Ethical Problems by Using a Declaration of Professional Services

When it comes to ethics, prevention is a far better strategy than having to solve the awkward or difficult problems that arise because someone didn't know the difference between right and wrong. Ethical challenges confront the Board Certified Behavior Analyst (BCBA) almost on a daily basis. Most are not crisis sized but rather are more like the daily meteor shower that our Earth experiences from outer space. Tiny pings on the radar of decision making can irritate, confuse, and confound the behavior analyst who is trying to do the right thing. These small challenges can sneak up on you just when you least expect them. They are

> Ethical challenges confront the Board Certified Behavior Analyst (BCBA) almost on a daily basis.

camouflaged in normal conversations in the form of requests of small favors or tiny slivers of gossip. Wouldn't it be great if everyone would just follow the rules? Or, in our terms, why can't we bring some stimulus control to this aggravating situation? Well, there is good news. It is possible to put up something similar to a video gamer's *deflector shield*. To prevent many ethics problems from occurring in the first place, the solution we are proposing is the use of a Declaration of Professional Practice and Procedures for Behavior Analysts. First suggested in one of our ethics workshops by Kathy Chovanec of Louisiana, this document is widely used in other professions to clarify rules and boundaries with clients at the initiation of services, before the meteor shower of ethical issues comes raining down.

Figure 18.1 shows a version of the full document that you can adapt to suit your particular situation. You might want to have more than one version for

> Clients have a right to know up front if you are practicing within the boundaries of your training and expertise.

different types of clients. For example, a declaration for in-home services will vary considerably from residential group home consultation procedures.

AREAS OF EXPERTISE

The declaration starts by informing your client, or better yet your prospective client, about who you are and your credentials. The client should know some basic academic information about you, where you got your degree, the field in which you earned the degree, and the specific degree (e.g., BA, MA, PhD). Some consultants might be uncomfortable about providing this information, particularly if the degree is in experimental psychology or pastoral counseling or was earned through a series of online courses. In any event, clients have a right to know about the education and training of their consultants. They should also know how many years you have been practicing and, most importantly, what you consider your specialty. Disclosing your specialty area is very important because clients have a right to know up front if you are practicing within the boundaries of your training and expertise. In a recent case, for example, a master's in applied behavior analysis (ABA), BCBA with 2 years' experience in autism and developmental disabilities (DD)

Declaration of
Professional Practices and Procedures
For Behavior Analysts[1]

[YOUR NAME, Degree]
Board Certified Behavior Analyst™

[Your mailing address & telephone number & email]

For My Prospective Client/Client's Family

This document is designed to inform you about my background and ensure that you understand our professional relationship.

1. AREAS OF EXPERTISE

[Basically, in this section you explain your area of expertise. This can be as long or as short as you want as long as the client is fully informed of your area(s) of competence.]

I have been practicing as a behavior analyst for _____ years. I obtained my degree in (field of study) in (year). My specialty is _____ (e.g., working with preschool children, parent training, etc).

2. PROFESSIONAL RELATIONSHIP, LIMITATIONS AND RISKS

What I Do

Behavior analysis is a unique method of treatment based on the idea that most important human behavior is learned over time and that it is currently maintained by consequences in the environment. My job as a behavior analyst is to work with behavior you would like to change. With your input, I can help you discover what is maintaining a behavior, discover more appropriate replacement behaviors, and then set up a plan to teach those behaviors. I can also develop a plan to help you acquire a new behavior or improve your skill level. Some of the time I will be treating you directly and at other times I may be training significant others as well.

How I Work

As a behavior analyst I do not make judgments about behavior. I try to understand behavior as an adaptive response (a way of coping) and suggest ways of adjusting and modifying behaviors to reduce pain and suffering and increase personal happiness and effectiveness.

You will be consulted at each step in the process. I will ask you about your goals, and I will explain my assessment and the results of my assessment in plain English. I will describe my plan for intervention or treatment and ask for your approval of that plan. If at any point you want to terminate our relationship, I will cooperate fully.

Please know that it is impossible to guarantee any specific results regarding your goals. However, together we will work to achieve the best possible results. If I believe that my consultation has become non-productive, I will discuss terminating it and/or providing referral information as needed.

---

[1] For clients/family members who would have a difficult time reading this document as written, you will need to explain each section in easy-to-understand language.

Figure 18.1 Declaration of professional practices and procedures for behavior analysts.

3. CLIENT RESPONSIBILITIES

I can only work with clients who fully inform me of any and all of their concerns. I will need your full cooperation as I try to understand the various behaviors that are problematic for you. I will be asking a lot of questions and making a few suggestions and I need your total honesty with me at all times. I will be showing you data as part of my ongoing evaluation of treatment and expect that you will attend to the data and give me your true appraisal of conditions.

One of the most unique aspects of behavior analysis as a form of treatment is that decisions are made based on objective data that are collected on a regular basis. I will need to take baseline data to first determine the nature and extent of the behavior problem that we are dealing with; then I will devise an intervention or treatment and continue to take data to determine if it is effective. I will show you this data and will make changes in treatment based on this data.

Under my code of ethical conduct I am not allowed to work with you in any other capacity except as your behavior therapist or consultant. If I am working in your home with your child it is not appropriate for you to leave the premises at any time or to ask me to take your child to some other location that is not directly related to my services.

I will need a list of any prescribed or over-the-counter mediations and/or supplements in addition to any medical or mental health conditions; this information is kept confidential.

Behavior analysis therapy does not mix well with non evidence-based treatments. If you are currently involved with other therapies please tell me now. If, during the course of our treatment, you should contemplate starting other therapies please let me know immediately so we can discuss the implications.

I expect that if you need to cancel or reschedule your appointment that you call as soon as you are aware of the change. If I do not receive 24-hour notification of your cancellation or you fail to show for an appointment, then you may be charged for the appointment.

4. CODE OF CONDUCT

I assure that my services will be rendered in a professional and ethical manner consistent with accepted ethical standards. I am required to adhere to the *Guidelines for Responsible Conduct* of the Behavior Analyst Certification Board®. A copy of these Guidelines is available upon request.

Although our relationship involves very personal interactions and discussions, I need you to realize that we have a professional relationship rather than a social one. According to my professional code of ethics, it is not appropriate for me to accept gifts or meals and it is not appropriate for me to be involved with your personal activities such as birthday parties, or family outings. [Modify this to suit your situation.]

Figure 18.1 (continued)

was asked by a parent to help with a suicidal and possibly homicidal teen on the autism spectrum. When she reminded the frantic mom that this was not her area of expertise, she was scolded for not being sensitive to the mother's needs: "I'm desperate here, can't you see that? I'm afraid he's going to hurt himself or someone else, and I don't know who else to turn to. You've got to help me." When the BCBA told the mother that a referral to a suicide counselor was needed, the mother replied, "I don't want anyone else to know

If at any time and for any reason you are dissatisfied with our professional relationship, please let me know. If I am not able to resolve your concerns, you may report these to the following: Behavior Analyst Certification Board, Inc., 288 Remington Green Lane Ste C, Tallahassee, Florida 32308; (850) 765-0902, www.bacb.com

5. CONFIDENTIALITY
In Florida, clients and their therapists have a confidential and privileged relationship. I do not disclose anything that is observed, discussed or related to clients. In addition, I limit the information that is recorded in your file to protect your privacy. I need you to be aware that the confidentiality has limitations as stipulated by law including the following:

- I have your written consent to release information.
- I am verbally directed by you to tell someone else situations.
- I determine that you are a danger to yourself or others.
- I have reasonable grounds to suspect abuse or neglect of a child, disabled adult, or an elder adult.
- I am ordered by a judge to disclose information.

6. APPOINTMENTS, FEES AND EMERGENCIES
[In this section you will describe how appointments are set and how fees are charged. It may also be necessary to indicate who to contact in case of emergencies.]

The current fee for my services is_____. Billing will be handled as follows:_____. [Modify this to suit your situation.]

7. This document is for your records. Please sign the attached form indicating that you have read and understand the information in this declaration.

_____   _____
WITNESS   CLIENT

_____   _____
BEHAVIOR ANALYST   DATE

Figure 18.1 (continued)

about this; I've got enough trouble as it is. Please don't tell anyone. Just tell me what to do."

Because behavior analysts have an obligation to keep current with new developments, this section of your declaration should be updated every year. If you lose clients because they do not feel comfortable with your expertise, consider this a blessing in disguise. Surely you do not want to get partway down the therapy road, have something go terribly wrong, and then have it revealed that you were not qualified to take the case.

PROFESSIONAL RELATIONSHIP, LIMITATIONS, AND RISKS

What I Do

This section begins the dialogue in which you explain the basis for behavior analysis services. This can be a challenge to explain in plain English, or Spanish, or H'mong, but it is here that you express your understanding of human behavior. In the sample declaration (item 2), we say that behavior analysis is "based on the idea that most important human behavior is learned over time and is maintained by consequences in the environment" (Declaration Sample, p. 261). It is critical to put this philosophy on the table to make sure your client understands where you are coming from. We also stress the notion that as behavior analysts we work with input from clients and that we develop a plan to acquire new behaviors. It is also important to let clients know that you work with significant others so family members will play a key role in the therapy partners if this is part of the treatment design.

How I Work

It is important to spell out for clients that we do not make judgments about behavior and that it is part of our belief system that "psychological" pain and suffering come from behaviors that do not adapt well to the current environment. We do consult with parents, teachers, and other individuals significant in the life of our client (with permission). This should be clearly spelled out at the initial meeting where the declaration is presented.

> Behavior analysts work toward achieving important life goals for the client.

This concept is not likely to be something parents or family members might understand otherwise. Most people would expect you to come in and work only with the individual child or adult, much like the individual session a psychiatrist would have.

It is a strong selling point of behavior analysis that we are not interested in changing only behavior per se, but rather we work toward achieving important life goals for the client. We refer to this as "increasing personal effectiveness and happiness," but you can explain this in your own terms in the declarations you develop.

Finally, in the last part of this section, we urge BCBAs to make clear to clients that we are not in the "cure" business and that we do not guarantee results. If clients don't understand from the beginning that results aren't guaranteed, they will surely become disenchanted when expected outcomes are not forthcoming.

CLIENT RESPONSIBILITIES

Up to this point, the declaration has been a clarification of your qualifications and how you operate. In this section of the declaration, you'll cover the possibly touchy subject of what your expectations are for the client. We need and expect their full cooperation and their total honesty in dealing with us. In a recent case, it was discovered that the mother-in-law did not approve of Association for Behavior Analysts (ABA) services for the child. In most circumstances this might not matter, but in this matriarchal family it did. Her position was that the tantrums, aggression, and noncompliance of the 7-year-old client were the result of poor discipline, and she blamed her son for not using his belt often enough. "He's just spoiled; he does not need psychologists poking around in his life. My son is to blame for treating a 7-year-old like a baby." The mother-in-law managed to cause so much trouble that the case was terminated abruptly midstream.

If you can accomplish buy-in to the behavior analysis approach, you will probably be asking parents or family members to take data. The success of the treatment depends on those who take the data being absolutely honest about it. There may be considerable pressure to make the behavior analyst happy by presenting data that show the problem is solved. Fake data are a behavior analyst's worst nightmare. Essentially the mediator—whether parent, teacher, or night shift supervisor—is saying they do not value data collection; it means nothing to them. The importance of accurate data should be brought up not only prior to the onset of services but also throughout the entire treatment process.

Behavior analysts need to know more about the client than what the data related to the target behavior show. Many people are surprised that we are interested in medications that the client might be taking. Of course, it is critical to know about drugs and medications because they could affect the client's behavior. A particular concern these days is the contamination of our evidence-based methodology with popular but confounding and potentially dangerous treatments or "cures" as they are sometimes billed. It is best to clarify when services begin if there are any procedures or substances in use such as strange or exotic vitamins, diets, or even "natural" products such as bee pollen as treatments. Data from the National Science Foundation biennial report (Shermer, 2002) shows us what we're up against when it comes to dealing with non-scientists. The Shermer report (2002, p. 1) states that "30 percent of adult Americans believe that UFOs are space vehicles from other civilizations, 60 percent believe in ESP, 40 percent think astrology is scientific, 70 percent accept magnetic therapy as scientific, and 92 percent of college grads accept alternative medicine." In a broader sense, there is a more fundamental problem, which is that "70 percent of Americans still do not understand the scientific process, defined in the study as comprehending probability, the experimental method and hypothesis testing" (Shermer, p. 1).

> A total of 40% of adult Americans think astrology is scientific; 92% of college graduates accept alternative medicine.

Finally, to prevent annoying requests for last-minute schedule changes, it is a good idea to include your personal, or your company's official, policy on appointments. Note that we indicate a 24-hour notification policy, but your company may prefer some other timeframe. If your policy is that missed weekday appointments cannot be moved to weekend days, this should be stated in the declaration.

CODE OF CONDUCT

Behavior analysts should be proud of their strict Guidelines for Responsible Conduct and should make sure that all clients are aware of these standards. We recommend making a copy of the Guidelines and presenting them to new clients, possibly with key sections highlighted. You should also inform clients that if they have any questions about your conduct they can contact the BACB directly.

One very important element we always recommend including in the declaration is a clear statement on gifts and invitations to dinners, parties, and celebrations. These small tokens of appreciation can start the unwary behavior analyst down the slippery slope to compromise of professional judgment and create dual relationships.

CONFIDENTIALITY

Breaches of confidentiality are among the most frequently occurring problems for BCBAs. Consultants are often asked to give out information that is confidential. They are also sometimes given confidential information by professionals who should know better. We recommend telling clients directly that you will keep any information given to you as strictly confidential and that you cannot give out information about any other clients. It is also wise to inform clients of the limits to confidentiality; that is, if you feel that the individual is a danger to himself or herself or others you can share this information (Koocher & Keith-Spiegel, 1998, p. 121).

Be sure to check your local laws regarding reporting of abuse or neglect and include this information in your declaration. At our ethics workshops, we've had at least two cases reported to us in the past year where a BCBA saw abuse or evidence of abuse, reported it, and then was quickly fired by the family. Abuse notification is supposed to be confidential, but often there are leaks or the family figures out who reported the incident. Avoiding possible loss of revenue from a dropped case is no reason to look the other way when it comes to abuse and neglect. To do so is not only unethical but is also a violation of the law.

APPOINTMENTS, FEES, AND EMERGENCIES

In this final section of the declaration, you'll need to spell out the details of how appointments are made, your fees, how billing is handled, and the method for dealing with emergencies. At a recent conference on ethics for itinerant teachers who work in the homes of DD clients, there was considerable discussion as to whether clients should be given the cell phone numbers of their therapists. Most of the teachers who gave out their cell numbers regretted the decision. However, after giving some thought about the implications in your particular situation, you should specify the rule for phone calls from your clients. As a final item in this section, billing is a topic that most behavior analysts would not discuss with clients. At a minimum, you must describe how this is done and who should be contacted if there are complications. Other than turning in their hours, under normal circumstances, BCBAs are not involved in billing and will refer questions to a bookkeeper or the client's case manager.

DISCUSSION, AGREEMENT, SIGNATURES, DATE, AND DISTRIBUTE

At the end of the declaration information session, which could take 30 minutes or so, the client and the behavior analyst should sign the declaration. A witness should also be present to ensure that signatures are authentic. Date the document, provide a copy to the family, and keep one for your files.

Four

Tips, Guidelines, Index, and Scenarios for Students

In Section IV, Chapters 19 and Appendices A–D, we present material that should be useful to students. Chapter 19 presents a dozen practical tips for your first job as well as several items to support the teaching of the Guidelines. These include the current Guidelines for Responsible Conduct plus a unique index that helps find key words in the code of ethics. We have expanded Appendix C with many new scenarios gathered from all over the country. Appendix D has suggested reading for those who want to learn more about ethics in behavior analysis.

19

A Dozen Practical Tips for Ethical Conduct on Your First Job

As a student, thoughts about ethical problems in your chosen profession probably seem far, far away and much more theoretical than practical at this point. However, in the not too distant future, perhaps just a few months from now, you will be taking your first job, and you will almost immediately begin to confront very real ethical dilemmas, some of which could affect the rest of your professional life. The purpose of this chapter is to outline some common issues that you are likely to encounter early on and to provide you with some practical tips for dealing with them.

CHOOSING A SETTING OR COMPANY

Your first big decision will involve choosing your first professional position. You might think that the primary considerations involve salary, location, potential for advancement, and matching your professional interests and behavioral skills. All of these are clearly important factors, but one additional choice involves consideration of the ethics and values of the company or organization itself. Currently, behavior analysts are a hot commodity in many cities across the country. For some agencies, hiring a Board Certified Behavior Analyst (BCBA) is essential for funding or to get relief from a federal lawsuit. In such cases, the agency may offer very high starting salaries and extensive benefit packages just to get you on board. Be wary, and ask lots of questions about these positions that appear too good to be true. There is some chance that you will be asked to sign off on programs that you have not written, to approve procedures with which you are not familiar, or to support agency strategies that are more public relations smoke and mirrors than behavioral methodology. It is appropriate to ask about the history of the agency, company, or organization. Who founded it? What is the overall purpose or mission? How does behavior analysis fit into this mission? Are there any political issues connected with the organization? For example, is this company currently the target of a lawsuit? Are there any "citations" from a recent state or federal survey? How many other behavior analysts are currently employed there? What does the turnover in behavior analysts look like? What is the funding stream? Who are the clients? Who will you be supervising? Are they Board Certified assistant Behavior Analysts (BCaBAs)? Will you be expected to attract and hire BCBAs?

You should be able to discern from the answers and the way the interviewer handles your questions whether there might be some ethical problems with the way that the company is run. In a recent case, for example, a small private school for children with autism that had been started by parents and initially headed by a Doctoral-level BCBA (BCBA-D) came under some scrutiny by parents and former employees when it was learned that the BCBA-D quit and was not replaced by another BCBA. Furthermore, two of the BCaBAs also left the organization and were not replaced by quali-fied professionals. The school, which originally attracted parents with its claim of a behavioral approach led by a certified person, still advertised itself as "behaviorally based" and still charged top dollar. It seems clear that going into this organization after more than 2 years without any behavior analysts could be a very chal-lenging situation where it is likely that your keen awareness of ethical problems will be required. In another case, a rehabilitation facility that was part of a national chain billed itself as behavioral but hired a nonbehavioral person as the administrator. This is quite common, but in this case the individual was "subtlety anti-behavioral" in her manner in dealing with the BCBAs and in her mode of operation. BCBAs were told that functional assessments did not need to be done on every client because it was obvious in some cases what the problem was, that data did not need to be taken—it took up too much time—and that she "trusted her staff's impressions" of client progress. In this case, the BCBA did not ask enough questions in the initial interview, did not actually meet the administrator who held these views, and was just a little too eager to start bringing home a fat paycheck.

WORKING WITH YOUR SUPERVISOR

In your job interview with the company or organization, it is a good idea to ask to meet your supervisor (this is rarely offered, but an ethical agency will comply if you make the request). Usually you will meet with the administrator, go on a brief tour, perhaps have lunch with some of the professional staff members, and then sit down with someone from the personnel office to negotiate your salary and benefits. However, meeting with the actual person by whom you will be supervised and report to is essential if you want to start your first job on a strong ethical foundation. There are many things you want to learn from potential new supervisors including their style—are they a reinforcing kind of person or somewhat negative or withdrawn? Are they interested in working with you, or do they want you do to their work? Is there any chance they are somewhat jealous of you (you might have a degree from a prestigious, well-known school) and you might be somewhat threatening? Ethically speaking, you would like to be assured that you will not be asked to do anything unethical: (1) you will be able to do your work responsibly; (2) you will have the time and resources to do a great, ethical job; and (3) your supervisor will be there to guide you through troubled waters should the occasion arise. Your supervisor sets the tone for your work: "Just get it done; I don't care how" is far different from, "Be thorough, get it right, we want what is best for the clients." So, in meeting with new supervisors, you might ask about their philosophy of management, about the most difficult ethical issue they have encountered in the last year and how they handled it. Or you might ask about any ethical issues you might encounter in your work. Just an open-ended question here should start the conversation going, and you can carry it from there with follow-up questions. When you're finished with this interview, you should have a secure, optimistic feeling about working for this person. If you feel apprehensive, think twice about taking the position, even if it is more money than you ever thought you'd see in a first job.

LEARN JOB EXPECTATIONS UP FRONT

If you have followed our suggestions up to this point, you will be happy and excited about your new position as a professional behavior analyst, making a good living, and helping people. Before you get too carried away, it would be a good idea to clarify exactly what you are supposed to do on a day-to-day basis. In your first 3 months on any job, you have a sort of grace period where you can ask questions without appearing to be dumb. If you are going to be analyzing behavior, doing functional assessments, writing programs, and training staff, you should be well prepared from your graduate work. However, each agency and organization has its own method for doing each of these tasks. Your first assignment is to find out how administrators want it done. So, ask for copies of "exemplary" intake interviews, case work-ups, functional assessments, and behavioral programs. You can avoid embarrassing and potentially ethically challenging situations if you know how your new consulting firm routinely handles complaints from consumers, inquiries from review committees, and issues with state agencies. You can make sure that your ethical standards match the other professionals if you review minutes of habilitation team meetings and take a look at behavior programs written by previous behavior analysts. You might also want to know in advance if you are expected to chair the weekly case review meetings or to simply attend and whether, in these meetings, there is open discussion of ethical issues. One of the most important job-related ethical issues involves whether you will be working within your level of competence or whether you will be asked to take on cases or tasks for which you are not fully qualified.

One freshly graduated BCBA joined some others in a mental health facility where she was assigned to the retarded-defendant program for which she was highly qualified. After a few weeks, she was asked to do some IQ testing on some mental health patients, on short notice and under short deadline pressure. She had avoided taking intelligence-testing classes in graduate school and pointed this skill deficiency out to her supervisor along with a question about why this requirement was not mentioned in the job interview. Then she pointed out how the Behavior Analyst Certification Board (BACB) Guidelines discourage behavior analysts from working out of their area. In some cases, this can brand a person as "not a team player," but really it is an ethical issue. Even if she did do the testing, it wouldn't be valid, and what if someone made a decision based on the test scores? This would surely be unethical. So, to avoid situations like this one, make sure that you ask plenty of questions early on, in the job interview and once you've started work, about what is expected, and establish the ethical boundaries necessary to protect yourself from engaging in unethical behavior.

DON'T GET IN OVER YOUR HEAD

Most people just starting out on their first job are excited to be doing what they've dreamed about for years: practicing behavior analysis as a professional and making a difference in people's lives. Early on you are likely to be so grateful to have a job that you will do nearly anything to please your supervisor and upper-level management. Your enthusiasm could actually cause some harm, however, if it turns out that you take on more than you can handle or take on cases without some recognition of their difficulty. Your most important goal is to do a first-class job on every case that you are assigned. If you put your heart and soul into your work and watch out for conflicts of interest and "do no harm," you will be fine. But if you take on too many cases, then the next thing that will happen is that something falls through the cracks and clients start complaining, or your supervisor notices that your reports are sloppy, or the peer review committee starts making negative comments about your programs. In behavior analysis, doing more is not always associated with doing better. Quality counts. This is especially the case because you are affecting the life of a person with your work. You owe it to your clients as well as yourself to take only the number of cases that you can do well.

This same philosophy holds for taking on cases for which you have no expertise. In your training, you may not have worked at all with clients who are sex offenders or who are mentally ill or who are profoundly physically disabled. You do not do yourself or the client any favors by taking these cases. You will no doubt be under a lot of pressure to do so from parents, teachers, or program administrators, but if you just think of the harm that could be done by taking a case and then handling it badly you will think twice about this decision. The easiest and most ethical stance to take is to always work within your range of competence. If you want to increase your range, the proper thing to do is to find another professional to serve as your mentor, someone who can give you proper training. You may also want to consider taking additional graduate coursework in a certain specialty area in addition to doing some practicum with supervision from an expert in that area.

USING DATA FOR DECISION MAKING

One of the distinguishing characteristics of the profession of behavior analysis is the reliance on data collection and data analysis. For us, data count. The Florida Association for Behavior Analysis has a new motto—"Got data?"—that is now available on T-shirts, coffee mugs, and key chains as a takeoff on the milk producers' "Got milk?" campaign. If there is anything that distinguishes us from other human services professionals, it is that we have a strong ethic in favor of objective data (not anecdotal, not self-report, not questionnaire) on individual behavior and the use of these data to evaluate the effects of treatments we devise and implement. Technically speaking, it is unethical to start an intervention without baseline data. And it is unethical to continue a treatment without taking more data to see if it was effective. Most behavior analysts agree to this, and, although it is procedural, it is written into our code of ethics (BACB Guidelines, 4.04). So, as long as you are taking data and using them to evaluate a procedure, you are ethically in the clear, right? Well, not exactly. It is actually a little more complicated than this. First of all, as you know, there are data, and then there are *data*. The latter is reliable (meaning reliability checks that are carried out under specified conditions with a second, independent, observer, and reach a certain standard) and socially validated (meaning that standards of social validity have been met, again under specified conditions). It can be argued that a practicing behavior analyst not only has to take data to be ethical but that the data have to be reliable and valid; after all, there is a lot riding on the data: treatment decisions, medication decisions, retain or discharge decisions. As an ethical behavior analyst, you would not want to use data that were tainted by observer bias or that had a reliability of, say, 50%. Furthermore, you wouldn't want to make treatment decisions if you thought the data had no social validity. So, what do you do as an ethical behavior analyst? You carry a burden to not only be data based in your decision making but also to assure the client, client-surrogates, and your peers that you have quality data (again, not self-report, not anecdotal, not questionnaire).

One final issue about the use of data in decision making; this has to do with whether your treatment was in fact responsible for any behavior change. Again, to be ethical, it would appear that it is your responsibility to know in a functional sense that it was your treatment that worked and not some outside or coincidental variable. This suggests that as a practical, ethical matter you should be looking for ways of demonstrating experimental control either with a reversal or multiple-baseline design. If you put in a treatment and the behavior changes, you cannot in all honesty say it was your intervention because you don't really know this for sure. Right about the time you instituted your treatment plan, the physician could have made a medication change, or the client may have developed an illness, or gotten some bad news, or perhaps someone else put in an intervention about the same time without your knowledge (e.g., the dietician cut back the person's calories, the client's roommate kept him up most of the night, etc.). In summary, as an ethical behavior analyst, you are obligated to be data based in your decision making and to develop a high-quality data collection system that allows you to address issues of reliability, validity, and demonstrations of experimental control. You will find that professionals in other areas don't take all of these issues into consideration, and you should be proud to be part of a profession that takes data so seriously.

TRAINING AND SUPERVISING OTHERS

As a behavior analyst, you are probably already aware that others—usually paraprofessionals, who are trained by you—do much of the actual behavior treatment. Your job as the behavior analyst is to take the referral, qualify it to make sure it falls into the behavioral problem area (as opposed to, e.g., being a nursing problem or education issue), and then perform an appropriate functional assessment to determine likely causes of the behavior. Once this is determined, you will draw up a behavior program, based on empirically tested, published, interventions, and then train someone to carry out the interventions. The ethical burden here is that you have to not only do the functional assessment according to accepted protocols but also to properly train the parents, teachers, residential staff, aides, or others. You are ultimately responsible for the program's effectiveness. This means that the program is carried out to your specifications. We know from the research literature that some methods of training work and that some don't. The most reliable form of training is not to simply give the parent a written program and then ask, "Are there any questions?" It is also not acceptable to explain the program and then leave a written copy. It is far more effective, and ethical, if you demonstrate the procedure, then have the parents practice, then provide feedback, have them try again, and so on until they do it right. Then you give them a written copy and maybe a videotape just to make sure, and then you may leave, but only for a short time because you need to make a spot check a few days later to observe to see if they are doing it right. If not, you will need to do some correction, some more role play, and some more feedback, and then another visit a few days later. This is ethical training. Anything less is unethical.

Probably within 6 months of taking your first job, you will be supervising others (in some positions it may be immediate). As a behavior analyst, you again have a high standard to meet in terms of the quality of your supervision. Because we have such an extensive literature on ways of changing behavior in the workplace (in fact, there is a whole subspecialty called performance management), you now have an ethical obligation to be an effective supervisor. It's not all that difficult for a person steeped in basic behavior analysis procedures. First, make sure you use the most effective antecedents. Don't lecture; demonstrate. After the demonstration, ask your supervisees to show you what they've learned. Then give immediate positive feedback. If you are training on written materials, for example, how to prepare a behavior program, show your trainee a sample of the best program that you can find. If necessary, break the task into smaller "bites" of material. And, consider using backward chaining if necessary. Practice giving positive reinforcement for work you see and receive every day, many times a day. You will soon discover that your supervisees and trainees seek you out for advice and assistance; they will want to show you their work and get your approval. If you are working in a large organization, you could easily become the most reinforcing person there without even trying hard. The time will come when you do have to give negative feedback or show disapproval. If you've worked hard to give out contingent reinforcers, the person who receives this punisher will initially be somewhat shocked (he or she might have gotten the initial impression that you were just a "goody-two-shoes"). Remember, the purpose of this correction is to change behavior, not punish the person, so you will also want to keep reinforcing the appropriate behavior. And don't forget your autoclitics (Skinner's [1957] *Verbal Behavior,* Ch. 12), those little comments that mean so much when you have to give someone negative feedback. "You know that I value what you do and that your work here has been excellent; now let me just point out something that is not quite right in this behavior program." One of the best books that can be used as a basic primer for business and professional skills is Dale Carnegie's (1981) *How to Win Friends and Influence People.* You should review this little gem as a supplement to what you have learned about behavioral supervision.

TIME KEEPING FOR BILLING AND SUPERVISION

An essential part of professional ethics is accountability. One of the most important aspects of accountability is that you keep track of how you spend your time. Time is your primary commodity. For your first position, you may find that you are working on a "billable hour" model of compensation. In this system, the agency or consulting firm you are working for has contracted for your services at a certain rate per hour and every documented hour that you work can be billed. You then receive a biweekly or monthly check based on your total number of billable hours. Although it may seem like a small matter, keep consistent, precise records of each and every billable unit—usually a quarter hour. Do not rely on your memory at the end of the day to reconstruct your activities, and do not average them out over a week. You will probably be able to set up a file on your personal digital assistant (PDA) that will allow you to note for each client the date, time, and duration of contact as well as a brief note of what you did. At the end of the billing cycle, all you then need to do is perform a few simple calculations to determine your billing to the agency or consulting firm. One important feature of this accounting is that you understand how critical it is to your firm that you actually match your hours of service to the contracted hours. If your agency or consulting firm has contracted with a facility for you to spend 20 hours per week onsite, it is inappropriate for you to provide only 16 hours of service. First, the determination was made by the facility and your consulting firm that 20 hours was needed. The facility has set aside a certain amount of money for your services, and they have mutually agreed that they need 20 hours of consulting or therapy. For you to decide on your own to take a day off is inappropriate and constitutes a violation of BACB Guidelines 2.03 and 6.01.

Needless to say, accurate and honest time accountability is essential to protect you from any allegation that you have been overbilling or that you have attempted to defraud a client or the government. This is especially urgent because there are cases being prosecuted at a high rate of physicians who are billing for clients they do not see or for services that are never rendered.

A related issue pertains to the need to keep close track not only of your billable hours but also your supervision hours. Many behavior analysts who take their first job after graduation are in need of hours of supervised experience to take the BCBA exam. The same procedure described earlier for billable hours is used to keep track of the service hours you have completed and an accompanying record of the number of hours of supervision that you have received. You should not rely on your supervisor to keep track of these data; it is your responsibility. Note in particular that you are required to complete either 18 months of "mentored" experience or 9 months of "supervised" experience and that this must be in units of at least 20 hours per week (i.e., at least a half-time job) for 80 hours per month. Many graduate school part-time positions are only 16 hours per week; if you were attempting to meet the requirement, you would then need to do at least 4 additional hours per week of pro bono work to meet the total of 20 hours. It is clear that you will need to document this so that at the end of your mentored or supervised experience there is no doubt as to whether you have met the requirement.

WATCH FOR CONFLICTS OF INTEREST

One of the subtlest unethical problems that can develop for any professional is that of a conflict of interest. Much is made in the clinical literature of the problem of the psychotherapist having sex with clients either during or after therapy as a prime example of a conflict of interest and exploitation of a vulnerable person (the client) by a more powerful person (the therapist). Another example is the therapist developing some sort of business or social relationship with a client or former client such as hiring that person to do work around the house or garden. In these cases, it is easy to see that such a relationship in our field could "impair the behavior analyst's objectivity" and affect his or her decision making. It would be a bad idea, for example, to take as a client someone you know, such as a friend, neighbor, or relative.

In behavior analysis, other relationships could be problematic that appear to be unique to our field. Behavior analysts are not restricted to the role of therapist. They are also supervisors, consultants, teachers, and researchers. Behavior analysts may sit on local or statewide human rights committees or peer-review committees. They may own a consulting firm or be an elected member of a professional association. The role of behavior therapist is also complicated by the fact that some therapy may be done in the home of the client as in discrete-trial therapy with autistic children. In this case, the family of the child client may develop a stronger bond with the behavior analyst than would be the case if the sessions were conducted in a clinic or at school. It has been reported often that parents under these circumstances begin to see the therapist as part of the family and will want to include them on outings or invite them to birthday parties or other family events. Surely participating in such events would begin to "impair the behavior analyst's objectivity" and would serve as a prime example of a conflict of interest when the time came to give an objective account of the child's progress or for a recommendation to be made to terminate the case. Serving on a peer-review committee where you are supposed to render an impartial judgment about the quality of a treatment program could present an objectivity problem if a friend or former student developed the case being presented. An owner of a consulting firm has a built-in conflict of interest when considering accepting a new client; the potential income from the case may cloud the judgment of the owner from determining that it would be in the client's best interest to refer to another behavior analyst who has more expertise with a special behavior problem. Of course, the same conflict exists at the individual therapist level when he or she must decide to take a client who has been referred. Decisions in all these cases revolve around the question of what is in the client's best interest (BACB Guideline 2.0: "The behavior analyst has a responsibility to operate in the best interest of clients") rather than what would benefit the therapist, the consulting firm, or the agency.

FIND A "TRUSTED COLLEAGUE" RIGHT AWAY

It is difficult to make ethical decisions in isolation. Without a sounding board, what appears to you to be an easy call may in fact be quite a complex dilemma. Determining whether some harm might come from a particular intervention is not that easy to establish in many cases. The effects could be delayed or subtle, and someone else with more experience than you could be a big help in making such a decision. Over time, you will feel more confident about your behavioral decisions, but in the beginning, to help build your confidence, we strongly recommend that you find a "trusted colleague" as soon as possible. Ideally this would be another behavior analyst who is easily accessible and who is not your supervisor or your employer. For political and other reasons, the colleague probably should not work for "the competition" in your geographical area. Your trusted colleague is someone that you will entrust some rather deep thoughts of yours such as (1) "Am I really prepared to take this case?" or (2) "My supervisor is telling me do to X, but it seems unethical to me. What should I do?" or, even more importantly, (3) "I think I've made a big mistake; what do I do now?" With luck you won't encounter any of these dilemmas in your first 3 months on the job, and you can use this time to try to find a person who is knowledgeable and whom you can trust. In your off-hours, your first 3 months on the job should be spent interacting with other professionals from your workplace and in your general locale. It's a good idea to get to know social workers, nurses, physicians, case managers, psychologists, and client advocates as well as any other behavior analysts in your area. This networking will serve other purposes also, such as making referrals; in this process of getting to know your colleagues you should make the acquaintance of someone who can be more than a casual business associate and become a confidant. You will want to size up this person's approach to ethics and make sure that his or her approach to dealing with complex issues appears to be sound, thoughtful, and deliberate, not glib or cavalier. A BCBA with 5 or more years of experience who is careful in what she does, has a good solid reputation, and who seems friendly and approachable would be a good candidate. You want to find your trusted colleague well before anything "hits the fan" because you will want to have a well-established rapport with the person and feel confident that you can in fact trust him or her with your urgent ethical situation.

TOUCHING PEOPLE

Unlike ordinary office-based psychotherapy, behavior analysis often involves getting up close and personal with your clients. Especially for those behavior analysts working with the developmentally disabled, the physically challenged, and the behavior-disordered client, our treatments may involve touching or holding the person. Innocuous procedures like graduated guidance involve putting your hands on the client to help him or her learn how to do some task like self-feeding or dressing. Toilet training can involve helping the person remove his or her clothes and tooth brushing requires the behavior analyst to stand behind the client and help manipulate the brush. Many behavior analysts routinely give "hugs" or brief shoulder massages as reinforcers without thinking of the possible adverse consequences. In all of these cases, even the most benign and well-intentioned action on your part could be misconstrued or misinterpreted as "inappropriate touching." This accusation could come from the client, the client's parents, a nearby caregiver, or even a visitor who just happened to be on the scene. Other more intrusive behavioral procedures are even more problematic: time-out almost always involves holding the client while taking him or her to the time-out room. Manual restraint, or attempting to apply mechanical restraints, can also present issues of potential misinterpretation or misperception (from "You hurt me," to "You hurt him deliberately," to "Were you groping her? I think you were, you pervert; I'm going to call the police!").

The ethical behavior analyst will always abide by the dictum "Do no harm," and will avoid at all costs doing anything to in any way physically or emotionally harm a client. But the cautious, ethical behavior analyst will also make sure that he or she is never the target of a mistaken or malicious accusation of physically inappropriate behavior toward a client. To this end, we make the following recommendations:

1. To avoid a false client allegation of inappropriate touching, always make sure to have another person (often called a "witness") present.
2. Make sure the witness knows what you are doing and why you are doing it.
3. If you are involved in any sort of physical restraint use, make sure that you have been properly trained and certified to do so.
4. If you know of a client who has a history of false reports of inappropriate touching, be wary of close contact with that person unless you have done (1) and (2).
5. Avoid cross-sex therapeutic interactions (male therapist–female client) unless there is absolutely no alternative (you will still want to follow rules (1) and (2), however).

The purpose of these recommendations is not to encourage you to become cold and impersonal in your interactions with clients but rather to promote some thinking about how your warm and affectionate behavior might backfire on you.

DEALING WITH NONBEHAVIORAL COLLEAGUES

Most of your professional time will be spent with colleagues who are not behavior analysts. Depending on the setting and the history of the agency or organization, this could present you with some serious ethical dilemmas. For example, if as part of a habilitation team you find that the consensus of the group is that your client should receive "counseling" you have an ethical obligation to propose a behavioral alternative (BACB Guideline 10.01) and to raise questions about whether there are any data on treatment efficacy (BACB Guideline 2.09a) for "counseling." This could make you somewhat unpopular on the team. Furthermore, if this treatment is actually implemented you have an obligation to request that data be taken to evaluate it (BACB Guideline 2.09c). To make matters worse, if you are ethical in following these guidelines, you are likely to be in the spotlight when it comes time to evaluate your proposed interventions. You will have to be ready with copies of published studies to justify your treatments and to be scrupulous about taking objective and accurate data to determine if they in fact work with this client.

You may soon discover that the other professionals with which you deal are not very aware of the ethics code for their field or pay it little heed. Or worse, you may discover that their code of ethics is not very clear on issues regarding client's rights, use of empirically based procedures, or the evaluation of treatments using data. New students working in the field for the first time are often shocked at the cavalier way meetings are conducted and decisions are made regarding clients. It is not unusual for one person to dominate the meetings with a clear motive of getting it over with as soon as possible. Often no data are presented and weak or no rationales are given for pushing certain treatment approaches. Convenience, a "just go along" attitude, and disregard for ethics in general are often the mode for these meetings that appear to be held more for show than for function. Initially, as a new and probably junior member of the treatment team, you will probably want to sit quietly and observe; try to determine who is in charge and what the custom is for handling decision making. You may need to consult with your supervisor about how best to handle these situations and to consult the BACB code of ethics for some key foundation points. Before you accuse anyone in public of engaging in unethical conduct, it would be wise to again check with your supervisor and then possibly meet with the professional in question outside of the meetings to discuss your concerns. This may also be a time for you to consult with your trusted colleague. In extreme cases, where you and your supervisor feel that you have done everything possible to have some impact but have been unsuccessful, it may be necessary to terminate your involvement. Guidelines 2.14a–2.14d address the circumstances for such a dramatic move and describe how this should be done.

So, to end on a positive note, it is important to point out that the vast majority of nonbehavioral colleagues are kind and caring, mean well, and will tolerate you if you will tolerate them. Most have never heard of behavior analysis, so you will have a chance to be an ambassador for the field and to educate them about current developments and how we are, in the utmost, concerned about the ethical, effective, and humane treatment of clients. Be patient with them, and give them a chance to educate you about their field. Be a good listener and a positive supportive person, and you will grow immeasurably as a professional yourself. Be honest about your own shortcomings (e.g., you may know very little about medications and how they work with certain behaviors) and open to other points of view. Over time, you will gain some perspective on how others view behavior and understand how you can nudge them toward a more behavioral perspective.

SEXUAL HARASSMENT

Sexual harassment is one of those awkward, ugly topics that few people want to discuss unless pressed to do so. Despite years of education, legal rulings, and company fines, it still exists (U.S. EEOC, 2009). As a behavior analyst, you might think that you might never be subject to this kind of treatment by others. Although you would never intentionally treat another person in this degrading way, nonetheless, a few behavioral aspects of sexual harassment should be discussed for the new behavior analyst.

First, we need to address unwanted sexual advances. If you have some special work circumstances, you might be more likely to encounter this problem. BCBAs who work in the client's home may find that there are occasions when they are alone with a single parent of the opposite sex (young female therapists seem most vulnerable if there is a divorced or single male in the house). It can start innocently enough with the person acting very interested in your work, perhaps sitting close, making exceptionally good eye contact, or smiling a lot. And you might take this as just a very involved person who thinks that you and your work are fascinating. An extra-warm greeting, a hug that lasts just a little longer than it should, or a touch to the arm or shoulder are the first clues that there may be something else afoot here. Behavior analysts are trained to be superb observers of behavior, and this is the skill that you want to bring to bear at this time. Behavior analysts also know how to use Differential Reinforcement of Other Behaviors (DRO), punish behaviors, put them on extinction, or bring them under stimulus control to reduce their rate of occurrence. So if you detect the early stages of unusually "familiar" behaviors, it is time to swing into action. Step one is to monitor your own behavior closely to make sure that you are not sending out any improper signals that advances might be welcome. This can be very difficult for a behavior analyst because another aspect of your training no doubt involved becoming a big reinforcer for those around you, particularly your clients; this can easily be misconstrued as having a personal interest in the individual. Having determined that you are not in any way encouraging the person, you need to begin working on ways of decreasing the behavior. You might use DRO by reinforcing the person for sitting a little farther away from you; for any "romantic" eye-contact responses, look at the floor or at your paperwork, appear distracted, or abruptly conclude the meeting. Inappropriate touching can be handled with a "cold stare" with no smiling and possibly a no-nonsense, "That's really not appropriate, Mr. Applegate." If you have caught this in the early stages and these tentative behaviors are punished, your problem may be solved. If it has gone further than this and the person is very inappropriate (e.g., calling you at home, leaving personal email messages), you need to make sure that you've got your extinction procedures memorized and are ready to put them into action. The prime foe of the victim of sexual harassment is intermittent reinforcement. If the person is calling you at home and you decide to use extinction, you will need to screen your calls and never pick up for these calls. Using extinction for a week and then in frustration picking up the phone to say, "I really don't want to talk to you; please don't call me here," is probably the worst thing you can do because, in fact, you just reinforced his or her making a run of 25 calls. When you start extinction, you must follow through. And you have to realize from your reading of the research literature that the behavior will probably escalate in some way (frequency, intensity, topography); be prepared to withstand this increase, and know that seeing such escalation is a sign that perhaps extinction is beginning to work. Nonbehaviorally trained people can be forgiven for making reinforcement, punishment, and extinction mistakes, but as a Board Certified Behavior Analyst, you have no excuse for not applying what you know to solve a serious personal problem like this one.

The second major concern regarding sexual harassment is the possibility that you will be accused by someone else of this behavior. We specifically train behavior analysts to be effective interpersonally, and this includes using head nodding, smiling, warm handshakes, and strong, effective verbal reinforcers. We encourage new consultants to "become a reinforcer" for those around you if you want to be effective. Different reinforcing behaviors are appropriate in different settings. In business and organizational settings, smiling, handshakes, and positive comments are all appropriate; on the shop floor, a pat on the back or shoulder hug might be acceptable. But you need to be careful that those you are "reinforcing" don't get the wrong idea and think that you are attracted to them. You might be working with a withdrawn child, for example, and trying to get her to stay on task or complete an assignment. At the first sign of success you break into a smile, give "high fives," and then a hug. Over time, this will probably work to increase the on-task behavior; however, you may begin to also increase your rate of hugs, or they may become a little more enthusiastic. The next thing you know you get called into the principal's office, and she says, "I've just gotten off the phone with little Lucy's mother. Lucy has complained that you touched her in her private areas. Is this true?"

The best advice to new behavior analysts is to be courteous, polite, even charming, but in all cases be professional. Do not let your enthusiasm for the progress of your client overwhelm you or the excitement of meeting a goal prompt you to get overly emotional and all "touchy-feely" with a client. Watch what you do with your hands at all times. As a check on your performance, ask yourself, "What if Channel Six Eyewitness News was here taping this? Would I still engage in this behavior?" If the answer is "no," then you need to modify your own behavior to prevent any misunderstanding or false accusations.

A FINAL NOTE

Most behavior analysts get so caught up in the intense minute-to-minute practice of their profession that it is difficult to stop and ask, "Is there an ethical problem here?" You might be caught off guard at the grocery store by someone who wants to know something about another client. It starts off innocently enough, but then the inappropriate question slips out: "I saw you working with Jimmy C., Marge's little boy. Why are you working with him?" Or, you are working hard to please your new supervisor and are right at your limit when she asks you to "drop everything and take charge of this now." Your tendency is to do what you are told, to try and be a compliant worker. But the task might be out of your range of competence or it might be unethical ("Bring your bottle of White-Out; we've got to fix some records. The review team is due here tomorrow.").

It is hoped that this volume will help you think about ethics not in a theoretical or purely moral sense but rather in the practical sense of doing the right thing; doing no harm; being just, truthful, fair, and responsible; affording dignity to your clients; promoting their independence; and in general treating others the way that you would like to be treated. The world would surely be a better place if everyone adopted the behavior analyst's ethical principles and put them to practical use every day.

Appendix A: Behavior Analyst Certification Board Guidelines for Responsible Conduct for Behavior Analysts[*]

*Revised June 2010 in Accordance With the Fourth Edition
Task List for Behavior Analysts*

Portions of the Behavior Analyst Certification Board (BACB) certification examinations relating to ethical and professional practices are based on the following Guidelines. The Guidelines address ethical and professional concerns particular to BACB certificants as well as concerns that are salient to the interactions among behavior analysts, the people they serve, and society in general. The Guidelines are provided for general reference to practitioners, employers, and consumers of applied behavior analysis services. For concerns about specific practices by a BACB certificant, please refer to the BACB Professional Disciplinary and Ethical Standards. The Guidelines may be referenced in complaints alleging violation of Section 6 of the BACB's Disciplinary and Ethical Standards; these Guidelines, however, are not separately enforced by the BACB.

1.0 RESPONSIBLE CONDUCT OF A BEHAVIOR ANALYST

The behavior analyst maintains the high standards of professional behavior of the professional organization.

1.01 Reliance on Scientific Knowledge

Behavior analysts rely on scientifically and professionally derived knowledge when making scientific or professional judgments in human service provision, or when engaging in scholarly or professional endeavors.

1.02 Competence

(a) Behavior analysts provide services, teach, and conduct research only within the boundaries of their competence, based on their education, training, supervised experience, or appropriate professional experience.

(b) Behavior analysts provide services, teach, or conduct research in new areas or involving new techniques only after first undertaking appropriate study, training, supervision, and/or consultation from persons who are competent in those areas or techniques.

1.03 Professional Development

Behavior analysts who engage in assessment, therapy, teaching, research, organizational consulting, or other professional activities maintain a reasonable level of awareness of current scientific and professional information in their fields of activity, and undertake ongoing efforts to maintain competence in the skills they use by reading the appropriate literature, attending conferences and conventions, participating in workshops, and/or obtaining Behavior Analyst Certification Board certification.

1.04 Integrity

(a) Behavior analysts are truthful and honest. The behavior analyst follows through on obligations and professional commitments with high quality work and refrains from making professional commitments that he/she cannot keep.

(b) The behavior analyst's behavior conforms to the legal and moral codes of the social and professional community of which the behavior analyst is a member.

(c) The activity of a behavior analyst falls under these Guidelines only if the activity is part of his or her work-related functions or the activity is behavior analytic in nature.

(d) If behavior analysts' ethical responsibilities conflict with law, behavior analysts make known their commitment to these Guidelines and take steps to resolve the conflict in a responsible manner in accordance with law.

1.05 Professional and Scientific Relationships

(a) Behavior analysts provide behavioral diagnostic, therapeutic, teaching, research, supervisory, consultative, or other behavior analytic services only in the context of a defined, remunerated professional or scientific relationship or role.

(b) When behavior analysts provide assessment, evaluation, treatment, counseling, supervision, teaching, consultation, research, or other behavior analytic services to an individual, a group, or an organization, they use language that is fully understandable to the recipient of those services. They provide appropriate information prior to service delivery about the nature of such services and appropriate information later about results and conclusions.

(c) Where differences of age, gender, race, ethnicity, national origin, religion, sexual orientation, disability, language, or socioeconomic status significantly affect behavior analysts' work concerning particular individuals or groups, behavior analysts obtain the training, experience, consultation, or supervision necessary to ensure the competence of their services, or they make appropriate referrals.

(d) In their work-related activities, behavior analysts do not engage in discrimination against individuals or groups based on age, gender, race, ethnicity, national origin, religion, sexual orientation, disability, socioeconomic status, or any basis proscribed by law.

(e) Behavior analysts do not knowingly engage in behavior that is harassing or demeaning to persons with whom they interact in their work based on factors such as those persons' age, gender, race, ethnicity, national origin, religion, sexual orientation, disability, language, or socioeconomic status, in accordance with law.

(f) Behavior analysts recognize that their personal problems and conflicts may interfere with their effectiveness. Behavior analysts refrain from providing services when their personal circumstances may compromise delivering services to the best of their abilities.

1.06 Dual Relationships and Conflicts of Interest

(a) In many communities and situations, it may not be feasible or reasonable for behavior analysts to avoid social or other nonprofessional contacts with persons such as clients, students, supervisees, or research participants. Behavior analysts must always be sensitive to the potential harmful effects of other contacts on their work and on those persons with whom they deal.

(b) A behavior analyst refrains from entering into or promising a personal, scientific, professional, financial, or other relationship with any such person if it appears likely that such a relationship reasonably might impair the behavior analyst's objectivity or otherwise interfere with the behavior analyst's ability to effectively perform his or her functions as a behavior analyst, or might harm or exploit the other party.

(c) If a behavior analyst finds that, due to unforeseen factors, a potentially harmful multiple relationship has arisen (i.e., one in which the reasonable possibility of conflict of interest or undue influence is present), the behavior analyst attempts to resolve it with due regard for the best interests of the affected person and maximal compliance with these Guidelines.

1.07 Exploitative Relationships

(a) Behavior analysts do not exploit persons over whom they have supervisory, evaluative, or other authority such as students, supervisees, employees, research participants, and clients.

(b) Behavior analysts do not engage in sexual relationships with clients, students, or supervisees in training over whom the behavior analyst has evaluative or direct authority, because such relationships easily impair judgment or become exploitative.

(c) Behavior analysts are cautioned against bartering with clients because it is often (1) clinically contraindicated, and (2) prone to formation of an exploitative relationship.

2.0 THE BEHAVIOR ANALYST'S RESPONSIBILITY TO CLIENTS

The behavior analyst has a responsibility to operate in the best interest of clients.

2.01 Definition of Client

The term client as used here is broadly applicable to whomever the behavior analyst provides services whether an individual person (service recipient), parent or guardian of a service recipient, an institutional representative, a public or private agency, a firm or corporation.

2.02 Accepting Clients

The behavior analyst accepts as clients only those individuals or entities (agencies, firms, etc.) whose behavior problems or requested service are commensurate with the behavior analyst's education, training, and experience. In lieu of these conditions, the behavior analyst must function under the supervision of or in consultation with a behavior analyst whose credentials permit working with such behavior problems or services.

2.03 Responsibility

The behavior analyst's responsibility is to all parties affected by behavioral services.

2.04 Consultation

(a) Behavior analysts arrange for appropriate consultations and referrals based principally on the best interests of their clients, with appropriate consent, and subject to other relevant considerations, including applicable law and contractual obligations.

(b) When indicated and professionally appropriate, behavior analysts cooperate with other professionals in order to serve their clients effectively and appropriately. Behavior analysts recognize that other professions have ethical codes that may differ in their specific requirements from these Guidelines.

2.05 Third-Party Requests for Services

(a) When a behavior analyst agrees to provide services to a person or entity at the request of a third party, the behavior analyst clarifies to the extent feasible, at the outset of the service, the nature of the relationship with each party. This clarification includes the role of the behavior analyst (such as therapist, organizational consultant, or expert witness), the probable uses of the services provided or the information obtained, and the fact that there may be limits to confidentiality.

(b) If there is a foreseeable risk of the behavior analyst being called upon to perform conflicting roles because of the involvement of a third party, the behavior analyst clarifies the nature and direction of his or her responsibilities, keeps all parties appropriately informed as matters develop, and resolves the situation in accordance with these Guidelines.

2.06 Rights and Prerogatives of Clients

(a) The behavior analyst supports individual rights under the law.

(b) The client must be provided on request an accurate, current set of the behavior analyst's credentials.

(c) Permission for electronic recording of interviews and service delivery sessions is secured from clients and relevant staff of all other settings. Consent for different uses must be obtained specifically and separately.

(d) Clients must be informed of their rights, and about procedures to complain about professional practices of the behavior analyst.

(e) The behavior analyst complies with all requirements for criminal background checks.

2.07 Maintaining Confidentiality

(a) Behavior analysts have a primary obligation and take reasonable precautions to respect the confidentiality of those with whom they work or consult, recognizing that confidentiality may be established by law, institutional rules, or professional or scientific relationships.

(b) Clients have a right to confidentiality. Unless it is not feasible or is contraindicated, the discussion of confidentiality occurs at the outset of the relationship and thereafter as new circumstances may warrant.

(c) In order to minimize intrusions on privacy, behavior analysts include only information germane to the purpose for which the communication is made in written and oral reports, consultations, and the like.

(d) Behavior analysts discuss confidential information obtained in clinical or consulting relationships, or evaluative data concerning patients, individual or organizational clients, students, research participants, supervisees, and employees, only for appropriate scientific or professional purposes and only with persons clearly concerned with such matters.

2.08 Maintaining Records

Behavior analysts maintain appropriate confidentiality in creating, storing, accessing, transferring, and disposing of records under their control, whether these are written, automated, or in any other medium. Behavior analysts maintain and dispose of records in accordance with applicable law or regulation, and corporate policy, and in a manner that permits compliance with the requirements of these Guidelines.

2.09 Disclosures

(a) Behavior analysts disclose confidential information without the consent of the individual only as mandated by law, or where permitted by law for a valid purpose, such as (1) to provide needed professional services to the individual or organizational client, (2) to obtain appropriate professional consultations, (3) to protect the client or others from harm, or (4) to obtain payment for services, in which instance disclosure is limited to the minimum that is necessary to achieve the purpose.

(b) Behavior analysts also may disclose confidential information with the appropriate consent of the individual or organizational client (or of another legally authorized person on behalf of the client), unless prohibited by law.

2.10 Treatment Efficacy

(a) The behavior analyst always has the responsibility to recommend scientifically supported most effective treatment procedures. Effective treatment procedures have been validated as having both long-term and short-term benefits to clients and society.

(b) Clients have a right to effective treatment (i.e., based on the research literature and adapted to the individual client).

(c) Behavior analysts are responsible for review and appraisal of likely effects of all alternative treatments, including those provided by other disciplines and no intervention.

(d) In those instances where more than one scientifically supported treatment has been established, additional factors may be considered in selecting interventions, including, but not limited to, efficiency and cost-effectiveness, risks and side-effects of the interventions, client preference, and practitioner experience and training.

2.11 Documenting Professional and Scientific Work

(a) Behavior analysts appropriately document their professional and scientific work in order to facilitate provision of services later by them or by other professionals, to ensure accountability, and to meet other requirements of institutions or the law.

(b) When behavior analysts have reason to believe that records of their professional services will be used in legal proceedings involving recipients of or participants in their work, they have a responsibility to create and maintain documentation in the kind of detail and quality that would be consistent with reasonable scrutiny in an adjudicative forum.

(c) Behavior analysts obtain and document: (1) Institutional Review Board (IRB), and/or local Human Research Committee approval; and/or (2) confirmation of compliance with institutional requirements when data gathered during their professional services will be submitted to professional conferences and peer reviewed journals.

2.12 Records and Data

Behavior analysts create, maintain, disseminate, store, retain, and dispose of records and data relating to their research, practice, and other work in accordance with applicable laws or regulations and corporate policy and in a manner that permits compliance with the requirements of these Guidelines.

2.13 Fees, Financial Arrangements, and Terms of Consultation

(a) As early as is feasible in a professional or scientific relationship, the behavior analyst and the client or other appropriate recipient of behavior analytic services reach an agreement specifying compensation and billing arrangements.

(b) Behavior analysts' fee practices are consistent with law and behavior analysts do not misrepresent their fees. If limitations to services can be anticipated because of limitations in financing, this is discussed with the patient, client, or other appropriate recipient of services as early as is feasible.

(c) Prior to the implementation of services the behavior analyst will provide in writing the terms of consultation with regard to specific requirements for providing services and the responsibilities of all parties (a contract or Declaration of Professional Services).

2.14 Accuracy in Reports to Those Who Pay for Services

In their reports to those who pay for services or sources of research, project, or program funding, behavior analysts accurately state the nature of the research or service provided, the fees or charges, and where applicable, the identity of the provider, the findings, and other required descriptive data.

2.15 Referrals and Fees

When a behavior analyst pays, receives payment from, or divides fees with another professional other than in an employer-employee relationship, the referral shall be disclosed to the client.

2.16 Interrupting or Terminating Services

(a) Behavior analysts make reasonable efforts to plan for facilitating care in the event that behavior analytic services are interrupted by factors such as the behavior analyst's illness, impending death, unavailability, or relocation or by the client's relocation or financial limitations.

(b) When entering into employment or contractual relationships, behavior analysts provide for orderly and appropriate resolution of responsibility for client care in the event that the employment or contractual relationship ends, with paramount consideration given to the welfare of the client.

(c) Behavior analysts do not abandon clients. Behavior analysts terminate a professional relationship when it becomes reasonably clear that the client no longer needs the service, is not benefiting, or is being harmed by continued service.

(d) Prior to termination for whatever reason, except where precluded by the client's conduct, the behavior analyst discusses the client's views and needs, provides appropriate pre-termination services, suggests alternative service providers as appropriate, and takes other reasonable steps to facilitate transfer of responsibility to another provider if the client needs one immediately.

3.0 ASSESSING BEHAVIOR

Behavior analysts who use behavioral assessment techniques do so for purposes that are appropriate in light of research. Behavior analysts recommend seeking a medical consultation if there is any reasonable possibility that a referred behavior is a result of a medication side effect or some biological cause.

(a) Behavior analysts' assessments, recommendations, reports, and evaluative statements are based on information and techniques sufficient to provide appropriate substantiation for their findings.

(b) Behavior analysts refrain from misuse of assessment techniques, interventions, results, and interpretations and take reasonable steps to prevent others from misusing the information these techniques provide.

(c) Behavior analysts recognize limits to the certainty with which judgments or predictions can be made about individuals.

(d) Behavior analysts do not promote the use of behavioral assessment techniques by unqualified persons, i.e., those who are unsupervised by experienced professionals and have not demonstrated valid and reliable assessment skills.

3.01 Behavioral Assessment Approval

The behavior analyst must obtain the client's or client-surrogate's approval in writing of the behavior assessment procedures before implementing them. As used here, client-surrogate refers to someone legally empowered to make decisions for the person(s) whose behavior the program is intended to change; examples of client-surrogates include parents of minors, guardians, and legally designated representatives

3.02 Functional Assessment

(a) The behavior analyst conducts a functional assessment, as defined below, to provide the necessary data to develop an effective behavior change program.
(b) Functional assessment includes a variety of systematic information-gathering activities regarding factors influencing the occurrence of a behavior (e.g., antecedents, consequences, setting events, or motivating operations) including interview, direct observation, and experimental analysis.

3.03 Explaining Assessment Results

Unless the nature of the relationship is clearly explained to the person being assessed in advance and precludes provision of an explanation of results (such as in some organizational consultation, some screenings, and forensic evaluations), behavior analysts ensure that an explanation of the results is provided using language that is reasonably understandable to the person assessed or to another legally authorized person on behalf of the client. Regardless of whether the interpretation is done by the behavior analyst, by assistants, or others, behavior analysts take reasonable steps to ensure that appropriate explanations of results are given.

3.04 Consent-Client Records

The behavior analyst obtains the written consent of the client or client-surrogate before obtaining or disclosing client records from or to other sources, including clinical supervisor.

3.05 Describing Program Objectives

The behavior analyst describes, in writing, the objectives of the behavior change program to the client or client-surrogate (see below) before attempting to implement the program. And to the extent possible, a risk-benefit analysis should be conducted on the procedures to be implemented to reach the objective.

4.0 THE BEHAVIOR ANALYST AND THE INDIVIDUAL BEHAVIOR CHANGE PROGRAM

The behavior analyst (a) designs programs that are based on behavior analytic principles, including assessments of effects of other intervention methods, (b) involves the client or the client-surrogate in the planning of such programs, (c) obtains the consent of the client, and (d) respects the right of the client to terminate services at any time.

4.01 Describing Conditions for Program Success

The behavior analyst describes to the client or client-surrogate the environmental conditions that are necessary for the program to be effective.

4.02 Environmental Conditions That Preclude Implementation

If environmental conditions preclude implementation of a behavior analytic program, the behavior analyst recommends that other professional assistance (i.e., assessment, consultation or therapeutic intervention by other professionals) be sought.

4.03 Environmental Conditions That Hamper Implementation

If environmental conditions hamper implementation of the behavior analytic program, the behavior analyst seeks to eliminate the environmental constraints, or identifies in writing the obstacles to doing so.

4.04 Approving Interventions

The behavior analyst must obtain the client's or client-surrogate's approval in writing of the behavior intervention procedures before implementing them.

4.05 Reinforcement/Punishment

The behavior analyst recommends reinforcement rather than punishment whenever possible. If punishment procedures are necessary, the behavior analyst always includes reinforcement procedures for alternative behavior in the program.

4.06 Avoiding Harmful Reinforcers

The behavior analyst minimizes the use of items as potential reinforcers that maybe harmful to the long-term health of the client or participant (e.g., cigarettes, sugar or fat-laden food), or that may require undesirably marked deprivation procedures as motivating operations.

4.07 Ongoing Data Collection

The behavior analyst collects data, or asks the client, client–surrogate, or designated others to collect data needed to assess progress within the program.

4.08 Program Modifications

The behavior analyst modifies the program on the basis of data.

4.09 Program Modifications Consent

The behavior analyst explains program modifications and the reasons for the modifications to the client or client surrogate and obtains consent to implement the modifications.

4.10 Least Restrictive Procedures

The behavior analyst reviews and appraises the restrictiveness of alternative interventions and always recommends the least restrictive procedures likely to be effective in dealing with a behavior problem.

4.11 Termination Criteria

The behavior analyst establishes understandable and objective (i.e., measurable) criteria for the termination of the program and describes them to the client or client-surrogate.

4.12 Terminating Clients

The behavior analyst terminates the relationship with the client when the established criteria for termination are attained, as in when a series of planned or revised intervention goals has been completed.

5.0 THE BEHAVIOR ANALYST AS TEACHER OR SUPERVISOR

Behavior analysts delegate to their employees, supervisees, and research assistants only those responsibilities that such persons can reasonably be expected to perform competently.

5.01 Designing Competent Training Programs and Supervised Work Experiences

Behavior analysts who are responsible for education and training programs and supervisory activities seek to ensure that the programs and supervisory activities:

- Are competently designed
- Provide the proper experiences
- And meet the requirements for licensure, certification, or other goals for which claims are made by the program or supervisor

5.02 Limitations on Training

Behavior analysts do not teach the use of techniques or procedures that require specialized training, licensure, or expertise in other disciplines to individuals who lack the prerequisite training, legal scope of practice, or expertise, except as these techniques may be used in behavioral evaluation of the effects of various treatments, interventions, therapies, or educational methods.

5.03 Providing Course or Supervision Objectives

The behavior analyst provides a clear description of the objectives of a course or supervision, preferably in writing, at the beginning of the course or supervisory relationship.

5.04 Describing Course Requirements

The behavior analyst provides a clear description of the demands of the supervisory relationship or course (e.g., papers, exams, projects, reports, intervention plans, graphic displays and face to face meetings), preferably in writing, at the beginning of the supervisory relationship or course.

5.05 Describing Evaluation Requirements

The behavior analyst provides a clear description of the requirements for the evaluation of student/supervisee performance at the beginning of the supervisory relationship or course.

5.06 Providing Feedback to Students/Supervisees

The behavior analyst provides feedback regarding the performance of a student or supervisee at least once per two weeks or consistent with BACB requirements.

5.07 Feedback to Student/Supervisees

The behavior analyst provides feedback to the student/supervisee in a way that increases the probability that the student/supervisee will benefit from the feedback.

5.08 Reinforcing Student/Supervisee Behavior

The behavior analyst uses positive reinforcement as frequently as the behavior of the student/supervisee and the environmental conditions allow.

5.09 Utilizing Behavior Analysis Principles in Teaching

The behavior analyst utilizes as many principles of behavior analysis in teaching a course as the material, conditions, and academic policies allow.

5.10 Requirements of Supervisees

The behavior analyst's behavioral requirements of a supervisee must be in the behavioral repertoire of the supervisee. If the behavior required is not in the supervisee's repertoire, the behavior analyst attempts to provide the conditions for the acquisition of the required behavior, and refers the supervisee for remedial skill development services, or provides them with such services, permitting them to meet at least minimal behavioral performance requirements.

5.11 Training, Supervision, and Safety

Behavior analysts provide proper training, supervision, and safety precautions to their employees or supervisees and take reasonable steps to see that such persons perform services responsibly, competently, and ethically. If institutional policies, procedures, or practices prevent fulfillment of this obligation, behavior analysts attempt to modify their role or to correct the situation to the extent feasible.

6.0 THE BEHAVIOR ANALYST AND THE WORKPLACE

The behavior analyst adheres to job commitments, assesses employee interactions before intervention, works within his/her scope of training, develops interventions that benefit employees, and resolves conflicts within these Guidelines.

6.01 Job Commitments

The behavior analyst adheres to job commitments made to the employing organization.

6.02 Assessing Employee Interactions

The behavior analyst assesses the behavior–environment interactions of the employees before designing behavior analytic programs.

6.03 Preparing for Consultation

The behavior analyst implements or consults on behavior management programs for which the behavior analyst has been adequately prepared.

6.04 Employees' Interventions

The behavior analyst develops interventions that benefit the employees as well as management.

6.05 Employee Health and Well-Being

The behavior analyst develops interventions that enhance the health and well-being of the employees.

6.06 Conflicts With Organizations

If the demands of an organization with which behavior analysts are affiliated conflict with these Guidelines, behavior analysts clarify the nature of the conflict, make known their commitment to these Guidelines, and to the extent feasible, seek to resolve the conflict in a way that permits the fullest adherence to these Guidelines.

7.0 THE BEHAVIOR ANALYST'S ETHICAL RESPONSIBILITY TO THE FIELD OF BEHAVIOR ANALYSIS

The behavior analyst has a responsibility to support the values of the field, to disseminate knowledge to the public, to be familiar with these guidelines, and to discourage misrepresentation by non-certified individuals.

7.01 Affirming Principles

The behavior analyst upholds and advances the values, ethics, principles, and mission of the field of behavior analysis. Participation in both state and national or international behavior analysis organizations is strongly encouraged.

7.02 Disseminating Behavior Analysis

The behavior analyst assists the profession in making behavior analysis methodology available to the general public.

7.03 Being Familiar With These Guidelines

Behavior analysts have an obligation to be familiar with these Guidelines, other applicable ethics codes, and their application to behavior analysts' work. Lack of awareness or misunderstanding of a conduct standard is not itself a defense to a charge of unethical conduct.

7.04 Discouraging Misrepresentation by Noncertified Individuals

Behavior analysts discourage non-certified practitioners from misrepresenting that they are certified.

8.0 THE BEHAVIOR ANALYST'S RESPONSIBILITY TO COLLEAGUES

Behavior analysts have an obligation to bring attention to and resolve ethical violations by colleagues.

8.01 Ethical Violations by Behavioral and Nonbehavioral Colleagues

When behavior analysts believe that there may have been an ethical violation by another behavior analyst, or non behavioral colleague, they attempt to resolve the issue by bringing it to the attention of that individual if an informal resolution appears appropriate and the intervention does not violate any confidentiality rights that may be involved. If resolution is not obtained, and the behavior analyst believes a client's rights are being violated, the behavior analyst may take additional steps as necessary for the protection of the client.

9.0 THE BEHAVIOR ANALYST'S ETHICAL RESPONSIBILITY TO SOCIETY

The behavior analyst promotes the general welfare of society through the application of the principles of behavior.

9.01 Promotion in Society

The behavior analyst should promote the application of behavior principles in society by presenting a behavioral alternative to other procedures or methods.

9.02 Scientific Inquiry

The behavior analyst should promote the analysis of behavior as a legitimate field of scientific inquiry.

9.03 Public Statements

(a) Behavior analysts comply with these Guidelines in public statements relating to their professional services, products, or publications or to the field of behavior analysis.

(b) Public statements include but are not limited to paid or unpaid advertising, brochures, printed matter, directory listings, personal resumes or curriculum vitae, interviews or comments for use in media, statements in legal proceedings, lectures and public oral presentations, and published materials.

9.04 Statements by Others

(a) Behavior analysts who engage others to create or place public statements that promote their professional practice, products, or activities retain professional responsibility for such statements.

(b) Behavior analysts make reasonable efforts to prevent others whom they do not control (such as employers, publishers, sponsors, organizational clients, and representatives of the print or broadcast media) from making deceptive statements concerning behavior analysts' practices or professional or scientific activities.

(c) If behavior analysts learn of deceptive statements about their work made by others, behavior analysts make reasonable efforts to correct such statements.

(d) A paid advertisement relating to the behavior analyst's activities must be identified as such, unless it is already apparent from the context.

9.05 Avoiding False or Deceptive Statements

Behavior analysts do not make public statements that are false, deceptive, misleading, or fraudulent, either because of what they state, convey, or suggest or because of what they omit, concerning their research, practice, or other work activities or those of persons or organizations with which they are affiliated. Behavior analysts claim as credentials for their behavioral work, only degrees that were primarily or exclusively behavior analytic in content.

9.06 Media Presentations and Emerging Media-Based Services

(a) When behavior analysts provide advice or comment by means of public lectures, demonstrations, radio or television programs, prerecorded tapes, printed articles, mailed material, or other media, they take reasonable precautions to ensure that (1) the statements are based on appropriate behavior analytic literature and practice, (2) the statements are otherwise consistent with these Guidelines, and (3) the recipients of the information are not encouraged to infer that a relationship has been established with them personally.

(b) When behavior analysts deliver services, teach or conduct research using existing or emerging media (e.g. Internet, e-learning, interactive multi-media), they consider any ethical challenges presented by media-based delivery (e.g. privacy, confidentiality, evidence-based interventions, ongoing data collection and program modifications) and make every effort possible to adhere to the ethical standards described herein.

9.07 Testimonials

Behavior analysts do not solicit testimonials from current clients or patients or other persons who because of their particular circumstances are vulnerable to undue influence.

9.08 In-Person Solicitation

Behavior analysts do not engage, directly or through agents, in uninvited in-person solicitation of business from actual or potential users of services who, because of their particular circumstances, are vulnerable to undue influence, except that organizational behavior management or performance management services may be marketed to corporate entities regardless of their projected financial position.

10.0 THE BEHAVIOR ANALYST AND RESEARCH

Behavior analysts design, conduct, and report research in accordance with recognized standards of scientific competence and ethical research. Behavior analysts conduct research with human and non-human research participants according to the proposal approved by a local Human Research Committee, and/or Institutional Review Board.

(a) Behavior analysts plan their research so as to minimize the possibility that results will be misleading.

(b) Behavior analysts conduct research competently and with due concern for the dignity and welfare of the participants. Researchers and assistants are permitted to perform only those tasks for which they are appropriately trained and prepared.

(c) Behavior analysts are responsible for the ethical conduct of research conducted by them or by others under their supervision or control.

(d) Behavior analysts conducting applied research conjointly with provision of clinical or human services obtain required external reviews of proposed clinical research and observe requirements for both intervention and research involvement by client-participants.

(e) In planning research, behavior analysts consider its ethical acceptability under these Guidelines. If an ethical issue is unclear, behavior analysts seek to resolve the issue through consultation with institutional review boards, animal care and use committees, peer consultations, or other proper mechanisms.

10.01 Scholarship and Research

(a) The behavior analyst engaged in study and research is guided by the conventions of the science of behavior including the emphasis on the analysis of individual behavior and strives to model appropriate applications in professional life.

(b) Behavior analysts take reasonable steps to avoid harming their clients, research participants, students, and others with whom they work, and to minimize harm where it is foreseeable and unavoidable. Harm is defined here as negative effects or side effects of behavior analysis that outweigh positive effects in the particular instance, and that are behavioral or physical and directly observable.

(c) Because behavior analysts' scientific and professional judgments and actions affect the lives of others, they are alert to and guard against personal, financial, social, organizational, or political factors that might lead to misuse of their influence.

(d) Behavior analysts do not participate in activities in which it appears likely that their skills or data will be misused by others, unless corrective mechanisms, e.g., peer or external professional or independent review, are available.

(e) Behavior analysts do not exaggerate claims for effectiveness of particular procedures or of behavior analysis in general.

(f) If behavior analysts learn of misuse or misrepresentation of their individual work products, they take reasonable and feasible steps to correct or minimize the misuse or misrepresentation.

10.02 Using Confidential Information for Didactic or Instructive Purposes

(a) Behavior analysts do not disclose in their writings, lectures, or other public media, confidential, personally identifiable information concerning their individual or organizational clients, students, research participants, or other recipients of their services that they obtained during the course of their work, unless the person or organization has consented in writing or unless there is other ethical or legal authorization for doing so.

(b) Ordinarily, in such scientific and professional presentations, behavior analysts disguise confidential information concerning such persons or organizations so that they are not individually identifiable to others and so that discussions do not cause harm to identifiable participants.

10.03 Conforming With Laws and Regulations

Behavior analysts plan and conduct research in a manner consistent with all applicable laws and regulations, as well as professional standards governing the conduct of research, and particularly those standards governing research with human participants and animal subjects. Behavior analysts also comply with other applicable laws and regulations relating to mandated reporting requirements.

10.04 Informed Consent

(a) Using language that is reasonably understandable to participants, behavior analysts inform participants of the nature of the research; they inform participants that they are free to participate or to decline to participate or to withdraw from the research; they explain the foreseeable consequences of declining or withdrawing; they inform participants of significant factors that may be expected to influence their willingness to participate (such as risks, discomfort, adverse effects, or limitations on confidentiality, except as provided in Standard 10.05 below); and they explain other aspects about which the prospective participants inquire.

(b) For persons who are legally incapable of giving informed consent, behavior analysts nevertheless (1) provide an appropriate explanation, (2) discontinue research if the person gives clear signs of unwillingness to continue participation, and (3) obtain appropriate permission from a legally authorized person, if such substitute consent is permitted by law.

10.05 Deception in Research

(a) Behavior analysts do not conduct a study involving deception unless they have determined that the use of deceptive techniques is justified by the study's prospective scientific, educational, or applied value and that equally effective alternative procedures that do not use deception are not feasible.

(b) Behavior analysts never deceive research participants about significant aspects that would affect their willingness to participate, such as physical risks, discomfort, or unpleasant emotional experiences.

(c) Any other deception that is an integral feature of the design and conduct of an experiment must be explained to participants as early as is feasible, preferably at the conclusion of their participation, but no later than at the conclusion of the research.

10.06 Informing of Future Use

Behavior analysts inform research participants of their anticipated sharing or further use of personally identifiable research data and of the possibility of unanticipated future uses.

10.07 Minimizing Interference

In conducting research, behavior analysts interfere with the participants or environment from which data are collected only in a manner that is warranted by an appropriate research design and that is consistent with behavior analysts' roles as scientific investigators.

10.08 Commitments to Research Participants

Behavior analysts take reasonable measures to honor all commitments they have made to research participants.

10.09 Ensuring Participant Anonymity

In presenting research, the behavior analyst ensures participant anonymity unless specifically waived by the participant or surrogate.

10.10 Informing of Withdrawal

The behavior analyst informs the participant that withdrawal from the research may occur at any time without penalty except as stipulated in advance, as in fees contingent upon completing a project.

10.11 Debriefing

The behavior analyst informs the participant that debriefing will occur at the conclusion of the participant's involvement in the research.

10.12 Answering Research Questions

The behavior analyst answers all questions of the participant about the research that are consistent with being able to conduct the research.

10.13 Written Consent

The behavior analyst must obtain the written consent of the participant or surrogate before beginning the research.

10.14 Extra Credit

If the behavior analyst recruits participants from classes and the participants are provided additional credit for participating in the research, nonparticipating students must be provided alternative activities that generate comparable credit.

10.15 Paying Participants

The behavior analyst who pays participants for research involvement or uses money as a reinforcer must obtain Institutional Review Board or Human Rights Committee approval of this practice and conform to any special requirements that may be established in the process of approval.

10.16 Withholding Payment

The behavior analyst who withholds part of the money earned by the participant until the participant has completed their research involvement must inform the participant of this condition prior to beginning the experiment.

10.17 Grant Reviews

The behavior analyst who serves on grant review panels avoids conducting any research described in grant proposals that the behavior analyst reviewed, except as replications fully crediting the prior researchers.

10.18 Animal Research

Behavior analysts who conduct research involving animals treat them humanely and are in compliance with applicable animal welfare laws in their country.

10.19 Accuracy of Data

Behavior analysts do not fabricate data or falsify results in their publications. If behavior analysts discover significant errors in their published data, they take reasonable steps to correct such errors in a correction, retraction, erratum, or other appropriate publication means.

10.20 Authorship and Findings

Behavior analysts do not present portions or elements of another's work or data as their own, even if the other work or data source is cited occasionally, nor do they omit findings that might alter others' interpretations of their work or behavior analysis in general.

10.21 Acknowledging Contributions

In presenting research, the behavior analyst acknowledges the contributions of others to the conduct of the research by including them as co-authors or footnoting their contributions.

10.22 Principal Authorship and Other Publication Credits

Principal authorship and other publication credits accurately reflect the relative scientific or professional contributions of the individuals involved, regardless of their relative status. Mere possession of an institutional position, such as Department Chair, does not justify authorship credit. Minor contributions to the research or to the writing for publications are appropriately acknowledged, such as in footnotes or in an introductory statement. Further, these Guidelines recognize and support the ethical requirements for authorship and publication practices contained in the ethical code of the American Psychological Association.

10.23 Publishing Data

Behavior analysts do not publish, as original data, data that have been previously published. This does not preclude republishing data when they are accompanied by proper acknowledgment.

10.24 Withholding Data

After research results are published, behavior analysts do not withhold the data on which their conclusions are based from other competent professionals who seek to verify the substantive claims through reanalysis and who intend to use such data only for that purpose, provided that the confidentiality of the participants can be protected and unless legal rights concerning proprietary data preclude their release.

Appendix B: Index for BACB Guidelines for Responsible Conduct for Behavior Analysts

Developed by Jon Bailey

INSTRUCTIONS

This index is designed to allow you to find exact references to key words in Ethics Scenarios for Behavior Analysts as well as for any other ethical situation that you might encounter. Start by identifying key words or phrases in the ethics scenario. Then look up each key word and reference the related principles in one of the 10 sections of the BACB Guidelines. If you are unable to find any reference in the Guidelines to cover your ethical issue you will need to fall back on the Nine Core Ethical Principles from Koocher and Keith-Spiegel (1998).

---

* "Best practice" is also known as "most
effective treatment procedures."
[†] See "disciplinary procedures."

---

[*] Please see "Disciplinary Standards" on the
BACB.com Web site.

_____

* Please see "Disciplinary Procedures."

---

* See "Disciplinary Procedures."

---

* Surrogate is used in place of "parent" in the Guidelines.

Appendix C: Fifty Ethics Scenarios for Behavior Analysts

INSTRUCTIONS

Read each scenario carefully. Each is based on an actual situation encountered by behavior analysts working in the field. We suggest that you first use a highlighter to mark key words or phrases in the scenario. Next, referring to your index for Behavior Analyst Certification Board (BACB) Guidelines, write in the code number for each key issue highlighted, and under "Principle" indicate in your own words what ethical principle is involved. Note that for each scenario there may be three to four such principles. Finally, after reviewing all the ethical principles involved, indicate what steps you should take to follow the guidelines. There may be several code numbers and principles for an individual scenario. For each scenario, answer the following:

Code number
Principle
What should you do?

PRACTICE SCENARIOS

1. I am an Applied Behavior Analysis (ABA) program supervisor. I have a preschooler who really needs lots of intervention. The family insists on mixing and matching
   approaches [e.g., floor time, gluten free and other diets,
   sensory integration]. This cuts down on the available ABA
   time to 10 hours. I don't feel that this is enough time but
   have been unsuccessful so far in convincing the parents.
   Should I drop this child from our ABA program or give
   what I believe is a treatment that is insufficient?

2. Is it always unethical to use testimonial information?
   What if a parent shares this information with a prospective client without your knowledge or permission?

3. When confronting another behavior analyst that you
   believe is doing something unethical, what should you do
   if the other analyst either disagrees with what you are saying or denies that it is occurring?

4. Kevin continues to bang his head when attempting to seek
   attention from his parents and teachers. The following
   approaches have been implemented: sensory integration
   recommended by the occupational therapist, deep pressure,
   joint compression, and jumping on a trampoline. Kevin
   continues to bang his head. Sign language was recommended by the speech therapist: Kevin is unable to discriminate between the signs; therefore he continues to bang his
   head. The use of a helmet was recommended by the physical
   therapist. Kevin continues to bang his head with the helmet,
   and he has now begun to bite his fingers. The behavior specialist has now recommended shock therapy, after reviewing all the interventions, or medication. Is it ethical to use

an aversive strategy at this point? How long should interventions continue to be in place before medication or shock therapy is considered?

5. Are we always obligated to use the best practices that are scientifically proven effective treatments with no exceptions? What happens if we are a member of a team [e.g., a school Individual Education Plan (IEP) team] and the team chooses to use and agrees on, despite your advice, an approach that is not supported by research?

6. An ABA consultant has been working with a child with autism and his or her family. As the child approaches the age of 3, a transition meeting is held between the early intervention program teacher and the school district. This meeting begins pleasantly, with sharing of information from both sides. However, a point comes when the ABA consultant and family actually become hostile and verbally attack school district personnel out of nowhere, and it becomes obvious during the meeting that the consultant has painted the school district as the enemy who has little to no concern for the best interest of the child. I would say that because this is the first time the district has encountered ABA, their impression of ABA, from the very beginning, is not a positive one. Does this not damage the school's perception of ABA, along with the parents' perception of a school district (which they will likely be working with for the next 20 years), and in fact distract from what is in the best interest of the child? Is this typical procedure in dealing with school districts?

7. As professionals in the field of education, we sometimes tend to forget that the children we work with have the right to privacy and their reports are deemed confidential. How can you politely tell another professional that to discuss a child's record without the family consent is not appropriate?

8. What do you do when you have one member of the family who constantly "sabotages" the positive impact the behavior intervention and your input has on his or her child? In particular, one parent refuses to keep data or to give you honest feedback and offers no encouragement or support to the other parent who is willing to at least attempt what is asked. The uncooperative parent feels that there is nothing wrong with his or her child and that this intervention is a waste of time. How far, ethically, can you become involved in this family dispute to convince the combative parent to become supportive of what you and the cooperative parent are trying to accomplish on behalf of their child? Is termination of the case a viable option?

9. Working in a home-based setting stirs up many ethical and boundary issues for therapists that do not occur in school or office settings. When working in a home, the family takes you into its "personal space." Additionally, when you work with someone's children, parents develop strong attachments to their children's therapist whom they are entrusting with their child's well-being. I have observed several of my colleagues develop "friendships" with the mothers of the children with whom they work. These relationships start out innocently enough. Usually it is a car ride to the grocery store, or perhaps the therapist and the parent may talk about shopping, and within a matter of a few sessions the two people have planned lunch and a day at the mall. These plans at times have included or excluded the child. Home-based therapy is very tricky, and without the proper supervision and without properly trained staff there are many opportunities to develop inappropriate relationships that can both jeopardize the child's treatment and engage the parent in an inappropriate manner. My question is actually a request for clarification of the boundary between therapist and the parent in a home-based situation. I am wondering if there are somewhat

relaxed criteria for the dual relationship rules in working with children and in working in a home environment.

10. Many of the requests for my services as a behavior consultant come when agencies or schools are struggling with families and are at odds with what to do to help a child with his or her behavior difficulties. The agency or school provides the funding to pay for my services and is the one who initiates my involvement with the student. At times, my review of the case and the analysis of the data I have gathered lead me to believe that previous interventions were not well thought out and were primarily of a reactive nature. Indeed, they may have actually caused the situation to become worse. Several times, families have asked me point-blank as to the cause of the student's behavior and my opinion of these previous interventions. How do I respond ethically, knowing that if I share my beliefs I risk alienating the agency or school and possibly giving the families more reasons not to trust the people involved with their child?

11. The client is a 19-year-old girl in high school (diagnosed with mild mental retardation). She has a history of sexual abuse and was a "crack baby" at birth. Last month there was an incident in which it was discovered that she was not riding the school bus and was instead walking to school. The problem is that she would meet with a man and have sexual intercourse in his front yard. At that point, they had an adult female talk to her about safe sex. My supervisor suggests she be provided condoms and given the money to go to a motel instead. The home group manager said she would allow her to have sex in her bedroom; however, there are foster kids present, and that may bring up other issues. I don't agree with directing her to a motel as a replacement behavior. I don't think she should be encouraged to have sex with strangers. She has in the past invited male strangers into the home. I am having a difficult time

coming up with a replacement behavior to suit her. She has excellent communication skills and gets great grades in school.

New Cases for the Second Edition

12. A Board Certified Behavior Analyst (BCBA) has been supervising an ABA educational program for a 3-year-old boy with autism for 6 months. The child's parents have recently gone through a long, bitter divorce. The BCBA has been subpoenaed to testify as to the child's custody and continued treatment. The BCBA has worked with the mother only during the home visits and knows of the home situation only from the mother's perspective. Despite ongoing parent training, the mother does not have good skills when it comes to managing the child. The father and his new girlfriend want custody of the child, and they have indicated they want no ABA program or therapist in the home. The BCBA deems the ABA program crucial but does not feel comfortable commenting on or recommending custody since she has met the father only once. The BCBA has been told she will be asked which parent would provide the better home for the child.

13. There is a BCBA in my area who often claims she was "trained" by well-known behavior analysts. I believe that to be "trained" by someone you should have been their student for a length of time or worked closely with them. This woman has goes to conferences where she sits in the audience and then says she was "trained" by well-recognized behavior analysts. She once received some advice from a leader in the field via email on a research project, and she now claims this person was her "mentor." I am really disgusted by this, and I feel she is misrepresenting herself to families and other professionals. Would it be unethical of me to email some of these well-known people, tell them what she is saying, and ask them about the "training" they

have given her? If you don't like this approach, how would you handle it?

14. In our district, there is a BCBA who charges the school district and other agencies a lot of money for providing services to children with autism—and I mean a lot of money. He tells people who are more than just a BCBA that he is one of the very few behavior analysts in the country nationally certified as a "Behavior Analyst for Verbal Behavior." What should I do about this? I am not inclined to approach him and would rather deal with someone else.

15. A BCBA works with a mother who homeschools her child. The child is a 6-year-old boy with autism. The BCBA has done a functional assessment and has identified the controlling variables for the child's target behavior. In the opinion of the BCBA, the best data collection system for gathering baseline data would require daily entries by the mother. A data-collection system has been designed that is easy to understand and score; however, the mother does not take the data despite the BCBA's best attempts to prompt and reinforce her. This child really needs help, but with no data it will be hard to provide treatment. Should the BCBA terminate services?

16. What are the ethics related to ending behavioral services because you have not been paid in several months? This happens frequently in my district. I started working with one client in October. It is now March, and I have never received a check. I have called the support coordinator, and she just says sometimes the system is slow. Everyone in our district thinks we have an ethical obligation to provide services so we can't terminate clients over lack of payment. Somewhere, on someone's desk, I am guessing our behavior analysis invoices are just piling up. Our clients have a "right to treatment." Do we have a "right to be paid?"

17. I am a BCBA working with a 30-year-old adult male client who moved from a large institution to a smaller 64-bed

residential facility. This client becomes dangerously aggressive to get access to his cigarettes. As a part of his behavior program, I set up a smoking schedule that spreads his allotted number of cigarettes out across his day in even, short intervals. Staff members went to the facility administrator and said they did not have time to manage the client's cigarettes throughout the day. The administrator listened to the staff and directed them to give the client all of his cigarettes in the morning along with a small chart showing him when he can smoke them. This has led to an increase of aggression because the client ignores the chart and smokes all of the cigarettes as soon as he gets them. He then tantrums throughout the day and demands more cigarettes. I would like to keep on working here, but I am ready to tell the administrator that I don't come in his office and work on his budget, so he should not be tampering with behavioral programs. What should I say to the administrator to let him know that his conduct is unethical and that it resulted in an increase in severe behavior problems?

18. One of the schools for which I provide BCBA services sent me a request to provide services for a 10-year-old girl who has been having multiple behavior problems in the classroom. She has been noncompliant (refusing to do what the teacher asks), frequently off-task and out of her seat, swearing at the other students on the playground, and not completing work in class. The parents are taking the child to a clinical psychologist. The psychologist has never seen the child in the classroom, but she created a "point sheet" for the teacher to use. I was told after I agreed to provide services that I should design a behavior plan around the point sheet designed by Dr. X. because she spends a lot of time with the child, the parents trust her and want her to be at the center of the therapy, and she is very well known in the community. The fact is, the point sheet is not effective, and the child's behavior is getting worse. I am a new

BCBA and don't want to present myself as a know-it-all, but I think I should be able to develop my own behavioral plan. Any advice?

19. My guess is that most of the people who ask ethics questions are BCBAs and Board Certified assistant Behavior Analysts (BCaBAs). My situation is somewhat different, as I am a professional who is responsible for approving behavioral services for clients. From time to time, I get a request for a significant amount of behavioral services. The consultant is requesting "prior service authorization," meaning I am being asked to pay for a certain number of hours before the work is actually done. This is a standard practice. In the most recent case, I was familiar with the client. The client was an adult male with a history of behavior problems. According to other professionals who work with the client, the behavior problems are under control at this time. I requested more information from the behavior analyst who requested that I approve consulting hours. All I got was a one-page document with suggestions for guidelines to follow when the behavior occurs. There were no data. The behavior analyst attached a note to his "guidelines" saying that, since the client was moving to the community after many years in an institution, there would probably be problems related to the transition and behavioral services should be in place.

20. The Medicaid waiver agency where I am providing behavioral services billed for behavioral services that were not provided to the client. I am sorry to say this was probably not just an error because this is not the first time it has done this. My ethical conflict is that the agency did provide another service the family desperately needed, so the family has not reported the agency. The family did not want to lose the best personal care attendant it has ever had. Does this balance out? The family and child really did need the personal care attendant. Can I get in trouble

for not reporting this? And I don't even know to whom or how I would report this.

21. Sometimes it is very clear when you are about to set yourself up to fail. I don't like to do that, but I want to do the right thing. I have been asked to take a case of a severely autistic child who has no language at all. She has never received services. The child is 6 years old. She wets her pants and has tantrums. She will throw food if she does not like it. She screams and cries at night when her parents try to put her to bed. The insurance company is willing to pay for only 2 hours of behavioral services each week. I feel like this isn't going to make any kind of difference. The parents are at a point where they are literally crying and saying they are desperate for any level of service. The service coordinator who has recently taken the case agrees with the parents. She says, "Something is better than nothing."

22. Where I live, many BCBAs working in the area of autism promote interventions that are ineffective or not based on research. Examples are casein-free diet, essential fatty acids, facilitated communication, auditory integration training, sensory integration therapy, secretin, megavitamins A, B6, and C, and chelation therapy. These BCBAs say, "I just don't want to argue with the parents; they want to try these things and are willing to pay for both them and behavioral services. As long as it is not hurting anything and my programs are working, I don't see this as an ethical issue."

23. A group of local behavior analysts gets together quarterly for a continuing education presentation followed by a group social and informal dinner. One of the members of our group is the owner of a large consulting firm. At a recent dinner, he mentioned that on Saturday morning he was having some parents of clients come to the office to have their photos taken for his new Web page. "We'll have a statement from each one about the great things we did for their child," he said. Someone at the table told him that

behavior analysts were not supposed to solicit testimonials. His response was that doctors, dentists, and other professionals did this and that there was no problem as long as the parents could choose to not participate. Was he wrong about this? Is there any situation under which testimonials would be acceptable? He said what he was doing was not what the Guidelines referred to in the section on testimonials.

24. A child in one of the schools where I am the new BCBA has multiple behavioral issues. I believe that he may need to be on medication for behavior control. I was called in to assess the child. I talked to the principal and told her we would be recommending a medical work-up to start with and a functional analysis. The principal said, "We just need to get him out of here. I need you to write a report that says this child can't be managed in a school setting like ours and that he needs to move to a special program." I am afraid that the principal's mind is made up and that if I tell her what I really think of her approach I won't be working at this school much longer.

25. In our district, a 12-year-old boy with severe developmental disabilities is in a foster placement. The client is ambulatory, and he roams at night. He will go in the kitchen and try to get knives to make a snack, and a few times he went outside and started walking down the road at night. The neighbor of the foster mother called one night at 3 a.m. to alert the foster mother that the boy was walking down the street in his underwear. The neighbor woke up when dogs started barking and looked out of her window to see what was happening. So, for now, to keep him safe, his "treatment" is a "cage" for sleeping. It looks like an old institution crib with a top that locks so he can't get out. A BCBA was involved in this intervention. Is something like this okay if it is used to keep the client safe?

26. I know the Guidelines say I should not accept gifts or socialize with clients and that I should not be giving

them gifts (e.g., meals). I understand this on a big scale—it could lead to a bad situation. But sometimes, there are some fine lines where I think it might be okay to do this. Are the Guidelines really just "guidelines" and not rules? Specifically, for one of my cases, I work in the home with a preschooler. The family is poor, and the mother is in a wheelchair. Sometimes, when I go to the home around dinnertime, I will take some burgers, pizza, or sandwiches so the mother doesn't have to cook dinner. I feel this helps me bond with this mom. Plus, if she doesn't have to cook and start getting dinner ready, she has more time to be with me and the child in our therapy sessions. Someone told me I should not be doing this. I believe that you should look at the results and if the food or gifts are not expensive and no one is getting beholden to the other person that this would be acceptable. If the mother started saying, "Can you bring some steaks the next time?" I would know I've gone too far.

27. In my consulting job as a behavior analyst, I have been working with a consumer who is a recipient of Medicaid waiver services. Recently, there was a breakdown in the service authority approval process, meaning that my upcoming hours were not approved in writing. Should I still provide behavior analysis and oversight even if I do not have a written authorization? I know it sounds like an obvious yes, but legally the rules say that if my hours are not approved in advance the agency does not have to pay me.

28. Third-party payers for services are starting to employ behavior analysts to review behavior programs provided by other behavior analysts. While this is better than having psychologists or bean counters reviewing behavior plans, are the behavior analysts who are employed to review the plans unethical because they are making decisions about services without observing the client, reviewing data, and so forth?

29. I work with clients who are developmentally disabled both in their homes and at school. There is a behavioral consultant in our area who will frequently recommend that a punishment procedure be implemented with a client without having seen the client himself. This professional basically hears from school staff of Board Certified assistant Behavior Analysts that the client has behavior problems, but he has never worked with or observed the child himself. I am fairly sure this is unethical, but I am not his supervisor, he doesn't work in the same consulting firm I do, and I am only a BCaBA. Should I do anything about this?

30. A BCBA is in business with a person from another field who was the lead author on a study that has been shown to have serious methodological flaws. The other authors have retracted its findings. The lead author was found to have a serious conflict of interest that was not disclosed when the study was published and is being investigated for scientific misconduct. Nevertheless, the BCBA continues to promote the person's unsubstantiated theory about the etiology of autism and treatments that have not been tested scientifically.

31. I am a BCBA working for a state-funded program. The problem concerns a BCaBA coworker and her relationship with a client who is a dependent caregiver. The relationship is not romantic; the two have become best friends. The BCaBA sees the client in her home on a weekly basis. My colleague asked if it would be appropriate to maintain a personal relationship with this client after she leaves her job with our program. I suggested that at the point that she ceases employment she cut the relationship and not try to treat her former client as a friend. I want to make sure that the client does not feel pressured into a relationship with my coworker. Should I follow up with the client to see if this was done, or is it okay for these two women to be friends once there is no longer a professional connection?

32. We have an 8-year-old client with a diagnosis of attention deficit disorder. According to her parents, the little girl has a history of "lying." We have not seen this behavior at our treatment center. Yesterday, she told two of our staff members that some time back she was roughhousing with her dad and that he squeezed her so hard that she fainted; she said that later she was sent to bed without dinner. This client also reported that her dad squeezed her wrists "really hard" on past occasions although we have not seen any sign of bruising. I documented all of this in her clinical file. Do I need to report this incident to the Florida Abuse Hotline, or should I just talk with the parents first and get their side of the story? I don't want to bother the hotline if this is just a case of a girl who fabricated a story.

33. When I was an undergraduate, I was given the opportunity to have a practicum in a classroom for children with autism. Basically, I was a volunteer who helped the teacher, but I was not responsible for any aspect of behavior programs. I was also permitted to observe treatment team meetings. The whole experience inspired me to go on to earn my master's degree in applied behavior analysis. One student who was very hyperactive was not doing very well on his goals. A therapist from another discipline came to a treatment team meeting and made the recommendation that the student be put in a weighted vest. She said it would help his "concentration, ability to learn tasks, reduce his behavior problems, and result in faster learning." This therapist was fast-talking and funny, and everyone liked her. I think she could sell snowballs to Eskimos, and that day she sold this concept to the whole team. I did not agree with this approach at all. I told my faculty supervisor later, and he told me, "You need to keep your mouth shut." I didn't say a word in any of these meetings, and the weighted vest was implemented a little later as the "treatment." Ever since then, I have felt guilty for not having

the courage to speak up on behalf of effective treatment for this child. After my supervisor warned me, was there anything else I could have done?

34. One part of my new job is to write up client progress notes. I use these notes and my data to keep track of where I am with my clients. My supervisor also uses my notes to determine if I am handling cases efficiently and effectively. If a client meets a goal, I record it in my notes. I became aware recently that my notes are also being used to document the need for continuing funding for clients. While I am excited that I have helped someone, the administration is upset that because I have written "Goal met" or "Case closed" the funding stream for this client will dry up. A recent conversation with my supervisor was quite disturbing—it was suggested to me in a somewhat roundabout way that rather than saying that the client had reached his goal I should indicate that there were other goals for him to work on and that further training was indicated. I thought about it and went back the next day for a clarification, just to make sure I understood; the answer was, "Yes, that's right." I have been following these directions now for a couple of months, but it doesn't feel right to me. If a client has met his goal, it seems to me that this should be a cause for celebration and an opportunity to take in a new client who needs our help. Am I missing something here? Am I harming the facility because it gets less funding when I terminate a client?

35. I am the supervisor for a team of behavior analysts who provide behavioral services in the homes of children. I have an unusual ethics question. One of my newly certified BCBAs was recently assigned to work in the home of a preschooler; the child lives in a rough neighborhood. After the second visit, the consultant came to my office and said she believes there is drug use in the home. The child's mother is single, and reportedly her boyfriend

and his friends come to the house often. The consultant said that she has seen evidence of drug activity (including use of drugs and dealing) in the home and that she feels uncomfortable going there. I am not sure what I should do. I have studied the BACB Guidelines very carefully. What I get from my common sense and my reading of the Guidelines does not match. For example, the Guidelines say a client has the right to effective treatment and that behavior analysts do not terminate services and leave a client with nothing. What would you advise me to do?

36. As a Board Certified Behavior Analyst, I am a member of a local peer review committee (LRC). The LRC looks at behavior plans for the clients in my area. I get along well with everyone on the committee. Here is my problem. The chair of the committee is also our regional Behavior Analysis Director. I have to review her programs, make comments, and present my review on the committee date scheduled. I am not sure if she is just overloaded or what, but this person's programs are very weak. The protocols she suggests are not behaviorally sound. She should stick to being an administrator because she is organized. I am in an awkward situation because this is the person who gives me cases and basically controls how much money I can make each month. My boyfriend is in law school. He told me to send a strongly worded letter about the quality of the programs to this woman. Other people on the committee have dropped subtle hints that the programs need to be improved, but she ignores the suggestions. One would think the chair would have the best programs of all of us, but she was trained in the early 1980s and is out of touch. Any ideas for an ethical and diplomatic solution?

37. I am a student in a behavior analysis program. I am not yet Board Certified at any level, but I would like to become a BCBA. I have gone to some conferences, and I know about the Guidelines although I am not an expert on them. To

get experience with children, I have been working at a private daycare center that has private clients as well as a few children with disabilities. We have one little boy who is very hyperactive. He does not speak well, and you can't understand him. He will spit on you, try to bite you, and kick you if he does not get his way. Sometimes, even when staff members are being nice to him he just "goes off." There is a program that involves the teacher giving him treats when he is good, putting stars on a chart, and using time-out. Here is my concern: I have seen one teacher's aide smack this child if he spits on her or tries to bite her. When she does this, he starts acting right and behaves himself. I know behavior analysts are not allowed to hit children; however, this is a private daycare, and parents will say, "Spank him if you need to." I have not reported this aide because one time when the child spit on me I grabbed him by the ear to take him to time-out. The aide gave me a little smile, and she did not report me. I am starting to feel nervous about all of this.

38. I am an assistant Behavior Analyst. I am in graduate school in psychology and work part time at a facility for people with developmental disabilities. I am lucky because several of us who are in school together also work for the same consulting firm and work at some of the same schools and facilities. One of our friends is more advanced than us in her graduate studies. She is working on a research project that has been all she has talked about for months. Our professor said if the study was done right and the data looked good, this was the kind of study that could be easily published. Our friend talked us into being observers for her. At the end of the study, when we were all out eating pizza and drinking beer, our friend proudly announced that our professor was going to help her submit her work for publication. She said the professor was impressed that the treatment she developed resulted in all of the clients in

the study having dramatic improvements in their behavior. "What about Participant #3?" I said. We all knew this participant's behavior got worse over the course of the study, and so did another one. Our friend got a desperate look on her face and admitted to us that she had thrown away the data for two clients who did not perform well. "This is probably done all the time in research; I *really* want to have a publication—you guys have got to stand by me on this. I need to graduate."

39. I am the behavior analyst who works with Jason, an 8-year-old boy who is in a third grade class for special needs children at an elementary school. This is the first year Jason has attended our school; his family moved here from another state. Jason's school records from first and second grades indicate that he has been "hyperactive," although there has been no formal attention deficit hyperactivity disorder (ADHD) diagnosis. In the past 6 months, teachers have noted that Jason has frequently appeared tired and irritable. Although he has lost some weight, Jason seems to be very motivated by food, often pushing and shoving other children out of the way to get to the head of the lunch line. The school requires a medical check-up at the beginning of the year. We have asked Jason's mother if we can see the results of his physical or have permission to talk to his doctors, and she says no. She will not share his medical information, and she says there is no need for a physical; he is just misbehaving. Is it ethical to proceed even though I have a strong hunch that Jason has a medical condition that is related to his hyperactivity? Can I tell the mother that I "have to have the records or he will get no services at all?" Or should I just drop the case altogether since I don't think Jason has a "behavior" problem?

40. I am a graduate student working part time in a facility for adults with developmental disabilities. For severe behavior problems, clients have BCBA services and behavioral

programs. But for all the clients who don't have behavioral services, the caregivers in the facility often make up their own behavioral interventions. They act as though the clients are their children and they are the parents. For example, they will say, "You can't go to (a scheduled special event) because you did (whatever the unwanted behavior was). Often, the punishment is too severe for whatever the misbehavior was. I know if I file a complaint, I run the risk of being ignored by staff. Or worse, they would dislike me, and it would be impossible to work with them. I am already a little different and seen as an outsider because they have all been there 20 years or more. Once when I tried to get them to do something a different way, a staff person told someone about me, "That little girl has never had any kids; she doesn't have to manage these clients 5 days a week, and she will be gone as soon as she graduates."

41. From a behaviorally trained Special Education Itinerant Teacher* (SEIT): A father had to go to the bank, which closed by the time my session ended. He wanted me to stay home with the child while he went. I told him "No, this is not allowed." He begged and said, "I trust you; I'll be right back," and started to leave. I again said, "No—this is against the law; if you have to go, we will end the session early." He said fine; I grabbed my stuff and left. The next day we discussed the situation, and he apologized for putting me in an uncomfortable position.

42. From a speech therapist: I have had many parents who suggest paying me for extra sessions over holidays and school breaks. I have also had parents who suggest that they bill and hold sessions to use on a holiday or school break.

43. Jane, a SEIT teacher, is providing in-home behavioral services to a 3-year-old girl, Mary P. The IEP goals include

---

* These are special education teachers who have been trained in the use of behavioral interventions.

increasing Mary's appropriate interactions with other children. Mrs. P., knowing that Jane has a 3-year-old child, has repeatedly asked Jane to bring her child to play with Mary. Jane told Mrs. P. that this was not professional. However, Mrs. P. stated that Mary does not really know any other children and that she needs to work on her social skills. When Jane suggested putting Mary into a pre-school, Mrs. P. stated that the family could not afford this financially. Jane has felt increasingly uncomfortable with the family's request for a play date. Last week Jane called Mrs. P. to cancel a session, saying that her babysitting fell through at the last minute. Mrs. P. insisted that Jane bring her own child to the session rather than cancel. Jane did not know what to do.

44. One colleague said that she gets pressure from families to do make-ups on Saturdays.

45. Another one of our team's therapists, a speech therapist, has a reputation as a "Chatty Cathy." It is her personality and her way of connecting, but she chats up a storm about her own personal life with her clients. Here's the dilemma: she is very funny, and the clients actually love the wild stories about her zany life. Should we intervene?

46. A parent is transitioning her child from Early Intervention to Committee on Preschool Special Education* (CPSE) funding and wants to get different services upon transition than she thinks the committee will approve. The child has a diagnosis of autism and is receiving extensive hours of applied behavior analysis as well as related services at home. The parent has exercised considerable control over the employment of providers in the home under early intervention. She and a lead member of the home-based team communicate to the speech/language therapist that she needs to write a progress report emphasizing

---

* This is a special funding source in New York State.

the child's weaknesses and not emphasizing the progress that the child is making. They want this report faxed to the committee chairperson right before the next meeting. The committee has not requested a progress report from this provider. The therapist feels uncomfortable with the parent's somewhat manipulative request. The therapist senses, however, based on past events, that if she does not please the parent and the lead member of the home-based team she will be removed from the case.

47. A child with a diagnosis of autism has been recommended by the Committee on Preschool Special Education for placement in a full-day center-based program designed to service children with autism. The parent has visited the program and accepted placement. The CPSE is planning to reconvene prior to transition, as was stipulated at the initial meeting, to ensure that the recommendations that were made earlier are still appropriate. The parent is now feeling that her child should not attend the center-based program but rather that the child should continue with extensive home-based ABA services under CPSE and also with a teacher accompanying the child to typical nursery school. The parent asks the lead teacher of the home-based team to contact the staff members of the center-based program to let them know that the parent does not really want their program. The home-based teacher knows that this may result in the center-based program not sending a representative to the Committee on Preschool Special Education meeting, which may make it easier to drive a change in the recommendation. There is a conflict between what we think the child needs and what the parent wants.

48. A behaviorally trained teacher providing services in the home is aware that the family is struggling financially and that it will not be able to provide even a simple birthday party for the child. The teacher would like to pay for

a modest party, because she feels sorry for the child. She knows that the family will accept this gift from her.

49. Guidance is needed for these three situations: (1) Currently, we have therapists and some teachers attending children's birthday parties or attending family parties. (2) They may also accept monetary gifts or gifts of high value (In our district occasional gifts with a token value of less than $50 are permitted). To skirt this rule, some parents try to give frequent gifts with a value of $50 or less, and the total of these gifts well exceeds $50. (3) Occasionally, to make a little extra money, therapists and teachers offer to babysit and get paid directly by the family.

50. Our consulting firm wants to make an ad for television. A few of our clients' parents have told others our services changed their lives. Since they are very vocal with no prompting from us, can we ask them to appear for a short sound bite in our TV and print ads?

Appendix D: Suggested Further Reading

Bersoff, D. N. (2003). *Ethical Conflicts in Psychology.* American Psychological Association, Washington, DC.

This third edition of Bersoff's text includes material on ethics codes, applying ethics, confidentiality, multiple relationships, assessment, computerized testing, therapy, and research. Additionally he covers supervision, guidelines for animal research, ethics in forensic settings, ethical practice within the boundaries of managed care, the American Psychological Association (APA) 2002 Ethics Code, and the revisions to the Rules and Procedures for adjudicating complaints of unethical conduct against APA members adopted by the APA's Ethics Committee in August 2002.

Canter, M. B., Bennett, B. E., Jones, S. E., & Nagy, T. F. (1999). *Ethics for Psychologists: A Commentary on the APA Ethics Code.* American Psychological Association, Washington, DC.

The three main sections of this volume are Foundations, Interpreting the Ethics Code, and Conclusions. The bulk of the book is the section on "Interpreting the Ethics Code," in which each ethical standard is analyzed and commentary is provided.

Danforth, S., & Boyle, J. R. (2000). *Cases in Behavior Management.* Prentice Hall, Upper Saddle River, NJ.

This book begins by presenting social systems theory; models of treatment including the behavioral, psychodynamic, environmental, and constructivist models; and information on analyzing cases. The second half of the book features 38 cases that illustrate behavior management issues faced by teachers, parents, and caregivers. A number of the vignettes are related to school settings (preschool through high school). Cases are very detailed with most being 3 to 4 pages in length.

Fisher, C. B. (2003). *Decoding the Ethics Code: A Practical Guide for Psychologists.* Sage, Thousand Oaks, CA.

The 2002 American Psychological Association's Ethical Principles of Psychologists and Code of Conduct is presented in this volume. After an introduction describing how the code came to be developed, the foundation and application of each ethical standard is discussed along with enforcement of the code. Other topics presented include professional liability issues, ethical decision making, and the relation between ethics and law.

Hayes, L. J., Hayes, G. J., Moore, S. C., & Ghezzi, P. M. (1994). *Ethical Issues in Developmental Disabilities.* Context Press, Reno, NV.

This volume is a collection of theoretical articles by a variety of authors. Some of the topics include choice and value, moral development, morality, ethical issues concerning people with DD, competence, right to treatment, ethics and adult services, and the pharmacological treatment of behavior problems.

Jacob, S., & Hartshorne, T. S. (2003). *Ethics and the Law for School Psychologists.* Wiley, New York.

This text provides information on professional standards and legal requirements relevant to the delivery of school psychological services. Topics covered include students' and parents' rights to privacy and informed consent, confidentiality, assessment, ethical issues related to Individuals with Disabilities Education Act (IDEA) and Americans with Disabilities Act, educating children with special needs, consultation with teachers, school discipline, school violence prevention, and ethical issues in supervision. *Ethics and the Law for School Psychologists* addresses the changes in the 2002 revision of the American Psychological Association's Ethical Principles and Code of Conduct.

Jacobson, J. W., Foxx, R. M., & Mulick, J. A. (Eds.). (2005). *Controversial Therapies for Developmental Disabilities: Fad, Fashion, and Science in Professional Practice.* Lawrence Erlbaum Associates, Publishers, Mahwah, NJ.

John Jacobson (to whom this book is dedicated), Richard Foxx, and James Mulick have done our field a great service in compiling this encyclopedia of fads, fallacies, "faux fixes," and delusions in the treatment of developmental disabilities. This must-have reference should be required reading for all behavior analysts. A few sample titles from the 28 chapters will give you some idea of the approach taken by nearly 30 experts—"Sifting Sound Practice From Snake Oil," "The Delusion of Full Inclusion," and "Facilitated Communication: The Ultimate Fad Treatment."

Koocher, G. P., & Keith-Spiegel, P. C. (1990). *Children, Ethics, and the Law: Professional Issues and Cases.* University of Nebraska Press, Lincoln.

Children, Ethics, and the Law outlines ethical and legal issues encountered by mental health workers in their work with children, adolescents, and their families. This volume addresses issues pertinent to psychotherapy with children, assessment, confidentiality and record keeping, consent to treatment and research, and legal issues. Case vignettes are provided to illustrate the ethical and legal dilemmas under discussion.

Lattal, A. D., & Clark, R. W. (2005). *Ethics at Work.* Aubrey Daniels International, Inc., Atlanta.

For behavior analysts who work in business settings, this is the book you want to use as your standard. Lattal and Clark discuss all the important issues including building moral integrity, achieving ethical sales, behaving ethically, and making ethics a habit. There are plenty of case examples that can be used to stimulate discussion in class.

Nagy, T. F. (2000). *An Illustrative Casebook for Psychologists.* American Psychological Association, Washington, DC.

An Illustrative Casebook for Psychologists was written to accompany the 102 standards of the American Psychological Association's Ethics Committee's Ethical Principles of Psychologists and Code of Conduct. Fictional case vignettes are used throughout the text to illustrate the key areas of the APA Code, which include General Standards; Evaluation, Assessment, or Intervention; Advertising and Other Public Statements; Therapy; Privacy and Confidentiality; Teaching, Training Supervision, Research, and Publishing; Forensic Activities; and Resolving Ethical Issues.

Offit, P. A. (2008). *Autism's False Prophets: Bad Science, Risky Medicine, and the Search for a Cure.* Columbia University Press, New York.

"Paul Offit, a national expert on vaccines, challenges the modern-day false prophets who have so egregiously misled the public and exposes the opportunism of the lawyers, journalists, celebrities, and politicians who support them. Offit recounts the history of autism research and the exploitation of this tragic condition by advocates and zealots. He considers the manipulation of science in the popular media and the courtroom, and he explores why society is susceptible to the bad science and risky therapies put forward by many antivaccination activists" (from the dust jacket).

Pope, K. S., & Vasquez, M. J. T. (1998). *Ethics in Psychotherapy and Counseling*. Jossey-Bass, San Francisco.

This text addresses areas in which ethical dilemmas occur in the work of mental health practitioners. Issues covered include informed consent, sexual and nonsexual relationships with clients, cultural and individual differences, supervisory relationships, and confidentiality. There are appendixes of codes of conduct and ethical principles for psychologists and guidelines for ethical counseling in managed-care settings.

Stolz, S. B., et al. (1978). *Ethical Issues in Behavior Modification*. Jossey-Bass, San Francisco.

In 1974, the American Psychological Association formed a commission to examine issues related to social, legal, and ethical controversies in psychology. The commission also provided recommendations regarding the use and misuse of behavior modification. This historic volume addresses the ethics of behavior modification in settings that include outpatient settings, institutions, schools, prisons, and society. The volume also addresses the ethics of interventions.

Van Houten, R., & Axelrod, S. (Eds.). (1993). *Behavior Analysis and Treatment*. Plenum Press, New York.

Van Houten and Axelrod persuaded over 30 experts in applied behavior analysis to give their assessment of the field and to suggest ways to create optimal environments for treatment and to provide assessments for quality care and state-of-the-art treatment. Chapter 8, "A Decision-Making Model for Selecting the Optimal Treatment Procedure," served as a foundation for Chapter 16 in this Second Edition.

Welfel, E. R., & Ingersoll, R. E. (2001). *The Mental Health Desk Reference*. Wiley, New York.

Part IX of *The Mental Health Desk Reference* is "Ethical and Legal Issues." This section of the text addresses procedures for filing ethics complaints, clients' rights to privacy, informed consent, responsible documentation, reporting child abuse, recognizing elder abuse, supervision, and responsible interactions with managed-care organizations.

References

American Psychological Association. (APA). (2001). *PsychSCAN: Behavior analysis & therapy.* Washington, DC: Author.

Animal Welfare Act. (1990). 7 U.S.C. § 2131 et. seq.

Axelrod, S., Spreat, S., Berry, B., & Moyer, L. (1993). A decision-making model for selecting the optimal treatment procedure. In Van Houten, R., and Axelrod, S., *Behavior analysis and treatment.* New York: Plenum Press.

Ayllon, T., & Michael, J. (1959). The psychiatric nurse as a behavioral engineer. *Journal of the Experimental Analysis of Behavior, 2,* 323–334.

Bailey, J. S., & Burch, M. R. (2002). *Research methods in applied behavior analysis.* Thousand Oaks, CA: Sage.

Bailey, J. S., & Burch, M. R. (2010). 25 Essential skills and strategies for the professional behavior analyst: Expert tips for maximizing consulting effectiveness. New York: Routledge.

BBC Radio. (1999, January 26). *Ten least respected professions* [Radio]. Available from www.bbc.co.uk/pressoffice/pressreleases/stories/2002/05_May/29/respected_professions.html

Behavior Analyst Certification Board (BACB). (1998–2010). Disciplinary standards, procedures for appeal. Retrieved January 2, 2005, from www.bacb.com/redirect_frame.php?page=disciplineapp.html

Beutler, L. E. (2000). Empirically based decision making in clinical practice. *Prevention & treatment,* Volume 3, Article 27. Retrieved from http://psycnet.apa.org.proxy.lib.fsu.edu/journals/pre/3/1/27a/

Binder, R. L. (1992). Sexual harassment: Issues for forensic psychiatrists. *Bulletin of the Academy of Psychiatry Law, 20,* 409–418.

Carnegie, D. (1981). *How to win friends and influence people.* New York: Pocket Books/Simon & Schuster, Inc.

Cooper, J. O., Heron, T. E., & Heward, W. L. (2007). *Applied behavior analysis, 2nd edition.* Upper Saddle River, NJ: Pearson Education.

Crouhy, M., Galai, D., & Mark, R. (2006). *The essentials of risk management.* New York: McGraw Hill.

Daniels, A. C. (2000). *Bringing out the best in people: How to apply the astonishing power of positive reinforcement.* New York: McGraw-Hill.

Daniels, A. C., & Daniels, J. E. (2004). *Performance management: Changing behavior that drives organizational effectiveness.* Atlanta, GA: Aubrey Daniels International, Inc.

Eliot, C. W. (1910). *Harvard classics volume 38.* New York: P. F. Collier and Son.

Frederiksen, L. W. (Ed.). (1982). *Handbook of organizational behavior management.* New York: Wiley.

Hill, A. (1998). *Speaking truth to power.* New York: Anchor.

Holland, J. G., & Skinner, B. F. (1961). *The analysis of behavior: A program for self-instruction.* New York: McGraw-Hill.

Iwata, B. A., Dorsey, M. F., Slifer, K. J., Bauman, K. E., & Richman, G. S. (1982). Toward a functional analysis of self-injury. *Analysis and Intervention in Developmental Disabilities, 2,* 3–20.

Jacobson, J. W., Foxx, R. M., & Mulick, J. A. (2005). *Controversial therapies for developmental disabilities.* Mahwah, NJ: Lawrence Erlbaum Associates, Inc

Kay, S., & Vyse, S. (2005). Helping parents separate the wheat from the chaff: Putting autism treatments to the test. In J. W. Jacobson, R. M. Foxx, & J.A. Mulick (Eds.), *Controversial therapies for developmental disabilities* (pp. 265–277). Mahwah, NJ: Lawrence Erlbaum Associates, Inc.

Koocher, G. P., & Keith-Spiegel, P. (1998). *Ethics in psychology: Professional standards and cases* (2nd ed.). New York: Oxford University Press.

Krasner, L., & Ullmann, L. P. (Eds.). (1965). *Research in behavior modification.* New York: Holt, Rinehart and Winston, Inc.

McAllister, J. W. (1972). *Report of resident abuse investigating committee.* Tallahassee, FL: Division of Retardation, Department of Health and Rehabilitative Services.

Neuringer, C., & Michael, J. L. (Eds.). (1970). *Behavior modification in clinical psychology.* New York: Apple-Century-Crofts.

O'Brien, R. M., Dickinson, A. M., & Rosow, M. P. (Eds.). (1982). *Industrial behavior modification: A management handbook.* New York: Pergamon.

Ontario Consultants on Religious Tolerance. (2004). Kingston, ON, Canada. Retrieved November 12, 2010 from http://www.religioustolerance.org/mor_dive3.htm

Shermer, M. (2002). Smart people believe in weird things. *Scientific American*, August 12, 2002.

Singer, M. T., & Lalich, J. (1996). *Crazy therapies: What are they? Do they work?* San Francisco: Jossey-Bass.

Skinner, B. F. (1953). *Science and human behavior.* New York: Macmillan.

Skinner, B. F. (1957). *Verbal behavior.* New York: Appleton-Century-Crofts.

Spreat, S. (1982). Weighing treatment alternatives: Which is less restrictive? *Woodhaven Center E & R Technical Report* 82-11(1). Philadelphia: Temple University.

Ullmann, L. P., & Krasner, L. (Eds.). (1965). *Case studies in behavior modification.* New York: Holt, Rinehart and Winston, Inc.

U.S. Department of Health & Human Services. (HHS). (2003). OCR Summary of the HIPAA Privacy Rule. Retrieved January 2, 2005, from www.hhs.gov/ocr/hipaa/privacy.html

U.S. Equal Employment Opportunity Commission. (EEOC). (2004). *Sexual harassment charges: EEOC & FEPA s combined: FY 1997–FY 2009*, p. 288. Retrieved November 12, 2010 from http://www.eeoc.gov/eeoc/statistics/enforcement/sexual_harassment.cfm

Van Houten, R., Axelrod, S., Bailey, J. S., Favell, J. E., Foxx, R. M., Iwata, B. A., et al. (1988). The right to effective behavioral treatment. *Journal of Applied Behavior Analysis, 21,* 381–384.

Wolf, M., Risley, R., & Mees, H. (1964). Application of operant conditioning procedures to the behaviour problems of an autistic child. *Behaviour Research and Therapy, 1,* 305–312.

Wilson, R., & Crouch, E.A.C. (2001). *Risk–benefit analysis, 2nd edition.* Cambridge, MA: Harvard University Center for Risk Analysis.

Wyatt v. Stickney. 325 F. Supp 781 (M.D. Ala. 1971).

Index